THE MOTHERHOOD CONSTELLATION

The
Motherhood
Constellation

A Unified View of
Parent-Infant Psychotherapy

DANIEL N. STERN

BasicBooks
A Division of HarperCollins*Publishers*

Library of Congress Cataloging-in-Publication Data
Stern, Daniel N.
    The motherhood constellation: a unified view of parent-infant psychotherapy / Daniel N. Stern.
        p.   cm.
    Includes bibliographical references and index.
    ISBN 0-465-02602-8
    1. Infant psychiatry. 2. Parent and infant. 3. Motherhood—Psychological aspects. I. Title.
RJ502.5.S74 1995
616.89'156—dc20   94-24388
                                                                        CIP

    96 97 98 ◆/HC 9 8 7 6 5 4

FOR NADIA

Contents

Part III
SYNTHESIS

Introduction

T HIS BOOK explores the nature of parent-infant psychotherapies, therapies that are a major segment of the rapidly growing, sprawling field of infant mental health. At present, this field consists of applications of and borrowings from well-known therapeutic concepts (including psychoanalysis, behaviorism, systems theory, social networks, and pediatrics) that have been modified for use with a new population. Most often these approaches try to remain faithful to their intellectual origins. At first glance, therefore, the field resembles a continent, previously unexplored, that has been divided into areas ruled by different colonial therapeutic empires. On closer examination, however, the established therapies are all undergoing modifications in their confrontation with this new setting and are converging. One can begin to see the general outlines of a future unified country, a single coherent field of psychotherapeutics with its own unique contributions to make to the general ideas of psychotherapy. This book will trace this evolution.

To put this inquiry into perspective, it is worth noting that the history of psychotherapy is, in large part, the story of encounters between existent therapeutic approaches and new clinical populations for whom the existing concepts and techniques were not designed. The specific psychopathology that is clinically addressed is of crucial importance to an understanding of the therapeutic approach that develops. Theories arise with specific clinical phenomena in mind. Freud's meeting, over one hundred years ago, with mostly female patients with hysteria, especially with phobias and symptoms of conversion reaction, gave rise to the psychoanalytic technique and (along with other psychoneuroses) to psychoanalytic metapsychology, in particular to the notion of the Oedipus complex as the central organizer of psychic life.

When psychodynamic therapies encountered schizophrenic adolescents enacting identifiable patterns of family interaction, family therapies emerged along with a systems theory perspective on psychopathology and technique. Similarly, when traditional psychodynamic psychotherapies met "new" forms of psychopathology such as narcissistic and borderline personality disorders, there arose Self Psychology and other important variations of psychoanalytic theory and technique that stress the pre-Oedipal rather than the Oedipal organizations of mental life and focus on deficits as well as conflicts (Green, 1983/1986; Kernberg, 1984; Kohut, 1971, 1977). The special relationship between depression and cognitive therapies may prove to be another such case of an approach largely shaped by a specific form of illness (Beck, Rush, Shaw, & Emery, 1979).

In brief, it seems that different forms of psychopathology are paradigmatic for different clinical approaches, both theoretically and technically. At each major new encounter with an unexplored illness or never-before-treated clinical population, new treatment approaches emerge. And these invariably have implications for the existing approaches. This book will examine the new psychotherapies that have emerged and are still emerging to deal with the "new" clinical population of parents with infants. It will also explore some of the implications of this encounter for the existing psychotherapies that address other clinical situations.

The population in question consists of very young infants (0–3 years) and their parents, largely mothers. The psychopathologies they exhibit consist largely of relationship disturbances that may present as eating or sleeping disorders, attachment disturbances, early conduct disorders in the infant, or as parental anxieties, disturbances in parenting, and other forms of parent-infant disregulations (Cichetti & Cohen, in press; Greenspan, 1981; Lebovici, 1983; Lebovici & Weil-Halpern, 1989; Lewis & Miller, 1990; Sameroff & Emde, 1989; Soulé & Golse, 1992; Weinberg & Tronick, 1994; Zeanah, 1993). They also include infant conditions that do not originate in the parent-infant relationship, such as developmental lag or specific handicaps. After all, the parent-infant relationship will have a powerful influence on how such illnesses are lived. This new clinical situation has of course been around for a long time, but only in the last decade has it greatly proliferated, with the result that a wide variety of treatment concepts and programs of intervention have emerged (see Fava Vizziello & Stern, 1992; Meisels, Dichtelmiller, & Llaw, 1993; Meisels & Shonkoff, 1990; Zeanah, 1993).

As a new terrain of encounter for the established therapeutic approaches, the parent-infant relationship offers several unique aspects that promise a fruitful meeting.

1. The new "patient," never before encountered, is not a person but a relationship, although a realistically asymmetrical one, between a young baby and his parents. This relationship is influenced by a rich and full past history on the parents' part and a quickly accumulating but still minimal one on the infant's part. We are not yet clear what a "relationship disturbance" is in this context (Sameroff & Emde, 1989).

2. It is not yet known how much of the infant's psychological nature is a construct of the parents' imagination (their wishes, fears, attributions, and so on)—that is, of the relationship.

3. Diagnostically the infant is neither neurotic, borderline, nor psychotic. Is he "normal"? He has an infant psyche, whatever that may be. (The DSM and ICD classification systems—as well as others—have been of little help for diagnosing infants under 3 years of age.)

4. The parents are psychologically "normal," in the vast majority of cases. If they carry a diagnosis it is a secondary or mediating variable. They tend to see themselves as having a problem rather than an illness. They usually do not choose or wish to see a psychiatrist, clinical psychologist, or psychoanalyst. Most often, referrals from medical sources must be done with some delicacy to avoid the stigma of mental illness.

5. Nonetheless, the mother (and perhaps the father) do have a special psychological condition, which I will later refer to as the motherhood constellation. This is a unique organization of mental life appropriate for and adapted to the reality of having an infant to care for. This special psychic organization makes the mother a "patient" who cannot be properly seen when viewed through the lens of a therapy designed for other sorts of patients.

6. The infant and his parents are in the throes of the greatest and fastest human change process known: normal early development. Furthermore, this life epoch is not simply another major "crisis," potentially conducive of change. Its cardinal function is to effect change, maturation, development, and growth. This engine for change operates with or without therapy. It is the milieu in which therapy takes place.

7. Rarely is it clear or permanent how to locate and identify the problem. The parent feels a kind of responsibility for who the infant is that is not found so strongly in adult relationships. Accordingly, the normal responsibilities and defenses of a targeted patient are different in this setting.

8. The relationship between parent and infant is conducted exclusively nonverbally and largely presymbolically. Pathology is thus the result of these preverbal interactions. How is that fact to be conceived and dealt with?

Some of these elements are not unique to the parent-infant situation; rather they are exaggerations of what may be found in other therapeutic situations. Exaggeration, however, can be illuminating.

The many therapies used to treat parents and infants must take into account these special elements. What search strategies are likely to reveal the convergences appearing among diverse therapies inspired from different sources? How can we best explore the fundamental aspects of these parent-infant therapies created in part by the special elements of the clinical situation, and discover if new concepts and practices are emerging, with relevance for all therapies in general, as well as for parent-infant disturbances in particular?

The approach to be adopted here is inspired by the impression that almost all the various parent-infant therapies work—and probably work equally well. This assumption is neither new nor surprising. The history of psychotherapy research (predominantly with adults) has continually shown that most therapies work—compared with no treatment—and that differences in outcome between different therapies are difficult to find. J. D. Frank and J. B. Frank (1991) have commented on this state of affairs with the suggestion that "the features common to all types of psychotherapy contribute as much, if not more, to the effectiveness of those therapies than do the characteristics that differentiate them" (p. 20).

My own work with infants and parents has led to similar conclusions. I have practiced several types and combinations of parent-infant therapies and have observed and read about many more. The commonalities seem to account for far more of the beneficial effects of therapy than do the differences, and there seems to be a rough equivalence among therapeutic approaches.

Many practitioners and theoreticians of one approach or another are not very comfortable with this situation for all the obvious reasons. (Some of the reasons for this discomfort are excellent. For instance, to get the expected positive therapeutic effect, it is necessary for the practitioner to have full confidence—even belief—in the specific approach and to be well trained and experienced in its application. Practically speaking, this usually means being relatively ignorant of the other approaches.)

The assumption, then, of rough equivalence among therapeutic approaches is unpopular and rests uneasy. There are several ways around it. The most appealing to committed practitioners is to search for clinically important exceptions to the basic assumption of equivalence. For example, if one only had a better description of a subpopulation that responded well or poorly to one or another of the therapies, then one could predict which therapy would work better for whom, when, and where. Such well-meant and necessary attempts to weaken or qualify the basic assumption of equivalence are usually of limited success, but they hold out the hope that if they were done better or carried further, the assumption would be compromised.

Others choose simply to ignore the assumption, even—or especially—those doing psychotherapy outcome research. They argue that since the common features are nonspecific to any of the therapeutic approaches being compared, there is no point in studying or even thinking about them. These features are always present and always acting; they do not constitute a potential variable (even if they do account for the largest share of the outcome effect). And in this spirit we tend to minimize or forget about the massive role of the nonspecific.

There is yet another way around the assumption: accepting that the different therapies have roughly equal outcomes but that they arrive there by different mechanisms of therapeutic action. Logically, then, therapies could be combined and get better results than could any one therapy alone. This approach is rarely used, however, except where the therapies have very different mechanisms of action, as when drug therapy is combined with talking therapy. This combination seems to offer the best of both worlds, but it is only a promise.

The strategy I will adopt here is to accept the assumption of the rough equivalence among therapeutic approaches (I was not crazy about it initially, either) and to put it to advantage in exploring the current situation, by identifying and examining in detail the commonalities among various parent-infant therapies. This is not a new strategy. It is what Frank and Frank (1991) have done for adult psychotherapies for over three decades.

There are two main reasons for such a strategy. First, it adheres closely to the empirical situation we find, namely, that nonspecific features (commonalities) shared by therapies account for more of the positive outcome effect than do the unique or specific features. Second, common features will best identify a general new form of therapy. The nonspecific features may appear to be less interesting—or even noise—when comparing different approaches within a well-known, defined clinical domain. But that is not our task. Ours is to define and map the nature of a new, unknown, and little-described clinical domain, parent-infant therapies. And the deepest way to do that may well be to see if there are commonalities used by all the various parent-infant approaches and to evaluate whether this set of commonalities is different from that seen in other domains (or populations or theories) of therapy. If it is, then we can start to talk about the unique and coherent features belonging to parent-infant therapy. And we can ask whether these features have something to teach the general field of psychotherapy in return.

In the course of examining different clinical approaches and exploring the features they hold in common, I have come to realize that a mother is not just another patient, nor only a parent to a young patient, nor simply another member of a system. She is a woman in a unique period of her own life, playing a unique cultural role and fulfilling a unique and essential role in the survival of the species. It has become apparent to me that any treatment of the parent-infant relationship has to take into account the special nature of most mothers' predispositions to think, feel, and act in certain ways. This realization has led to the concept of the *motherhood constellation*, which makes more comprehensible many of the commonalities seen in the different approaches and draws together many of the strands that start to describe a common direction in parent-infant psychotherapies. While the basic idea of a motherhood constellation is present in a vast array of writings, it is pulled together here in the service of understanding a domain of psychotherapy. Because of this key role, this book carries it in the title.

In part I, the nature of the parent-infant clinical situation will be described. Separate chapters will examine the different elements that make up the parent-infant clinical system: the parents' representations of the relationship with their baby, the overt interactions occurring between parent and infant, the infant's representations of these overt interactions, and the place of the therapist in this clinical system.

In part II, different therapeutic approaches to parent-infant disturbances will be discussed in terms of the elements of the clinical situation described in part I. Different chapters will focus on approaches that single out different elements of the system—for example, the parents' representations or the parents' overt behavior—as the preferred locus of therapeutic action. The discussion of these various approaches is not exhaustive; rather it highlights the major therapeutic features that will permit the development of the themes of the book. The commonalities among the different approaches are identified and explored.

In part III, a synthesis is attempted in which the parents (mostly the mothers) are viewed as having a unique form of organized mental life, the motherhood constellation. This constellation determines the optimal form of the therapeutic alliance and permits a fuller use of the commonalities that have been identified. Whether or not a new form of psychotherapy is indeed emerging and what practical and theoretical consequences it may have for the general field will be considered.

I hope that by identifying and developing several central ideas that are fundamental to parent-infant psychotherapies—especially the notion of the motherhood constellation—this book will be helpful to those who practice these therapies as well as to those who theorize about and practice other forms of treatment with different populations.

PART I

THE CLINICAL
SYSTEM IN PARENT-INFANT
PSYCHOTHERAPY

CHAPTER 1

An Overview of the Clinical Situation

THE MAIN CHARACTERS in the clinical situation in parent-infant psychotherapy are one infant and one or two parents. If only one parent participates, it is invariably the primary caregiving parent—usually, but not necessarily, the mother. Thus, the "patient" is generally the mother[1]-infant dyad or the mother-father-infant triad. And there is the therapist. In the same vein, for the sake of clarity, I will generally use the masculine pronouns in referring to the infant. This device is not intended to suggest that problems are more common with male infants but simply to avoid confusion and clumsy expressions in referring to mother and baby.

This clinical situation consists of many different elements, its working parts. To visualize the elements of this system, I will use a model that is an elaboration of a schematic presented earlier (Stern-Bruschweiler & Stern, 1989). The relevant elements will be assembled by progressively adding them to the model. Separate chapters will later be devoted to detailed descriptions of the individual elements. Here I want to give an overview.

I will start with the bare minimum. At the very center of the model is the interaction between the infant and the mother. (Less often the triad is at the center. Whether it is the dyad or the triad that belongs at the center will be taken up later in this chapter.) This mother-infant interaction consists of the overt behaviors performed by each in response to and in con-

---

[1]Hereafter, whenever the word *mother* is used, it will mean the primary caregiver, except when otherwise specified. I use this shorthand because it is overwhelmingly the case that the mother is the primary caregiver.

cert with the other. The interaction is visible and audible to a third party, such as the therapist, as well as to the participant-observers.

For the purposes of schematization, let B stand for the baby and M for the mother, and the subscript $_{act}$ stand for their actions—that is, their overt behavior.

The observable interaction can be modeled as:

FIGURE 1.1

The basic elements for a purely behaviorist approach are now in place. A behavioral treatment based solely on what the two partners do could be implemented with these elements.

So far, however, we have only an interaction and not a relationship. A relationship is, among other things, the remembered history of previous interactions (Hinde, 1979). It is also determined by how an interaction is perceived and interpreted through the many lenses particular to the participant of the interaction. There are the lenses of fantasies, hopes, fears, family traditions and myths, important personal experiences, current pressures, and many other factors. For the purposes of the model, I will summarize this amalgam of remembered history and personal interpretation as the *representation* of the interaction. Thus we can add to the model the mother's representation (M_{rep}), consisting of how she subjectively experiences and interprets the objectively available events of the interaction, including her own behavior as well as the baby's.

This added element can be modeled as follows. (Hereafter, all phenomena that are externally observable events will be in bold block letters inside the ovals, and all intrapsychic, unobservable phenomena will be in lighter type outside the ovals.)

FIGURE 1.2

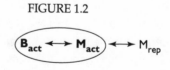

With this addition, the basic elements for a cognitive therapeutic approach or a limited psychodynamically inspired approach are now in place.

But the mother is not alone in forming a representation of what is happening during the interaction. As we shall see in chapters 5 and 6, the baby is avidly involved in constructing a representation of this interaction from the memory of its past occurrences. He too is building an interpretative and guiding representational world to deal with the current interaction. We must add an infant representation, the counterpart of the mother's representation. We thus add B_{rep} to the model:

FIGURE 1.3

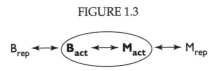

The therapist is the final member of the minimal cast of characters of this clinical situation. The therapist, like the others, not only has objective interactions with the primary caregiver and infant, but also has a representational world in which such interactions take on part of their meaning and in which the therapeutic intervention takes on its specific form. So we must add the therapist (T) to the model as follows:

FIGURE 1.4

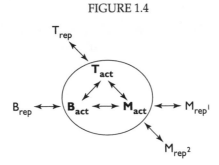

Note that I have added a M_{rep}^2, which is different from the M_{rep}^1 discussed above. When the mother is in the therapeutic process, that is, actively in the presence of the therapist, she may see her infant, and herself-as-mother, and what is happening between them in a different light than when she is alone. M_{rep}^2 is the view she acquires while in the therapeutic relationship. This parallel view can play an important therapeutic role as will be discussed below. In addition, the M_{rep}^2 will contain the mother's views of the therapist, and the T_{rep} will contain the therapist's views of the mother.

Now all the elements are in place for a psychoanalytically inspired approach via the mother and infant, including the provision of a role for transference and countertransference. It is now also possible for the mother's fantasy life to be seen to influence the infant's fantasies, and vice versa.

For the present, I will say no more about the therapist and temporarily leave that role out of the schematization for the sake of visual clarity. Just assume that the therapist is there as schematized. (A discussion of the therapist as a separate element follows in chapter 7.) Instead, I will now expand, schematically, the clinical situation beyond these minimal characters.

Some therapists consider the mother-father-infant triad as the "central patient." Others reserve this place for the mother-infant dyad, with the father playing a supporting and framing role. And yet others leave this question open, to be decided on a case-by-case basis. In any event, the father or his counterpart must be brought into our model. In actual practice the father's presence is variable unless it is made a condition for a session. Assuming he is there, he interacts with the mother and the infant (and the therapist), and he too evolves representations of his relationship with these others. So we can expand the model as follows:

FIGURE 1.5

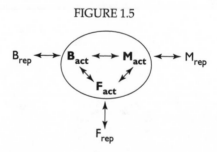

We now have present all the basic elements for a family-systemic approach, with or without an emphasis on individual psychodynamic past history—that is, the representations.

Often, especially in nontraditional, nonnuclear families, the complex of characters playing relatively important caregiving roles may be expanded and variable. Accordingly, the system can be opened up to include other crucial caregivers whose biological relation to the infant is not a criterion. The elements for a larger general system approach are now in place.

Finally, there are the levels of secondary and tertiary caregivers, support systems, social networks, and other factors at large, which are also always present, always acting, and always available as routes of therapeutic intervention. For the moment, I will collapse all these into the term *support system*, without recognizing the discrete potential influence of each of these factors, which include preschool nurseries, other parent-infant groupings, the medical care system, home visits, family networks, financial realities, and many others.

Support systems, in the above sense, can act as a continuous maintaining force or as an episodic influence on almost any (or several) elements of the basic model. The relationship of the support system to the basic model can be schematized as follows:

FIGURE 1.6

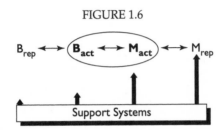

This schematic tries to capture the fact that the support system will have its greatest direct effects on the mother's representations (largely those of herself-as-mother and herself-as-person) and perhaps an equally great effect on what the mother does, behaviorally, with the baby. The direct effect of the support system on the baby's overt behavior will be much smaller and on the baby's representations almost negligible, because the efforts of the support system are mainly directed at the mother's maternal functioning.

Four basic points are highlighted by this model. First, almost all the elements are always present and acting. Second, all the elements are interdependent. Third, all the elements are in a dynamic, mutually influencing relationship. Finally, and most relevant, a successful therapeutic action that changes any one element will end up changing all the separate elements. For instance, if one can change how a mother subjectively experiences herself as a mother—that is, her representation of herself with her infant (M_{rep})—she will end up behaving differently with her infant in at least some of their interactions (that is, M_{act} will also change). The infant then will have to alter his behavior (B_{act}) to adjust to the new interactive reality. Since the infant's representation of the interaction (B_{rep}) depends on what happens during repeated interactions, he will be forced to take his changed behavior and that of his mother into account by readjusting his representation of current and future interactions; that is, his representation (B_{rep}) will have changed. And so the chain reaction occurs no matter where the first change was made. It could have occurred with the mother's interactive behavior (M_{act}) rather than with her representations (M_{rep}) with the same ultimate spread of changes throughout the model.

From this point of view, the different therapeutic approaches can be viewed as utilizing different ports of entry into a single dynamically interdependent system. To the extent that this is true, the nature of the system is a most powerful nonspecific commonality that transforms specific clinical interventions into general clinical outcomes. Therapeutic action will spread throughout the system so that it matters little how or why or where the initial change was brought about. In this way, the interrelated elements of the clinical situation will forge common outcomes from what were, initially, different approaches. We will explore in chapter 10 the extent to which this is true.

There is another reality of this clinical situation that tends to produce common outcomes. The nature of the system is such that in actual clinical practice it is hard, if not impossible, to restrict therapeutics to one port of entry alone. This "impurity" of approach is not due to any lack of trying on the part of practitioners, who work hard to direct their efforts into the one port of entry designated by their chosen approach. But the system does not allow for absolute purity. For instance, if one is therapeutically focused on the mother's fantasy life (M_{rep}) as the privileged port of entry, the actual interaction with the baby ($B_{act} \leftrightarrow M_{act}$) will of necessity intrude frequently, whether for feeding, changing, calming, paying attention to, or a coda of play. To ignore the interaction would be artificial and bad therapy, the interaction might end the session on practical grounds anyway. Or from the other side, if one's approach is primarily interested in the overt interaction and not at all in the mother's representational world, one will constantly be taken unawares by the profusion of fears, fantasies, memories, and so on, evoked by the parent-infant encounter. Again, ignoring these factors is therapeutically perilous, if not impossible. The therapist is forced to cross and recross the boundaries between the interpersonal and the intrapsychic. Similarly, regardless of the therapist's persuasion, the therapy is simultaneously an individual psychotherapy (with the primary caregiver), a couples therapy (with the husband and wife), and a family therapy (with the triad), either all at the same time or in sequence.

In spite of these difficulties in holding strictly to traditional perspectives and techniques, and in spite of the inevitable impurities in each approach, one element—that is, one port of entry—is privileged and receives most of the therapeutic attention and action.

Theoretically and technically, the situation seems to be quite complex, even messy. And so it is, as measured by the standards of other therapies with other populations. (It is compounded by the unavoidable confusion between therapeutic change and developmental change.) This situation introduces a theme that will reappear over and over in this book. What look like impurities, difficulties, messiness, oddities, and outright failures from standard perspectives are, in fact, intrinsic to the parent-infant clinical situation. It is not a compromised normal clinical situation. It is a *different* clinical situation, with its own imperatives and opportunities. It must be seen on its own terms, not as an imperfect or pale application of another established therapy. Let us now proceed to explore "its own terms."

CHAPTER 2

The Parents' Representational World

T HE REPRESENTATIONAL world of the parents is the first element of the clinical situation to be examined. The parents representations have played a key role in the history of parent-infant psychotherapies influenced by psychodynamic considerations. The parents' representations of the baby and of themselves-as-parents may be given the highest priority in the mind and practice of the therapist, or they may be more or less ignored. In either case, this mental world exists and plays an important role in determining the nature of the parents' relationship with the baby. It is useful to think of the clinical situation in terms of two parallel worlds: the real, objectifiable external world and the imaginary, subjective, mental world of representations. There is the real baby in the mother's arms, and there is the imagined baby in her mind. There is also the real mother holding the baby, and there is her imagined self-as-mother at that moment. And finally, there is the real action of holding the baby, and there is the imagined action of that particular holding. This representational world includes not only the parents' experiences of current interactions with the baby but also their fantasies, hopes, fears, dreams, memories of their own childhood, models of parents, and prophecies for the infant's future.

But what are such representations made of? How are they organized and how are they formed? No one knows exactly. They remain largely

Parts of this chapter and the following chapter have appeared in a less developed form in *The Infant Mental Health Journal,* 12(1991):174–186.

mysterious.[1] Rather than explore the nature of these representations here, I will defer that discussion until chapter 5, on the infant's representations, where we can proceed with a cleaner slate, since we will be trying to understand such representations as they develop in the infant. Until then, we can assume that we know well enough what we mean that we can proceed.

One preliminary comment, however, is needed. I will assume that these representations are mostly based on and built up from interactive experience—more precisely, from the subjective experience of being with another person. Accordingly, I will also describe these representations in terms of *schemas-of-being-with*. The interactive experience can be real, lived experience, or it can be virtual, imagined (fantasized) interactive experience. There is, however, always an interaction somewhere underneath. The reasons for this insistence on an origin in interactive experience are several. Object-related representations are not formed when the outside is taken inside, as is suggested by such terms as *internalization* and *introjection*. They are formed from the inside, on the basis of what happens to the self while with others. It is in this sense that these representations are not of objects or persons (now inside), or images, or words; they are of interactive experiences with someone. (The representational world is probably more like a montage of film clips than a collage of photographs or words.) I will assume that this is equally true when we speak of a parent's wishes, dreams, fears, and fantasies for their infant or for the self-as-parent. These, too, form around real or imagined pieces of interactions, as we shall see. It is with these reasons in mind that I refer to both representations and *schemas-of-being-with*.

As a provisional help. I will adopt the following terminology. It will be revisited in chapter 5.

1. A *schema-of-being-with* is based on the interactive experience of being-with a particular person in a specific way, such as being hungry and awaiting the breast or bottle or soliciting a smile and getting no response. It is a mental model of the experience of being—with—someone in a particular way, a way that is repetitive in ordinary life.

2. A *representation-of-being-with* is a network of many specific schemas-

---

[1]In the discussion of representations that follows here and in chapters 3 and 5, several points must be kept in mind. First, we do not know whether representations, especially nonverbal ones, are to be viewed as the product (some kind of entity) of various processes or as a procedure, a process itself to permit a kind of reexperiencing. Second, I will not, at this point, discuss representations in terms of introjections, internalization, projective identifications, and so on, because all these terms are for the most part historically associated with the formation of representations in the service of defense. Here, I will be concerned, as a starting point, with representations as a necessary and normal part of modeling the world of experience with others.

of-being-with that are tied together by a common theme or feature. Activities that are organized by one motivational system are frequently the common theme—for example, feeding, playing, or separation. Other representations are organized around affect experiences; they may be networks of schemas-of-being-sad-with or happy-with, for example. Yet other representations are assemblies made up of many representations that share a larger commonality such as person (all the networks that go with a specific person) or place or role. Representations thus are of different sizes and hierarchical status. I will make no attempt here to distinguish these or to signal the nature of the commonality that organizes the networks; these features can, I believe, be intuited from the context.

A Brief Historical Perspective

The conviction that the mother's representations can influence how she acts with her infant is as old as folk psychology. And for almost a hundred years the psychodynamic literature has commented richly on such influences as yet another example of the pervasiveness of conflictual themes in all domains of life, including the parent-infant relationship.

With the work of Donald Winnicott (1957, 1965, 1971) and Wilfred Bion (1963, 1967), among others, the fantasy life of the mother took on special, even unique importance. Her reveries, preoccupations, fantasies, and projective identifications (as forms of representations) involving the baby became of great interest to the psychic development of the infant. In fact, the mother's fantasies about her infant took on the status of one of the major building blocks for the infant's construction of a sense of identity. (This view will be examined further in chapter 5.)

Against this background, Selma Fraiberg revolutionized the perception of this situation by placing maternal fantasies and memories at the very center—practically (that is, clinically) speaking—of a pathogenic process that results in a disturbed parent-infant relationship or in the formation of an infant symptom (Fraiberg, 1980; Fraiberg, Adelson, & Shapiro, 1975). Her "ghost in the nursery" acting in the mother's mind is the example par excellence. This placing of the maternal representation at the core of the parent-infant clinical situation marked the beginning of "infant psychiatry" of a psychoanalytic inspiration. In a sense, a field was born (Call, Galenson, & Tyson, 1983; Rexford, Sander, & Shapiro, 1976).

Soon after, the same shift in focus took place in Europe, pioneered by Serge Lebovici (1983) and Leon Kreisler (Kreisler & Cramer, 1981; Kreisler, Fain, & Soulé, 1974). The prior work of Winnicott and Bion on maternal reveries certainly set the stage for these shifts in perspective on both sides of the Atlantic. At present, the importance of the mother's representations is evident in the attention given to the "imaginary baby" and the "phantasmatic baby" in the early problems of infancy (Cramer & Palacio-Espasa, 1993; Gautier, Lebovici, Mazet, & Visier, 1993; Lebovici, 1988).

There continues to be an explosion in psychoanalytically inspired therapies and research that focus on the maternal and (less often) the paternal representational world. Critics have been concerned that this movement runs the danger of becoming a new version of "blaming mother," since it is her representations that are the pathogenic agent. What is at issue, however, is the weight given to parental representations as a contributing cause of psychopathology, not whether they contribute at all. (This question will be taken up again in chapters 8 and 11.)

In the recent past, developmentalists and others became more intrigued by the representational world, particularly as it applies to parents and infants. They became convinced that broader and more systematic efforts were needed to explore these worlds. Different avenues of approach have resulted, such as role-relationship models (Horowitz, 1987), working models (Bowlby, 1980), and, at a more fundamental level, generalized event representations (Bretherton, 1984; Mandler, 1979, 1983, 1988; Nelson, 1986, 1988; Nelson & Greundel, 1981; Stern, 1989). As a result of these innovations, there now exists a growing and diverse body of ideas and data about the representational worlds involved in being an infant or parent.

I will take up the task of putting this body of information into some order, as it concerns one of the main elements of the clinical situation, and I will do it in terms of networks of schemas-of-being-with. What follows, then, is a partial list of different sets and subsets of parental representations that may be clinically pertinent. This list is too long and unwieldy to be directly usable, but it gives a sense of the mental worlds that may be candidates for clinical relevance and may require selective exploration in a psychotherapy.

The Mother's Networks of Schemas-of-Being-With

I will first briefly sketch the range of maternal representations that are potential candidates to become the (M_{rep}) of our diagrams.[2]

---

[2]For the rest of this section I will use the term "maternal" when referring to the mother or the primary caregiver and reserve the term "paternal representation" for a father who is not the primary caregiver.

SCHEMAS ABOUT THE INFANT

The mother's infant-centered schemas include the baby as the particular son or daughter who belongs to her-as-the-mother and to her husband-as-the-father; to her other children, as a sibling; and to her parents as a grandchild. Each of these is a slightly or very different baby who may look different and act differently. These schemas include the prediction of the baby at various older stages. There is also the baby as a person—that is, as a type of personality or character. This is largely a judgment about temperament, to the extent that it describes the natural tendencies the baby brings into a relationship.

One could ask, are these schemas-of-being-with really based on interactions? Two examples may suffice to address this question. The representation of the baby-as-the-particular-daughter-to-her-as-a-mother is likely to be made up of a network of schemas that could, for example, include such real or fantasied interactive experiences as someone's looking back and forth between mother and daughter and saying, "Oh, how much she resembles you," as the mother feels herself swell with love and perhaps pride; or a moment of complicity between daughter and mother laughing together; or a fantasy of the interaction on showing her daughter the house she grew up in; or the feeling of narcissistic satisfaction in caring for her. All these moments are based on interactions. A type of personality or temperament may seem harder to put into the form of an interactive schema-of-being-with, but it is not. Such a network for, say, a very active baby could include such schemas as the way he moves around in the mother's arms when she is trying to feed him or the way he is always trying to get out of the baby seat as she watches with vigilance, some fear, and perhaps some admiration, but always with her muscles ready to jump. The point is that these networks consist of schemas that are founded on interactive experience. They are not pieces of abstract knowledge that has moved beyond the specificity of particular instances.

These many overlapping represented babies must also be viewed in a historical perspective, leading up to the present time and proceeding into the future (for the elaboration of the represented "baby" continues for the rest of the mother's life). The represented baby has a long prenatal history. As the fetus grows and develops in the mother's uterus, the represented baby undergoes a parallel development in her mind. The two developmental courses are not truly parallel, however, since the networks of schemas about the fetus develop under the influence of psychic and social factors as well as biological ones. For instance, at around 4 months of gestation there is a leap in the richness and specificity of the maternal representations of her fetus-as-infant. These days, this quantum leap is likely to have been triggered by an echography, when the parents see an image of the fetus (Piontelli, 1992). If not, there will probably be a big spurt around 4 months anyway, because that is when mothers start to feel the fetus move and the reality of the existence of the baby-to-be suddenly becomes palpable and more imperative. Recent studies (for example, Ammaniti, 1991, 1994; Ammaniti et al., 1992; Benoit, Parker, & Zeanah, in press; Fava Vizziello, Antonioli, Cocci, & Invernizzi, 1992; Fava Vizziello, Antonioli, Cocci, Invernizzi, & Cristante, 1993; Zeanah & Barton, 1989; Zeanah & Benoit, in press; Zeanah, Keener, & Anders, 1986; Zeanah, Keener, Stewart, & Anders, 1985) are starting to provide fascinating information about this "morphogenesis" of the represented baby. There is a general agreement that between the fourth and seventh months of gestation there is a rapid growth in the richness, quantity, and specificity of the networks of schemas about the baby-to-be.[3]

At first glance, one might expect this growing elaboration of the represented baby to continue right up to birth. But that is not what the researchers have found. The elaboration of the networks peaks at about the seventh month. The studies suggest that between the seventh and ninth months there is a kind of undoing of the reported representations. The representations about the baby decrease and become progressively less clearly delineated, less specific, and less rich. Why? The most plausible answer is that mothers intuitively protect their baby-to-be and themselves from a potential discordance between the real baby and a too specifically represented baby. After all, birth is the meeting place for the baby now in her arms and the one in her mind. As far as possible, she needs to keep the real situation unburdened with the past so that she and her real baby can start to connect, with a minimum of interfering baggage.

With the birth of the baby, the mother starts to rebuild her representations of who her baby is and will become. But now she normally does so along the general outlines provided by the real baby (such as the baby's sex and temperament) and by who she is turning out to be as a real mother. Many of the old schemas she held during pregnancy will reappear, but they will be varied and reelaborated to fit the given reality.

Many (for example, T. B. Brazelton, personal communication, 1993) have found that what mothers really do between the seventh and ninth months is to undo their more positive representations in order to prevent disappointments but that their negative ones involving fears of deforma-

---

[3]Different aspects of the representation, such as the concern with the baby's activity and assertiveness, each may develop at different times during the pregnancy (Ammaniti, 1994).

tion and death flourish underground, remaining or becoming largely unconscious. In any event the mother adjusts her representational world as best she can to create a constructive mental work space for her future representations.

The represented baby did not, in fact, begin at conception, but long before, in the whole life history of the doll play and fantasies of the mother as a girl and an adolescent. This early history of the representations of a baby may be of clinical utility, and it may not. Many excellent mothers were quite uninterested in motherhood and all its aspects until well into reproductive adulthood. I don't believe that this early history is predictive in general, but it may be clinically useful in a given case and thus falls among the potential candidates to play an influencing role in the current clinical situation.

SCHEMAS ABOUT HERSELF

With the birth of her first baby, the mother's basic status and identity in life are changed overnight. A sweeping reappraisal of the organization and priority of most of her self-representations begins. Some of these changes may have been well anticipated and planned out by the mother before the birth; others will have been unforeseen and will sneak up on her. But all these changes will have to be reworked constantly under the pressing realities of daily life with baby during the next several months. While the mother is behaviorally organizing the baby's world—his cycles of sleep and hunger—the baby is helping her to reorganize her own representational world. He is turning her into a mother and forcing her to construct new networks of schemas for herself (Lebovici, 1988).

The networks of schemas that undergo reworking are the mother's self as woman, mother, wife, career-person, friend, daughter, granddaughter; her role in society; her place in her family of origin; her legal status; herself as the person with cardinal responsibility for the life and growth of someone else; as the possessor of a different body; as a person "on call" 24 hours a day; as an adventurer in life, a creator, a player in evolution's grand scheme, and so on—in short, almost every aspect of her life. All these networks are thrown by events into the postpartum crucible, potentially to be reforged. It will happen again with the second and third babies, but with less intensity and usually with less mutation in the representational world.

These major reorganizations are well known and widely written about. Nonetheless, it is perhaps worthwhile to enlarge upon some that are often less discussed, as we will need them later.

There exists within most women an important identity as the daughter of her parents. Even if she is an autonomous, independent woman, well engaged in her work and marriage, this life-long identity as daughter occupies a kind of historical center of gravity. With the birth of her own daughter she must shift that center of gravity from being primarily the daughter-of-her-mother to being the mother-of-her-daughter. In one blow, part of the fixed representational world has shifted irreversibly.

The new mother must give up, in large part, whatever long-held fantasies she has safeguarded about repairing, correcting, or redoing her childhood or being able to return there when she needs to. Now, all the faults, disappointments, and omissions that occurred in her girlhood in relation to her parents become fixed forever as past history. She can perhaps repair the past, but never again as a girl. A world (even if part of it is illusion) is gone. And there is often a profound sense of loss that runs beneath the sense of worlds gained. Several clinicians have commented on this sadness that may, in some cases, contribute to the normal postpartum blues (Manzano & Palacio-Espasa, 1990).

This reappraisal of primary roles is sometimes delayed by a grace period after the birth, when the mother's mother again takes on a maternal role to her daughter. Sometimes this permits repairs in the old relationship. As often as not, no such opportunity presents itself.

One of the reasons I have chosen to use as an example that network of schemas-of-being-with involving mother and daughter is because of its importance as a spawning ground for so many of the positive and negative fantasies, hopes, and fears elaborated by new mothers: "I will be just like" or "I will be the exact opposite of the way my mother was with me." The representation of her relationship with her father is often less immediately and violently challenged (as it may have been when she got married) but will eventually have to undergo a similar reappraisal.

A second challenge to the new mother's representational status quo is presented by the realistic need and desire to put the baby's interests before her own (Winnicott, 1957). Altering the balance between narcissism and altruism is not easy, especially when some of her central life goals—such as a career—may suffer. This representational shift demanded of the primary caregiving mother is almost always of some clinical importance and may comprise the nexus of the clinical problem.

The creation or adjustment of the many networks of schemas mentioned above provide potential candidates to influence the actual mother-infant interaction. The list is only indicative, not complete.

SCHEMAS ABOUT HER HUSBAND

The shift in going from a couple to a triad (couple plus baby) inevitably alters the mother's networks of schemas of her husband—as husband, as father, and as man. The new practical realities and priorities imposed by the baby day and night put her previous representations about the couple under constant pressure to be modified. The opening up of the couple to include the baby is an obvious potential source of conflict between husband and wife, with sequelae for the parent-infant relationships.

Many of the representations that the mother may evolve about the baby imply a complementary representation about her husband. For instance, the representation of the baby as "marital glue," holding the marriage together, implies a representation of the husband as potentially leaving her and now being stuck in the marriage. The schema of baby as "her lover" implies that the husband is now—what? her provider? her protector? her parent? her enemy? The representation of the baby as the one person in the world who will, finally, love her unconditionally has implications about how her husband now loves her. The representation of the baby as a threat to the survival of the marital couple implies that the husband is unable to cope with his own needs and demands for exclusive care—that is, the husband as the "other baby." The baby can be the fantasized offspring of another man (such as a lost lover or the mother's father); in this case the complementary representation is of the husband as second choice and cuckolded unto the second generation. There is the baby who is a "gift" from her to her husband, implying that he is being rewarded for something or receiving his rightful due. Or the baby can be viewed as a gift to her from her husband, with similar implications.

Often the shape of the representation for the baby (for example, as her lover) takes its form along the existing fault lines in the couple (she had really wanted to marry another man who left her and whom she has not yet gotten over). In this way the representation concerning the husband can become exaggerated or made manifest, when before it was unimportant or latent.

Viewed in this light, how are these representations to be interpreted? Are they dyadic—that is, about two interdependent dyads (mother-baby, wife-husband)—or are they best conceived of as triadic?

There are two related issues here. The first is clinical. Different therapeutic approaches make different assumptions about what is the basic unit of the represented relationships. A nuclear family consisting of mother, father, girl, and boy will be seen and treated by many therapists as six separate dyads, each potentially requiring attention. More psychoanalytic therapists will reorganize the six dyadic representations into two basic or predominating Oedipal triads. And a family therapist will see and treat a single composite unit, collapsing all the dyads and triads. Different treatment experiences result from these diverse assumptions, which raise a second and more fundamental issue. Leaving clinical utility aside, are there natural or basic, hierarchically privileged units by which humans tend or prefer to organize multiple relationships? This is an open question. One could argue that developmentally the dyad is the earliest and most basic unit. Attachment is dyadic, not triadic; two people, but not three, can mutually gaze into one another's eyes. One can also argue that a third person is always present (in reality or imagination) as the necessary context to define and bound a dyad. In that sense there are only triads (the Oedipal triad being only a special case). Finally, there is the systems theory view, in which dyads and triads are the lower order sub-units that are contextualized by the higher order composite unit.

In any event, with the advent of the baby the mother's network of schemas of her husband as father, lover, husband, man, and so on, will be altered. And these shifts will be largely determined by the imperative construction of the family unit. In this sense the mother's representation of her mate becomes "triadified," a term suggested by Serge Lebovici (1993; see also Corboz-Warnery, Fivaz-Depeursinge, Gertsch-Bettens, & Favez, 1993; Corboz-Warnery, Forni, & Fivaz, 1989; Fivaz-Depeursinge et al., 1994; Gertsch-Bettens, Corboz-Warnery, Favez, & Fivaz-Depeursinge, 1992).

Just as the maternal networks of schemas of the baby underwent ontogenetic changes during the pregnancy and the postpartum period, so do her networks about her husband. Massimo Ammaniti and Graziella Fava Vizziello have independently reported that as the pregnancy progresses the soon-to-be-mother's representations of her husband—as a person, mate, and potential father—become more positive in general (Ammaniti, 1991, 1994; Ammaniti et al., 1992; Fava Vizziello, Antonioli, Cocci, & Invernizzi, 1992; Fava Vizziello, Antonioli, Cocci, Invernizzi, & Cristante, 1993). During this phase she is more likely to imagine more resemblances between the future baby and the future father than between herself and the future baby. After the birth of the baby, there is a reversal. The mother tends to see the father/husband more negatively between birth and the baby's third month. Also, she now sees the baby as being more like her and less like her husband. (The mother's representations concerning her own mother suffer the same negative fate after birth as those concerning the husband, as I will describe later in this chapter.) In a sense, the mother pushes the others away during this initial phase and takes the baby into her own positive sphere of influence, perhaps better to forge the necessary attachment bonds. But even when the mother does do this (it is more likely to occur in a traditional family structure, especially when breast-feeding and maternal leave join together to privilege the mother's primary parental role, at least during this initial phase) another network of schemas for the husband takes on greater importance: the husband as the keystone of the support system that facilitates the mother's primary role. The mother's representation of this paternal role can have enormous clinical relevance. This point will be taken up in more detail in chapter 11.

SCHEMAS ABOUT HER OWN MOTHER

With the arrival of the baby, the new mother is likely to start, consciously or unconsciously, to reevaluate her own mother. Here, too, well-established representations are drawn into that postpartum crucible of change. Most often new or at least more elaborated and understood networks of schemas of her own mother emerge. These include her own mother as mother to her when she was a child, as a wife, as a woman, and as the grandmother to the new child.

Folk wisdom and clinicians have long suggested that the mother's representations of her own mother-as-mother-to-her-in-childhood will greatly influence how she will be as mother to her own infant now. Recently there has been an explosion of research on just this point (Fonagy, Steele, Steele, Moran, & Higgit, 1991; Main & Goldwyn, 1985; Main, Kaplan, & Cassidy, 1989; Zeanah & Barton, 1989). This research not only supports the notion of a strong intergenerational influence but goes even further and suggests that the nature of the mother's current representation of her own mother-as-mother may be the single best predictor of the pattern of attachment that the mother will establish with her own infant at 12 months of age (secure, ambivalent, avoidant, or disorganized). It must be recalled that the pattern of attachment (Ainsworth, Blehard, Waters, & Wall, 1978) seen at 12 months is proving to be one of the best predictors of a child's general adaptation during the preschool and early school years (see, for example, Grossmann & Grossmann, 1991; Parks, Stevenson-Hinde, & Marris, 1991; Sroufe, 1983).

It is not surprising that in large part women learn how to mother from their mothers. We have the concepts to help understand this process, such as modeling, identification, and internalization. A woman can learn from a negative model ("I will never act as she did") as well as from a positive one. The research on adult attachment, however, has added a new and unexpected dimension to the issues involved in this intergenerational effect. The aspect of the mother's representation of her own mother that is most predictive of her future maternal behavior is not necessarily what happened in the past—whether she had a good or bad mothering experience—but rather the way in which she thinks and talks about her own mother now. Does she talk about these networks of schemas with coherence? with too much or not enough emotional distance? and with what degree of current involvement or dismissal? In other words, the form of the telling may be as important as—or even more important than—the content of what she tells. The narrative of the past history may be more relevant than the past history itself, and the narrative is one exposition of the representation.

For example, a new mother could describe her past history with a terrible, inadequate mother, where there is every reason to believe that her mother was, in fact, quite bad. If, however, she has evolved a representation of this unhappy early experience that is coherent, balanced, involving but not overinvolving, she is likely to contribute to a secure attachment pattern on the part of her infant. Or the reverse could occur. A mother could describe a wonderful early experience of being mothered but in a narrative exposition of her representation of these happy events that is overinvolved, incoherent, and imbalanced. That mother is more likely to contribute to an insecure attachment pattern with her child. Narrative coherence has won out over historical truth as the stronger predictor.

This finding is counterintuitive. Yet it opens the door for a woman to overcome a bad past or escape the fate of repeating it by way of the psychological work she has accomplished in understanding, putting into perspective, and rendering coherent her past, especially her experience of being mothered (see Fonagy, Steele, Steele, et al., 1991).

It may be that this is true for all such representations. Research is just beginning on this issue, and it has begun on the maternal networks of schemas about her own mother. Further implications of these findings will be taken up in other chapters.

SCHEMAS ABOUT HER FATHER

Occasionally the father has been the most stable "mothering" and attachment figure in a woman's life. In such a case, do the same basic issues apply as we have noted for the representations of the mother's mother? This is an open question that raises other issues. For example, is the real mother unique for a girl-as-future-mother because of identification along sex identity and sex role lines? Is there a problem of incompatibility in that the father is the main object of both a mothering dyad and an Oedipal triad? These issues are beyond our scope here, but they require attention.

When the father occupies a more traditional role, there are a host of representations of him that may assume clinical relevance. For instance, has he been over idealized as a model and standard, or has he been devalued? After all, the mother in imagining the future life course for her child, especially for a son, will use her husband, her father, and perhaps a brother as the main navigational points to steer toward or away from.

SCHEMAS ABOUT THE FAMILIES OF ORIGIN

Family therapists and those interested in transgenerational continuity have also begun to explore the clinical situation in which disturbances of the parent-infant relationship provide the motive for seeking therapy (e.g., Byng-Hall, 1986; Byng-Hall & Stevenson-Hinde, 1991; Fivaz-Depeursinge, Corboz-Warnery, & Frenck, 1990; Hinde & Stevenson-Hinde, 1988; Lamour, 1988; Stoleru & Moralès-Huet, 1989). From this systemic perspective, different representations are highlighted. For instance, there is the infant whose role it will be to maintain family continuity (e.g., carry on the family name, perpetuate the family business, or become the fourth generation of lawyers). The power of these representations over the infant's development can be enormous. Or there is the infant who will avenge an ancient but still active family wrong or feud or disgrace. There is the infant who legitimizes his parents' previously unacceptable marriage by opening the family door of the rejecting generation of his grandparents. There is the infant who must play a crucial role in the upward mobility of the family. This representation is especially strong in immigrant families (which include no small number of families in the United States and more and more in Europe); it will last for several generations after the actual immigration and can be an all-pervading influence. The resulting pressures on the infant and child to play an important role in the family's assimilation and success may make it impossible to see who the child really is and to recognize his natural gifts and tendencies. In communist and other highly collectivist societies, the baby is seen as belonging primarily to the state rather than to the mother or family. This too is a powerful parental and societal representation, with consequences for the baby's emotional life and social experience.

There are also the specific types of characters recognized within families. These create slots to place the infant within the typology of the family, which is particular to each family. For instance, the little girl may be a "beauty" like Aunt Claire, who was also promiscuous and "bad"; being beautiful is risky in that family. Or the little girl may be "brilliant," a "natural student" like Aunt Jeanne, who was a professor at the university but never married and was labeled an "old maid" at an early age. Family types carry much extra (sometimes hidden) baggage for a child, with inevitable implications for prophesied relationships.

Representations of the family of origin also play a major role in influencing how each new parent acts as a member of the new nuclear triad. For instance, the boy who played the role of conciliator and diplomat in a turbulent family may slip into the same role in his own new nuclear family, keeping the peace and framing the dyad of his wife and child.

Thus the parents each carry networks of schemas-of-being-with that include their own families of origin and their unique organizations. This situation can be schematized as follows, borrowing and adapting a schema developed by Joan Stevenson-Hinde (personal communication, 1993) for a nuclear family of four in which the mother was the second child and the father was the first child in their original nuclear families of four.

FIGURE 2.1

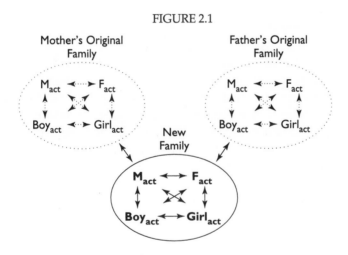

In other words, the family interactions of one generation provide some of the representations that guide the interactions of the new nuclear family.

These considerations bring us back to the question of how such a complex composite unit may be represented. The work of family systems analysts such as David Reiss (1989) and John Byng-Hall (1986, in press) helps answer this question. They suggest that the multiple, interconnected, complex family interactions are reorganized into units such as family scripts, myths, legends, stories, paradigms, and secrets. Such representational units are generalizations and abstractions of interactional events. For instance, Byng-Hall and Stevenson-Hinde define a "family script" as "shared [by all members] working models of who does what, where, when and how in specific contexts" (1991, p. 189) such as when mother and father argue, when grandma visits, when father drinks too much, or when mother has a migraine. In our terminology a "family script" would be a network of schemas-of-being-with that is shared by all members.

When an attachment theory viewpoint is added to this family perspective, one gets a different reading of what, in other viewpoints, were dyadic or triadic units. For instance, in a nuclear family with a girl and a boy, Byng-Hall and Stevenson-Hinde (1991) speak of one member (in this case the girl) successfully "capturing an attachment figure" (in this case the father). The girl not only establishes a strong, exclusive dyadic relationship with father but actively prevents the father from functioning as an attachment figure to brother and mother. What might have been described as an Oedipal triangle in a psychoanalytic perspective is here viewed as a four-member family interactive pattern maintained by shared scripts.

Reiss (1989) has also introduced the concept of "family practices" such as "rituals" (e.g., Christmas dinner), "hallowed grounds" (father's reading chair), and "sacred [to the family] objects" (a special photo album). "Practices" replace representations as the key to providing the continuity in family functioning. Stated differently, acting in concert in the present replaces memories from the past (reorganized as representations). There is a kind of group memory where each member has intimate knowledge of only his or her piece of the whole. And only when all the members come together can the group memory operate to permit the enactment of a family practice.

I do not believe that this notion of practices profoundly alters or diminishes the principal role I have given to representations, but it does qualify it in some situations. Exploring this idea further, unfortunately, is beyond the scope of this book.

SCHEMAS ABOUT SUBSTITUTE PARENTAL FIGURES

The group of representations about substitute parental figures can be of great importance therapeutically, especially when the substitute figure (a grandmother, an aunt, a sister) has made up for negative experiences with the parents. In such cases it can be helpful to identify positive "parenting" experiences that can be used therapeutically as alternative models around which to build modifications. We will return to this issue in part III.

SCHEMAS ABOUT FAMILY OR CULTURAL PHENOMENA NEVER
ACTUALLY EXPERIENCED BY THE MOTHER

So far, I have stressed the fact that representations are largely based on real interactions that have been experienced. Some representations, however, including some powerful ones, can be based on cultural or historical events never experienced directly but represented nonetheless in terms of narratives or semantic knowledge. For instance, there may be a long-dead family member whose positive or negative influence lives on, such as the celebrated great-grandfather who founded the family business and whose qualities remain the reference and standard. While the mother never knew or directly experienced this person, he has a "narrative reality" for her and perhaps for her new son, the great-great-grandson. This concept is no different from a family myth or legend, discussed earlier, but it stresses the narrative nature of some representations and opens a way for conceptualizing how the ideals and standards of the larger culture (via the media, education, or the grapevine) become represented.

It is important to note that representations can change in the absence of the interactions of which they are composed. Robertson's classical work with children experiencing brief separations from their parents provides an example (Robertson, 1958). The children first began to avoid photographs of their parents and later, on the parents' return, the parents themselves. This shift in representations does not, however, occur in an interactive vacuum. There are many repeated interactions, of less than optimal success, with secondary caregivers that by comparison may contribute to the alteration: "I never knew what I was missing or what I really wanted until. . . ."

Today, the media provide more and more of the representations of who the baby and mother ideally are and ought to be and what constitutes competence, age appropriateness, and so on. The power of this source of maternal representations cannot be underestimated.

The Father's Networks of
Schemas-of-Being-With

The father's representational world is largely parallel to the maternal representational world we have just explored. The extent to which the two worlds are different or need to differ remains an open question, but two differences are clearly seen in families where the mother is the primary caregiver during the first year or so of the baby's life. First, the father's representational world is often less violently shaken by the birth of the baby, and the work of reorganizing multiple networks of schemas is carried out over a longer time period. Fathers often say that the irreversible shift in center of gravity from son-to-his-own-father to father-to-his-own-son may not occur until the boy is several years old. This lag, so to speak, may put the new parents out of synch with each other as parents, a potential source of conflict.

The second difference concerns the supporting role the father must play in sustaining and framing the mother-infant dyad. This role involves a special subset of representations with sources in the father's individual and family past, as well as important cultural directives. This topic will be discussed in more detail in chapter 11.

Four Clinical Models of the Representational World

The list of maternal and paternal representations could go and on. In fact, to account for all the clinical possibilities it could end up being synonymous with the parents' entire representational world. That is why I said at the outset that the list was too big and too unwieldy. It is, nonetheless, helpful in that clinicians who do take into account the parents' representations scan most of those just described when taking a complete history.

Once this vast representational material has been scanned, in whatever completeness or detail, some model of psychopathology is needed to organize and reduce it and to estimate the nature and extent of the problem at hand. Four main models for doing so seem to be used. Each has advantages and problems, both for clinical conduct and for conceptualizing the research and theoretical issues at stake.

THE DISTORTION MODEL

The first model evaluates to what extent subjective reality—that is the representation—has been distorted from some objective view of reality. The measure in this model is the distance between these two realities. Many diverse clinical examples leap to mind: situations of risk and handicap, such as the developmentally lagged baby who is seen by the parents as completely normal and in need of no special interventions, or situations of mismatch, such as the objectively normal baby who is seen as hyperactive by a mother who wanted a temperamentally more passive baby, or situations of psychodynamic distortion, such as the baby who is seen by the divorced mother to be not at all like—in fact, the opposite of—the estranged father-husband whom she now hates.

In such cases, the distortion model is useful and even necessary. There are however, two major problems with this model. First is the assumption that there is an objective reality that can be used as a meaningful reference point. Most parental views of their babies are constructions, as we have seen, not objective observations taken from a few steps back. Researchers on infant temperament using parental reports and objective measures constantly run up against this situation. Are the parents' views wrong? Not necessarily. In the case of a developmentally lagged baby, a distorted optimistic view on the part of the parents may predict better than any objective measure, by fulfilling its prophecy. (I am not arguing against objective testing, only suggesting that it be viewed in the light of the actual psychic environment of development, which is formed in great part by parental constructions.)

The second problem with the distortion model is that clinicians tend to see all distortions from objective reality as negative and thus potentially psychopathogenic. But that is not at all the case. Most parents create a set of positive distortions about their baby. Parents joke when they say that their baby is the most beautiful, fascinating, captivating, lovable baby in the world, but emotionally they experience these distortions as powerful subjective reality.

Charles Zeanah and his colleagues (Zeanah et al., 1985) conducted a study of the parents' perceptions of their offspring before and after birth. They found that parents overwhelmingly tended to attribute positive qualities to their fetuses and newborn babies. In fact, the absence of such positive distortions is a grave prognostic sign in new parents, for they are part of what is meant by "maternal love" or, in Winnicott's term, the "primary maternal preoccupation."

Another good example of positive distortion is the maternal tendency to work in the child's "zone of proximal development" (Vygotsky, 1962). Mothers intuitively teach the child to speak or act at a level that is just a little ahead but not too far ahead of where the child currently is. The child is thus drawn forward, so to speak. To do this, the mother must act as if the baby can do something he is not yet capable of but will be soon. She is interacting, now, with her future baby. She is working within the framework of an optimistic future-oriented construction.

THE DOMINANT THEME MODEL

In another model, inspired mostly by the psychodynamic orientation, the baby is represented in the mother's eyes as taking part in and being woven into themes that have been ongoing, conflictual, and problematic throughout the mother's life or that at least predate the life of the baby. These themes are dominant in that they take up too much representational space and time. The networks of schemas devoted to such a theme are so large and constantly activated that they command too much of the parents' behavior. Here, the measure is the pervasiveness and intrusiveness of the theme. How much representational room is left to view the baby in the many possible ways the baby offers, other than the ways dictated by the dominant theme?

Multiple examples of dominant themes fill the clinical literature. There is the "replacement baby" to take the place of a child who was aborted or died or to replace a recently dead family member—Selma Fraiberg's "ghost in the nursery." There is the baby who is needed as an antidepressant to activate and animate a depressed mother. There is the baby who will provide unconditional love. The baby may be seen as avenger, as family saviour, as gift, as marital glue or, conversely, as a marital wedge. There is the baby whom one of the parents can narcissistically identify with. The theme may be the baby as a stranger, or the baby who was switched with another baby right after birth; the baby as companion, or complement to an older sib; the baby as a "normal" child or a "perfect" child or as a genius, and so on.

Several questions arise concerning these themes. How many such dominant themes are commonly found in the culture? across cultures? within an individual mother? Psychoanalysis traditionally assumes that in each person's life there are only a few central, conflictual themes (e.g., the Oedipal theme, separation, and sibling rivalry), which are simply reedited to embrace new situations and new people, such as a new baby. The recent research of Luborsky and Crits-Christoph (1990) on psychotherapy transcripts supports this view in finding that in any therapy, very few core conflictual themes—only one or two—are in play. Is this also true for the kinds of dominant themes we see in mothers?

In a related vein, is the content of these dominant themes concordant with the predictions of psychoanalytic theory, attachment theory, or any other theory? Or are we dealing here with a population of dominant themes that has not been adequately classified? We may well be, and that should not come as a great surprise. Motherhood as a cardinal psychobiological life situation has never been the focus of a systematic search for central themes. It may introduce themes that are unique to itself and not derivatives of other general psychodynamic themes, or only so in a secondary sense. (The unique situation of being a new parent and the specific themes that arise are discussed in chapter 11, as part of the motherhood constellation.) Such a classification might prove heuristic and should be attempted. Graziella Fava Vizziello has attempted an adaptational classification of these themes for prognostic purposes. She asks whether they are "reparative," "maintaining," or "destructive" to the adaptational status quo. Future work here will be interesting.

THE NARRATIVE COHERENCE MODEL

The narrative coherence model is a version of what in psychoanalysis has come to be identified as the hermeneutic model, psychoanalysis as narrative coconstruction between patient and therapist (Ammaniti & Stern, 1991/1994; Ricoeur, 1977; Schafer, 1981; Spence, 1976). In this view, the story that one constructs, believes, and tells about the past has a "narrative coherence" that is thought to have more of an influence on current psychological life than does the "historical truth," which can be known only by way of the narrative anyway.

As I mentioned earlier, the mother's representation of her own mother-as-mother-to-her-as-a-child is proving to be of great clinical interest and predictive power regarding the kind of mother she will be to her own child. Research in this area has unexpectedly opened the door to a narrative coherence model. One of the more striking findings from this research, as I have noted, is that in many cases what is most predictive of the current pattern of attachment between mother and her new infant is not necessarily the kind of attachment experience that the mother herself had as a child (the historical truth) but rather the nature of the narrative that she tells about her own mother-as-a-mother (the narrative coherence). In effect, the narrative coherence of the mother's representation can be more predictive than what actually happened to her as a child.

That is the essence of a hermeneutic-narrative model. The predictive power is not whether the mother's representation is true or distorted or dominated by a particular theme. It is the coherence, comprehensibility, continuity, consistency, plausibility, and emotional balance of the narrative told—that is, of the representation as narrated. This is entirely different from a dominant theme model. And it is curious that attachment research in the tradition of developmental psychology, on the one hand, and psychoanalysis in its most minimalist hermeneutic form, on the other, have approached one another to this extent.

One major challenge of the narrative model is what to do with historical truth—that is, "objective truth"—especially in a psychological domain such as attachment, which is so grounded in objective behavioral observation. The great advantage of this dilemma is that the interface between these two models will now have to be more fully explored around a well-defined issue.

One could argue that the Adult Attachment Interview (Main & Goldwyn, 1985) is really evaluating the current situation of attachment between the mother and her own mother and that the narrative coherence and style are only the window into this current relationship. In other words, the interview tells more about the current mother-daughter relationship than about the past one. In that case, the current attachment status of the mother to her own mother is what has the greater predictive power than the historical, past attachment status of the mother as a child. If this is so, our notions about "sensitive periods" in attachment will have to take this into account.

Or, even more probable, narrative coherence is measuring the mother's ability to put together a mental model—a kind of psychological sketch—of her own mother. This ability, which includes insight, emotional perspective, and organizing capacity (ego strength), among other things, may permit the mother to transcend the potential fate of the historical truth of her attachment history as a child (Fonagy, Steele, Moran, Steele, & Higgit, 1991).

In summary, it is not yet clear how much each of the following contributes to the predictive value of the Adult Attachment Interview: the current attachment status of the mother with her own mother, or the coherence with which she tells about it, or her ability to achieve a certain emotional perspective via self-reflection. Each implies a different model. The answer to this question is important, as it may tell us much about the manner in which psychotherapy may operate to effect changes. After all, psychotherapy can change a life narrative; it cannot change the past.

The Out-of-Developmental-Phase or Ontogenetic Model

As we saw earlier in the chapter, the mother's representations of her infant, herself, and her husband undergo a regular pattern of changes during pregnancy and after. These phases provide yet another way to organize and view potential indices of psychopathology. Researchers are beginning to be able to describe a sort of "normal growth and development curve" for many of the mother's networks of schemas-of-being-with. The ontogenetic model would address the out-of-phaseness of representations, rather than their distortedness, theme predominance, or narrative coherence. For instance, if a mother gives birth to a premature infant with a gestational age of 7 months, she has not had the normal time allotted to undo the specificity of her representations of the fetus-as-baby-to-be appropriate to the seventh month of pregnancy; her representations will be out of phase, with possible pathogenic implications. The baby is thus doubly disadvantaged, being hit with a developmental lag in his own functions and unfinished representations in his mother's mind.

In a similar but less dramatic fashion, representations (of infant, self, or others) well after birth that are appropriate for one period may not be so for another. Sometimes mothers remain stuck on a phase-specific set of representations long beyond the phase (e.g., the "dependent baby"). Sometimes their representations are in advance of things (e.g., the baby who is seen as autonomous long before he is).

Perhaps the most distressing situation of all is when the parents cannot design and elaborate a developmental course for their represented baby. I am thinking, in particular, of those situations where the parents are prevented by a medical reality from knowing or imagining what the future of their infant will be like. This happens whenever there is a significant developmental lag, such as with considerable prematurity, and with almost all handicaps or pervasive disabilities, such as cerebral palsy. The sure guidelines of normal development are no longer applicable. This uncertainty covers the relatively small (Will my baby be able to sit up "on time"?) to the enormous (Will my child ever walk, talk, be able to go to school, marry, have children, earn a livelihood?). If there is a medical uncertainty about any of these, the parents are put in an impossible situation in which they cannot elaborate a meaningful representational structure of the future. They are in a representational vacuum. And when you cannot imagine the future, you cannot evaluate the present. One of the main pillars of the whole enterprise of representation has been taken away.

This situation also happens often with straightforward, well-defined handicaps such as deafness or blindness. For example, it is only in a small minority of cases that the doctors can and do say to the parents of a newborn, "Your baby is totally blind; he will never see" and that the parents accept, assimilate, and act on that information. Instead, the doctor is more likely to say—or be forced to say, because of legitimate uncertainties—"There is a severe problem with your baby's eyes and sight. The worst scenario is that he will never see. On the other hand we do not yet know the full extent of the impairment or its future course. We must evaluate it. There are, at present, no cures for this condition." The evaluation then takes several months, ending in a slight but potentially important difference of emphasis or nuance between what the pediatrician and the ophthalmologist have said. Another opinion is sought. A little later the parents hear of a new operation or treatment just developed and performed on two cases in Madrid, or New York, or Tel Aviv; a correspondence begins, and a visit is arranged. By now the baby is one year old. In such cases involving blindness, deafness, and some sensorimotor deficits, the uncertainty regarding the future drags on for years and years. And of course it can be exacerbated very early by professional mismanagement, lack of coordinated care and advice because of failures of interdisciplinary organization, and resistance and denials on the parents' part. The result is a failure in the ontogenesis of the parents' representation of the future and present child (and a corresponding failure in the child's representation of himself).

A family in such a situation cannot be treated effectively unless the ontogenic model is consulted and used. Much of their anguish is best understood by this developmental model. They can probably not be well treated or guided unless it is openly recognized that they are in a representational vacuum. Several treatment approaches that rely heavily on this model have been developed, such as "previewing" (Trad, 1990), in which the parents and therapist spend much time working on the parents' representations of the baby-in-the-future.

These four models not only help organize the material about representational worlds for clinical intervention but also provide guidelines for the search and discovery of relevant clinical information. Most experienced clinicians probably use an eclectic mix of all four models without thinking much about it, depending on the clinical material presented. Nonetheless, specifying the models they use may clarify and facilitate their clinical endeavors.

CHAPTER 3

The Parents' Representations Enacted

IN THE LAST CHAPTER, I described the huge cast of representations (the networks of schemas-of-being-with) that can appear in the parents' internal world. It remains to see how these networks work—how they influence the interaction. After all, the representation must have an impact on the interaction if it is to produce a symptom or problem with the baby or if the mother's personal past is to influence the baby's future for good or ill. Two questions are involved. First, how does one schema-of-being-with or one network of such schemas, among many possible, get activated into a state in which it can exert an influence? Second, in what way are activated schemas enacted in the interaction? That is, how are they translated into corresponding acts? We will address only the second question.

Our model insists that maternal representations can influence the observable maternal behavior with the baby; that is, they can be enacted. What would serve as evidence that an effective transformation from a mental model to concrete acts has occurred?

It is not enough to find a correspondence between the mother's representation and how her actions appear to adult observers; it is necessary to describe those actions that are discernible by and potentially meaningful to the infant. For instance, imagine a mother who represents herself as someone who is always rejected by those she loves; to protect herself, she tends to reject first and hold back until unequivocally invited. It is not enough to state that with her infant she is also rejecting and somewhat aloof. We must be able to describe in concrete behavioral terms how the mother manages to be rejecting and aloof such that her rejection and aloofness can be perceived by the baby and have an impact on him. Can "rejecting" be translated into behaviors such as breaking mutual gaze, putting the baby down when he still wants to be in her arms, or refusing to pick him up when so solicited? Can "aloof" be translated into behaviors such as selectively ignoring some of the infant's vocal signals or being unable to smile until the baby has done so?

Many therapists, working in the psychoanalytic tradition, have obscured the above point. In the immediacy of the clinical moment and with their eyes on the world of representations they may forget that the maternal representation or fantasy cannot influence the baby magically. The baby cannot grasp the substance of a mother's mental life except through her overt behavior. A great deal of mystification still abounds concerning this reality. For instance, Wilfred Bion's writings (1963, 1967) on the impact of maternal fantasy on the infant are highly sensitive and of great clinical value, yet his explanation of the mechanism of this influence remains very unclear—almost as if there were an ether medium through which the fantasies of mother and infant could communicate and affect one another. Overt behavioral interactions get short-circuited. Françoise Dolto, another important influence on clinical practice, suggests another way for the maternal mental life to influence the baby, almost directly, without recourse to overt behavior, namely that the baby from birth can understand the contents of what is said, when it is said right (1971).

In spite of the past decades of infancy research, this mystification persists. It has recently been stated that maternal fantasies, via projective identification, are the basic building blocks of the infant's psychic development (Cramer, 1993). But this cannot be so. The mother's fantasies and representations must first take a form that is perceivable, discriminable, directly influential, and potentially meaningful to an infant. In other words, they must first be transformed into interactive behavior. Thus what should have been said is that the maternal fantasies are the basic starting point for the *clinician's* construction of the key psychological problem of the case, but not for the *infant's* constructions. This is not splitting hairs. The scientific basis of the whole inquiry rests on these distinctions.

Perhaps neglecting overt behavior in favor of the intrapsychic, as psychoanalysis has historically done, has helped maintain this particular form of unneeded mystification. Nonetheless, there is a puzzle close at hand: how to conceive of continuity of theme or meaning in the passage from a mother's representation to her overt interactive behavior, and then from the infant's experience of that overt behavior to his construction of his own representational world. The issue becomes, what are the rules of transformation across these domains? But a question remains. Can we chase a phenomenon into and out of several domains or levels of description and across the borders of different minds and at the end of the chase be sure we are still following the same phenomenon? Let us begin such a chase anyway.

An Initial Glimpse at Parental
Representations in Action

Almost twenty-five years ago I was studying a mother and her 3½-month-old fraternal twins (Stern, 1971). I called them Mark (M for mother's twin) and Fred (F for father's twin). What struck me was that when the mother played with the two of them on the floor, Fred would get progressively more distressed and after five minutes would be in tears. Mark, on the other hand, remained quite happy. It was not at all clear to me how or why this happened. Since these were weekly televised home observations, I had plenty of time to talk to the mother. The following clinical picture emerged. When she was pregnant and knew she would have twins, she made a distinction between them while they were still in the womb. One kicked more and was thought to be more active; the other was slower and less lively. The mother saw herself as a very lively, energetic, fast-starting person—qualities that she liked in herself. She also saw her husband, in comparison with her, as slower, more lethargic and phlegmatic. While the twins were still fetuses, she identified the active, lively one as more like her—the one who would become Mark—and the passive, phlegmatic one as more like her husband—he would become Fred.

After delivery, she assumed that she had correctly assigned the twins to the two categories she had identified during the pregnancy. Indeed, by the time I met the twins at 3 months of age, Mark ("her twin") was the more active, alert infant of the two. It is commonly observed in mothers of twins that some of the normal ambivalence, heightened by having twins, is split so that more of the positive feelings and identifications are initially attached to one baby and the more negatives ones to the other. This normal tendency to split attributions was certainly amplified in this situation, because the couple was going through a difficult period in which the wife was feeling more than usually negative about her husband. This hostility got played out with the twins.

The result was that the mother identified Mark as the one who had been more active in the womb, was more active now, and was more like her. He was "her baby." Fred was her husband's baby. She experienced an easier and happier rapport with Mark and a more turbulent and difficult one with Fred, but she could not explain how or why that was so.

Given this situation, I set myself the task of discovering what the mother and infants were doing in their interactions during those five minutes of play every morning so that her fantasies were fulfilled. A microanalysis of the play interaction revealed, in brief, the following main differences in how the mother interacted with each twin. (For the full findings and illustrations, see Stern, 1971.) The mother acted differently toward gaze aversions during face-to-face play, depending on who performed it. If Mark averted his face, the mother accepted this signal as a temporary cutoff and either looked away or stayed still. If Fred averted his face, the mother did not accept it as a cutoff signal and moved closer to him, as if to force a fuller contact but succeeding only in forcing him into a position of greater aversion.

The pattern of steps between Fred and the mother traced a repeating sequence. If Fred and the mother were facing one another in a moment of mutual gaze—usually a moment of short duration—Fred would invariably avert his gaze slightly as the mother moved toward him. Instead of considering Fred's face aversion as a signal to back off (as she did with Mark), she treated it as a signal to approach closer. One reason she may have acted differently with Fred is that even when Fred averted his gaze, unlike Mark, he continued to monitor her every move peripherally. She may have sensed this fact through the responsivity of his movements to hers, and it may have given her the impression that he was still in contact with her. She would move closer to establish full face-to-face and eye contact, sending Fred even farther away into an exaggerated face aversion. Then as Fred turned back toward her, she would withdraw and turn away. It was still a mutual approach-withdrawal flow but now in the other direction, Fred approaching and the mother withdrawing. By the time she was fully withdrawn and facing away from Fred, he would be facing her again and still executing small approach and withdrawal movements that were dependent on her motions, even though her motions were no longer directed to him. She would be looking elsewhere, but the combination of his gazing at her and his moving with her would quickly recapture her attention. She would again turn to Fred, and as she moved toward him he would avert and they would be retracing the same sequential steps. This mutual approach-withdrawal pattern was mutually frustrating. At each successive round, Fred got progressively more upset, until he was fully distressed and the interaction broke down.

One of the striking features of this pattern of "missing" was that the mother and Fred could never get together fully for long and never stay completely apart for long. Yet they spent much more time and effort working—or rather failing—at getting together than Mark and the mother, who spent less time interacting but more time in mutual gaze and face-to-face contact.

One of the interesting outcomes of this interactive pattern was that through the second year of life Fred continued to have more trouble than Mark did in both establishing and maintaining mutual gaze with his mother and others and also more trouble in disengaging from the mother and wandering off alone without checking back. In general, he remained less attached and less separated, an example of paradoxical stimulation.

One important lesson from this case was that a mother's enactment of a representation with her baby is not a unilateral event. It requires some form of reciprocal or complementary actions on the part of the baby to permit its enactment. For the discussion that follows, it is necessary to hold in mind that the baby is not the passive victim of the mother's representations but becomes a partner in some manner.

This single case left a deep impression on me concerning the influence of representations on interactive behavior, but it was only an initial glimpse. A long time went by in which I became more knowledgeable about the workings of mother-infant interactions and more convinced of the importance of the mother's representational world. This appreciation grew from clinical work and from the work of the many authors cited in this chapter.

A Pilot Attempt to Link Behavior and Representation

Ten or so years ago, Bertrand Cramer and I undertook a pilot study of one mother-infant dyad to explore these issues (Cramer & Stern, 1988). The work was divided so that Cramer identified the mother's interview-activated representations, and I described her overt behavior in the interaction with her son. Cramer practices a form of brief, psychoanalytically inspired psychotherapy with mother-infant dyads (Cramer & Palacio-Espasa, 1993). This therapy is ideally suited to identifying the mother's interview-activated—and sometimes interaction-activated—representations. In fact, that is the aim of this therapeutic approach, which could also be called representation-oriented brief psychotherapy. The

> inquiry remains directed at the nature and history of the mother's representational world as it may have relevance for the infant and the interaction. No therapeutic effort is made to alter directly the mother's overt behavior. In fact, it is

not commented upon. The therapy is directed squarely at the mother's representations of herself and her infant. (Cramer & Stern, 1988, p. 23)

A discussion of this approach as a form of therapy is discussed in chapter 8. Here we are concerned with it only as it bears on the question of how the mother's representational world may be enacted in the interaction.

I conducted a behavioral analysis of the interactive behaviors of mother and infant consisting of proxemics, body orientation, gestures, gaze, and vocalizations. The overt behaviors were observed during the same five sessions that made up the course of brief psychotherapy and that provided the interview-activated representational themes.

Five different representational themes (or networks of schemas-of-being-with) were identified, and a behavioral correspondence was sought. For example, one representational theme could be called "fear of bodily damage due to the child's aggressiveness." The mother complained that her son was aggressive with her, and was constantly hurting her; she found the child's contact with her body as harmful. This was a recurrent theme. Further inquiry about this representation revealed that she saw her son

> as aggressive and threatening ... that he really wanted to hurt her ... and was having fun doing so; he bit, hit, and scratched and was never soft or affectionate. ... She had felt pain from him even when she was pregnant; he was born by Caesarian section. Right from birth, he pulled her intravenous drip and when she put him to the breast he hurt her so much that she fainted. (Cramer & Stern, 1988, pp. 25, 26)

These were some of the schemas-of-being-with him that were drawn into the same network.

In addition, we found that this representation of fear of bodily damage was a core-conflictual theme that arose early in her own past history. We were witnessing a reanimation of the old theme, reedited for her interactions with her own son.

> She had had a severe infection with dehydration as a baby that had required two long-term hospitalizations with painful treatments; her life had been in danger. Since then, she always had been treated as a sickly, vulnerable child. Moreover, she had a series of illnesses that required five surgical interventions up to the age of 18. Her representational theme centered around a core of body harm and vulnerability and created a continuous fear of body damage. This central anxiety from her past now was influencing the conflictual relationship that she was having with her son. He was experienced as aggressively intent on damaging her body, as he became the present-day incarnation of people who, like the doctors of her past, contributed to painful bodily experiences. (Cramer & Stern, 1988, p. 26)

To find behavioral correspondences in the interaction with this relational script, we made a list of all of the infant's behaviors that could reasonably be called aggressive: poking fingers in mother's face, eyes, or mouth, forcefully exploring the mother's body, threat gestures, hitting, pushing or pulling vigorously (outside of a play context), banging his head against her body, banging an object (toy) against her, pulling her hair or earrings, and so on. We were not, in fact, very impressed by the "aggressiveness" of this boy. At times, he was clearly aggressive, but often that was after she had ignored his behavior and he was forced to repeat it at a higher level of intensity to get her attention. The percentage of time that she ignored these acts was considerable. Most striking, however, was that when she did not ignore these acts, potentially interpretable as aggressive, she responded to them by turning away, protecting herself physically, putting the child down or away from her, or becoming aggressive with him. The picture emerged of an infant who was probably normally assertive physically but whose mother (as influenced by her activated representation) interpreted his assertion as aggression and acted accordingly with self-protection, rejection, or counteraggression. On such occasions the infant would, indeed, become progressively more aggressive in response to her response. Over the five sessions, the situation improved considerably, but not because the boy changed the level of his aggressiveness. He did not. Rather, the mother began to interpret his behavior differently and started to respond to his assertiveness with more positive behavior.

A network of schemas-of-being-with was clearly identified. Its enactment in behavioral terms during the mother-infant interaction was described. And the level of behavioral description was such that the behaviors were conceivably discernible and meaningful to the infant. So far, so good. While this pilot study was promising, however, it had many shortcomings. The most obvious limitations were that it was only one case and that Cramer, in defining the mother's representations, and I, in describing the specific interactive behaviors, did not work blindly one from the other. Because it was a pilot study, we tolerated much contamination of our knowledge of what was being found at the other level of analysis. There was, however, an even more important limitation. We have no idea whether the interactive behavior is specific to the thematic material. If the mother has a fear of and aversion to physical contact/harm, as this mother did, how many different specific behaviors could that fear and aversion be translated into? Did we uncover only a small subset? And could the subset we did reveal also be related to other themes that we did not uncover? The issue of specificity is crucial and unanswered in spite of appeals to plausibility.

There is a final problem. The themes described were culled from material from many sessions or many minutes during the whole session, as were the interactive behaviors. They are presumably general, pervasive themes.

Does that mean that they are acting all the time, or, more to the point, were they acting at the very moment that the related interactive behaviors were enacted? We had no way to know. We never asked the mother, either at the time or afterwards. Were the correspondences only in the minds of the researchers?

To state the problem differently, we had failed to differentiate between interview-activated and interaction-activated representations. At that time, the distinction was not being made, and Cramer's interview technique was aimed almost exclusively at the interview-elicited representations. Accordingly, we did not really know much about the mother's representational experience in the interaction at the time when the themes supposedly being enacted appeared. Nonetheless, a small step forward had been taken, even if it did not do much more than document the kind of clinical material that was becoming more familiar to the field.

Methodologically, one thing, at least, was apparent. It was necessary to evaluate the mother's interaction-activated representations. And to do that the usual clinical interview had to be altered or supplemented.

The Microanalytic Interview Technique

How does the representation influence behavior? What is the mechanism of such a process? To begin to study such questions, it is necessary to start at the microanalytic level and inquire about the state of the representation and its articulation with behavior at the instant that the behavior is performed, or right before. One must have a way of examining what goes on mentally in a short stretch of time—what is, or was once, the "present moment." And knowing "what happens" in the present moment is very difficult; a long and honorable history attests to its elusiveness. Not only is the present moment always dissolving into the immediate past, but it is constantly being reconstructed when it is brought forward. A concept such as the "emergent moment," which will be developed in chapter 5, is needed to deal with this question.

What I mean by an emergent moment in this situation is the momentary experience of having an action emerge from the felt background of an activated representation that shapes and guides the emerging action.

It is true that the subjective experience of an emergent moment is, almost by definition, not seizable. The separate components are being processed locally and unconsciously, and the synthesis of these separate pieces into a larger whole, which can be conscious, is of the nature of an intuitive leap. There are also the considerable methodological problems of viewing the subject matter through both time- and content-distorting lenses. Still, it seemed worthwhile to try to get even a small, cloudy, partial glimpse of the manifest actions of a representation in operation at the moment of the formation of an enactment.

To get some hints for asking what is going on subjectively during an emergent moment, I first looked into the clinical literature. It proved disappointing, because therapists identify one or two more therapeutically salient events in a "moment" (often described at a split-second level) and then immediately pursue that event with respect to its meanings, its precedents, its correspondence to other such moments in other life spaces and times. In a sense the event they choose (among many) is followed, via associations, across many therapeutically useful levels of abstraction and generalization. (The therapist may of course return to the moment to pick up another thread and follow its associative chain.) This way of proceeding is a large part of therapeutic work. It is well suited to understanding the patient's life, but not necessarily well suited to seeing what goes into an emergent moment.

With this in mind, I began an exercise that I called the "breakfast interviews," later to become the microanalytic interview. The goal was to get a more detailed notion of what is potentially recountable about what goes on in a "moment" (and later to use that information to explore the problem of representations and their enactment). Family, friends, and colleagues were asked, "What happened this morning at breakfast?" Breakfast was chosen because it was a recent, ordinary event, probably lacking in psychodynamically important moments. (The idea was to avoid a "clinical" interview.) One moment was then singled out among the sequence of moments that made up breakfast. The chosen moment was a short stretch of time (usually lasting many seconds, but rarely more than 20 seconds). It was a well-bounded episode with clear starting and ending markers. For example, "From the moment I picked up the teapot and was at that instant thinking . . . until after pouring I looked into the pot to see if I needed to add more water." This chosen moment then became the sole subject of an interview that lasted between 1 and 1½ hours. The choice of the moment was influenced by the question, "Was there a moment that stands out?" That was the sole question influencing a choice.

Subjects were asked everything that they could remember or reconstruct about what they saw, heard, felt, thought, or did during that moment. They were asked to divide the moment into intuitive units on the basis of shifts in scene, time, action, cognition, posture, or feeling. To help in this parsing process, a number of techniques were used. One of the most helpful was to ask the subject to be a director/cameraman and to film a montage of the moment. Each change in camera angle or closeness of shot helped to subdivide scenes and actions. Where possible, the subject was asked to describe the shifts in cinematographic terms, such as abrupt cut, fade in or out, or superimposition. Another helpful technique was to ask about changes in the speed of the passage of time. Yet another was to determine at which points the subject changed position or posture. This helped to parse the passage into discontinuous units.

Once units were established, the subject was asked to order them sequentially. It turned out that many of the units were roughly simultaneous or overlapped in time, so that several time lines were required. The notation system came closer to a musical one that is designed to render co-occurrences as well as sequences.

There was no attempt to make links between this moment and the rest of the subject's life. The subjects, nonetheless, did so frequently. (For instance, "Now that I am telling you the story of the teapot, I wonder if it isn't like me to constantly go looking in life's teapots to see if. . . .") They were not stopped immediately, but a short while after some connections with events outside the moment were made, they were brought back into the chosen moment. I was examining a reconstructed moment, not the subject's life.

Both the subjects and I found the interviews fascinating, with several surprises: that so much had happened in such a short period of time; that one can be in several time frames and places simultaneously; that many acts were clearly triggered by thoughts, fantasies, and memories; conversely, that acts can clearly trigger mental events; and—what was most striking—that a central theme emerged that loosely organized the moment. This theme was of considerable importance to the teller and was a currently dominant concern in that person's life, even though it was not being experienced, per se, in the moment.[1] The breakfast scenes invariably became anything but banal events, and the clinical potential of the technique was evident.

With these breakfast interviews as a form of pilot, a group of us at the Sackler-Lefcourt Center for Child Development in New York—Ilene Lefcourt, Steven Bennett, Wendy Haft, Patricia Nachman, and I—set about to adapt this microanalytic interview to mothers, to see if we could examine more closely the interactive enactment of a maternal schema-of-being-

---

[1]The richness of a moment is actually lost if one asks about an emotionally charged moment (either positive or negative). It is as if the idling brain, going through automatic actions, permits a greater array of subjective occurrences happening simultaneously than one focused by affect or by a sharp cognitive goal. This idling also gives to internal themes a greater role in the construction of apparent coherence to the moment.

with. Mothers and their 3- or 4-year-old children first interacted freely for 15 to 20 minutes in the nursery of the center, which was familiar to the children. After the interaction, a "moment" was chosen; the mother was asked what had happened and whether there was a particular moment that stood out. (For details of this microanalytic interview, examples of the data collected, and preliminary results, see Bennett, Sackler-Lefcourt, Haft, Nachman, & Stern, 1994 and Nachman, Sackler-Lefcourt, Haft, Bennett, & Stern, unpublished manuscript.)

Several problems were encountered. The first was the paradoxical one that all members of the research team are good, experienced clinicians. By training and long interest, they were drawn to explore the associative chains and networks that relate the chosen moment to the rest of the subject's life. It took great effort to restrain and redirect them to explore more deeply the moment, not the subject's life story. What makes this interview different from the kind of clinical interview described by Fraiberg (1980) is that in the interests of enriching and deepening the clinical material, Fraiberg encourages and follows the associative chains that lead out from the actual interaction into the patient's past life. We do not encourage or follow this widening (it is not discouraged, either) but lead the subject back into the interactive moment to flesh it out as much as possible.

Second, because the subjects associated quite freely and spontaneously beyond the confines of the moment, it was necessary to ask them frequently if the thought or memory that they just recounted was actually part of the experienced moment. That is, was it an interaction-activated experience or an interview-activated experience?

The results-in-progress of this pilot work suggest the following picture. When the mother is interacting with her infant, some of her networks of schemas-of-being-with are almost always activated. Exactly which ones are activated can shift from moment to moment, depending on what is happening. Subjectively, the mother's experience is very rich and multilayered. As the active network of schemas shifts, she can move back and forth (every few seconds, even) between the past, present, and future; between here and elsewhere; between distance from the action and immersion in it; between identification with her child and experience fully centered within herself; between herself-as-child as the subject and her child as the subject; between viewing with her eyes and her mother's eyes, and so on. The currently active network of schemas provides a meaning and feeling to the current interactive moment. It also acts, in part, to determine which subsequent events in the stream of the interaction will be noticed and found salient—that is, what the next emergent moment will be.

This kind of circular dialogue between the events and the schemas seems to be going on all the time, at least unconsciously. Mothers report, however, that at least subjectively, it feels as if they can sometimes discon-nect the representational flow from the interactive flow of events for a while. At times they go "inside of themselves" and focus their attention on their representational world while they execute actions in the interactive world semiautomatically with only peripheral attention. At other times they do the opposite. Sometimes they are equally aware of both, but more often on reconstruction one world seems to be more attended to but not exclusively. One of the reasons mothers can spend so much time occupied, or partly occupied, by their representational life is that they are smarter than their babies. Even when feeding or playing with her baby a mother can be elsewhere in her mind and still maintain a good interaction that requires the infant's full attention. Often the interactions with baby are boring, and the mother's mind is idling—partly in the world of represen-tations.

This is a rather complicated way of describing the everyday experiences of daydreaming or distraction or preoccupation. People are generally good at parallel processing at the subjective level. What I want to capture is that the mother, in the parenting situation, is necessarily operating in at least two subjective spaces: the behavioral interaction and her representa-tional life. The shifting dialogue between the two is what the experience is largely about for her.

This shifting dialogue is so rich, varied, dynamic, and mobile, however, changing in seconds and at times microseconds, that it proved impossible to study in a satisfying way the interaction between an activated schema and the actions indicating its enactment. Neither one could be pinned down or sufficiently disembodied from the other. Nonetheless, the study did illustrate well how an external event can trigger a schema and how an activated schema can identify and define an interactive event. While the microinterview has proved to be fascinating and useful clinically, other, complementary approaches to the problem are clearly needed.

Before leaving the microinterview, it is worth explaining further in what ways it may be useful. First, it seems to be valuable in exploring the subjectively lived aspects of experience. And, after all, that is what we are ultimately most interested in clinically. Although this kind of interview-led, introspective approach is fraught with difficulties and dangers, some further exploration of the nature of subjective experience is badly needed. The psychoanalytic enterprise has carried us far into this domain of expe-rience, but it has done so largely via free associations and immediate transference experiences elicited within the very special psychoanalytic framework. While valuable, this approach is not sufficient.

The microinterview is an attempt to cut free from the exploration of associative chains that lead out from—but are not the same thing as—the initiating lived experience that began the chaining process. A fuller focus on the subjectively lived present may prove fruitful in several ways. One such way concerns the further understanding of certain mental operations that are clinically indispensable, such as identification. Identification can be seen largely in terms of its functions, one of which is to make a child become more like a parent in certain respects. Traditionally, the mental operations to fulfill this function have been viewed as general, pervasive processes that occur over a long time period, as in a boy-child's progressive identification with his father. Identification has also been described abstractly as the process whereby the self-representation is altered to become more like the representation of another—that is as a process that occurs intrapsychically (Sandler, 1987). These views are certainly true, but there must also be small, discrete, and concrete mental acts that make up the process. Using the microanalytic interview, Nachman et al. (unpublished) describe how a mother interacting with and watching her infant interact undergoes many shifts in her position of being "in her child's skin" or in her own. She can also subjectively occupy positions somewhere between these two poles. Furthermore, mothers describe that they often have shifts in their identificatory position every few seconds. What emerges from this picture is a very active dynamic process made of sequences of mental acts in real time. Identification thus becomes a live process as well as a psychic function. It is reasonable to suppose that an approach such as the microinterview, carried further, may teach us more about identification.[2]

If one explores the moment of interactive experience more deeply on its own terms and within its own boundaries, rather than following the associative networks elsewhere, will one have missed or avoided what is of clinical value? Originally I practiced the microanalytic interview only on research subjects, not on patients, because I was afraid that it was only satisfying my scientific curiosity and not necessarily following the clinical needs of the case. More recently, I have come to use the microanalytic interview clinically—not in its pure long form, but in order to stay longer

[2]Meltzoff has recently suggested that for infants, imitation is one process for identifying and getting to know about people, just as manipulation is the analogous process for identifying and getting to know about inanimate objects (1994). To take a step further, identification requires a virtual imitative act whereby the represented self is brought to imitate some aspect of the represented other. These virtual imitative acts are discrete and brief. The larger process of what we usually mean by identification is made up of the accumulation, perfection, and automation of just such smaller acts. This appears to be Sandler's view of the process as well (1987).

in the lived experience before going off on the associative chains. I have done so because I am now convinced that a different perspective on psychic life can be gained, a perspective that also has much therapeutic value. The utilization of the microinterview in parent-infant psychotherapies is now being studied by Bennett et al. (1994).

A final potential value of this type of interview is in providing the descriptions that are needed for the cognitive neurosciences to know where to look in the domains of experience that most interest us clinically. For instance, the cognitive neurosciences have presented elaborate parallel distributed processing (PDP) models of mental functioning (described in chapter 5). The descriptions of a lived moment that emerge from approaches such as the microanalytic interview provide one of the more convincing (to me) pieces of evidence that the experience of the "stream of consciousness" is approachable with a PDP model. Ultimately, the horizon of the cognitive neurosciences may be limited in certain directions without more progress in describing and understanding subjective experience.

Activation and Enactment of Schemas

In the single-case study mentioned earlier (Cramer & Stern, 1988), we worked from representation to interaction. That is, we first identified a representational theme in the mother and then sought to find its behavioral manifestations in the interaction. We acted as if the mother's most clinically charged schemas were in a constant state of activation (much as one might expect of a "core conflictual theme" [Luborsky & Crits-Christoph, 1990]). This kind of notion assumes that the representation is, so to speak, hovering in the air, waiting and looking for an opportunity to be enacted. Indeed, this could be the situation for a while, but our experience with the microanalytic interview makes it clear that an event can activate a dormant network of schemas just as well and that changing events elicit changing schemas. The influence is bidirectional and dynamic. The bidirectionality of influence is clear but the question of how a representational theme can be "translated" from one level of description to another still remains.

With this question in mind, a research study was designed to compare the form of the representational theme as it appears in the enacted interaction and in the representations at different levels of description.

In Lausanne, Elisabeth Fivaz and I assembled a diverse group, each of whom worked at a different level of description and inquiry. The group consisted of Dieter Bürgin (Basel), John Byng-Hall (London), Antoinette Corboz and Elisabeth Fivaz (Lausanne), Martine Lamour and Serge Lebovici (Paris), and myself. A family was then chosen with whom to work: a culturally mixed couple, multilingual (English, French, German, Russian), and their newly born first son. The parents, healthy volunteers, were extremely cooperative. They agreed to allow multiple interviewing by several people and also to participate as active members of the collaborating research team (see Fivaz-Depeursinge et al., 1994 for details).

The decision was made to choose, a priori, a particular interactive event that would serve as our "anchor point." This point was the moment when the father joined in to change the configuration of the triad from two actively interacting members with one member at the periphery to all members equally engaged. We called this transition going from "two plus one" to "three together." This moment was chosen because it promised to be relevant to many important networks of schemas (e.g., ethological, Oedipal, cultural, intergenerational, personal). Each colleague then conducted an interview or observation to see if the theme of going from two plus one to three together was manifested at that researcher's level of analysis, and if so, what form it took.

First, Antoinette Corboz and Elisabeth Fivaz performed a detailed microanalysis of the behavior and proxemics on the basis of the televised recording of the interactive transition from two plus one to three together. The shift itself took 20 seconds and was divided into six phases: the initiation of the transition; partial disengagement of the old triadic configuration; partial reengagement of the new triad—that is, configuration; complete disengagement of the old triadic configuration; and the end of the transition. The entire transition was over when the triad was completely reconstituted.

Next, I conducted a variation of the microanalytic interview described above, with the differences that it was given to the parents together and was confined to the chosen anchor event as viewed on video. The purpose of this interview was to search for the relationship between the interactive anchor event and any activated schemas. John Byng-Hall then conducted a family interview, with particular focus on the family scripts and intergenerational themes that related to the same interactive anchor point. Serge Lebovici then conducted a psychoanalytically informed interview to assess the meaning to both parents of the triadification process. Martine Lamour then did a psychodynamically informed behavioral analysis of the televised triadic interactions that surrounded the anchor point. Finally, Dieter Bürgin conducted a psychoanalytically informed interview of both parents, with a particular focus on the issue of cultural identity as it was involved in the anchor transition. This procedure was done at 13 and 52 weeks of infant age.

The most striking finding was that each of us felt confident that we could recognize the anchor theme of "triadification" (going from dyad plus one to three together) at our separate levels of description. Furthermore, we began to consider the idea that such themes, or motives, permeated all levels of organization and that the structure of the motive at each level was basically the same. In this sense the notion of "enactment" as I have used it so far may be too narrow. It has up until now referred only to the transformation of an activated schema into overt interactive behavior. Our experience with the anchor theme, however, suggests that the activated schemas (related to a theme) can potentially be enacted at any or all levels of organization: interactive behaviors, autobiographical narratives, fantasies, memories, scripts, and practices. The enactment into interactive behavior is just one form of expression. The issue of the transformation of themes across the different expressions at different levels becomes the less mysterious problem of understanding the language, rules, and constraints intrinsic to each level of expression.

The level of organization at which the schema is expressed seems to be determined by the needs of the "present context." If a mother finds herself in the present context of interacting with the baby, rather than talking to someone about how things are going with the baby or talking about how it was for herself when she was a baby, then the enactment will occur at the level of interactive behaviors, rather than in a verbal description of the present or an autobiographical narrative of her past. The parent who is interacting with a baby is simply locked into a powerful present context.

We need a concept of a working space similar to that implied in the notion of a working memory. We could call such a time-space a *working representation space*, similar—perhaps finally identical—to the working memory.[3] In a working representation space, the different elements of the activated schemas could be rearranged so as to be best adapted to the mode of enactment dictated by the present context.

We now know that the exact form of a memory or the precise execution of an enactment is greatly dependent on the present context that influences its formation. One of the important recent notions in the cognitive sciences is the idea that representations, memories, and motor programs need not exist in a fixed, absolute, and complete form, waiting to be "trig-

---

[3] This conception borrows from the research on working memory (Baddeley, 1986; Case, Marini, McKeough, Dennis, & Goldberg, 1986; Pascual-Leone, 1987; and, for developmental aspects, de Ribaupierre & Bailleux, 1993).

gered" or "elicited." Rather, each time they are brought into the working memory or working representation space, they are composed or constructed anew, according to the demands of the present, unique context (see, e.g., Edelman, 1989).

Such an arrangement is likely to have an adaptive advantage. It assures that whatever is happening now (the local conditions of adaptation) will recruit all the networks of schemas at all the other hierarchical levels that are related to the present ongoing activity, mentally or physically. Thus, networks of representations can contribute flexibly to the process of organizing behavior around functional goals.

It is important to note the speed at which such a system must operate. Each time an act is committed or a memory is retrieved, the present context may change and the process will be repeated.

The enactment of maternal representations in the behavioral interaction can be summarized as follows.

1. Interactive behaviors unfold under the influence of activated schemas-of-being-with. Just as there are few motor actions without ongoing guidance from sensorimotor schemes, few interactive behaviors occur without guidance from activated schemas-of-being-with. These schemas help select the interactive behaviors that will be performed and their exact manner of performance.
2. I will not try to position "consciousness" relative to activation or enactment. Activated schemas may be conscious or preconscious. Similarly, enactment may be conscious or not.
3. Conversely, interactive behaviors activate schemas-of-being-with. As the interaction proceeds and changes—and it continually does—new behavioral features appear to activate different schemas. Accordingly, as the interaction goes forward, some schemas-of-being-with are maintained in an active state, others become deactivated, and new ones are activated.
4. Accordingly, the activated schemas and the interactive behaviors are constantly acting upon one another and continually changing one another, so that a shifting dialogue between them is maintained all the time.
5. More than one such shifting dialogue may be occurring at any one time between activated schemas and interactive behaviors. The relative attention given to one or the other of these dialogues may also shift frequently. The subjective landscape is much like that of music in which several melodic themes intertwine; each may surge forward for a while, then fade or disappear, only to appear again.
6. Once a schema is activated, the exact manner in which it will be

enacted depends on the present context. If the activated schema occurs within the present context of the demands of an interaction—a very powerful, rich, and constraining context—the schema will be expressed in overt behavioral acts. The same activated schema can be expressed in narrative or other verbal form. From the clinical point of view, the expression of an activated schema-of-being-with in a behavioral mode is not seen as more or less revealing or profound or basic than its expression in any other mode.

What is relatively new and different in this view is the emphasis on the moment-by-moment interaction as a present remembering context to activate different representations. Traditionally, we tend to think in clinical terms of one or two central themes or representations (such as core conflictual themes) that are constantly activated internally, or maintained in a state of semireadiness by internal forces such that their threshold for activation from external events is so low that the representations are, in effect, almost constantly activated. While this may be the case for certain representations, I am more impressed by the role of the shifting interaction in evoking specific representations that were latent. A shift toward a greater role for interactive reality compared to purely intrapsychic events in the regulation of the subjective landscape has been made.

Since the present context that interests us most for clinical reasons is the interaction with the baby, let us turn at this point to an examination of the parent-infant interaction for a better understanding of its language, rules, and demands as a present context for the parents, as well as for the baby's representations.

CHAPTER 4

The Parent-Infant Interaction

THE NEXT ELEMENTS of the clinical system that we will take up are the mother's overt interactive behavior with the infant (M_{act}) and the infant's overt interactive behavior with the mother (B_{act}). Together they make up the parent-infant interaction.

The Central Place of the Interaction

The parent-infant interaction is the centerpiece of the clinical situation. It is the key element to be understood, for several reasons.

First, the parent-infant interaction is the arena in which the parents' most critical representations, wishes, fears, and fantasies about the infant are played out. Certainly, only a part of the parents' representational world concerning the infant is played out here, but it is exactly that part that most concerns us clinically, because only those parental representations, fantasies, and so on, that are enacted in the interaction will directly influence the baby. They thus occupy a special place clinically. Ultimately, we cannot understand how a parental representation acts clinically unless we understand the interaction through which it acts. Similarly, the interaction is the arena for the enactment of the infant's representations, which directly influence the parents.

The interaction is thus the bridge between the parent's and the infant's representations. As I have discussed earlier, there is no magic ether connecting representations across two separate minds. The influence must be transmitted by way of the concrete interaction between them.

The interaction is also the path for most of the influences that ultimately impinge on the very young infant from the world at large—such as social, economic, and cultural factors—because of the highly asymmetrical nature of this relationship. The parent has a huge volume of interactive traffic with the world, but the young infant's interactive traffic is overwhelmingly with his primary caregiver, especially during the first months and first year. The parent filters and regulates the growing but still relatively limited traffic with the world external to direct parent-infant interactions. In the beginning, then, pathogenic influences can arise from anywhere, but they will impact on the baby only to the extent that they influence the privileged caregiving dyad or triad. This general rule applies to all the factors we know to have powerful influences on the later mental health of the child. Socioeconomic status is the example par excellence, having more predictive power than any other single influence (see, e.g., Sameroff, Seifer, Barocas, Lax, & Greenspan, 1987). This list of external (i.e., to the dyad) factors includes malfunctioning social supports, the nature of the intervening mental health care system, if there is one, the parental culture, minority status, level of education, and so on. When the infant is still quite young, these factors can have no conceivable meaning or influence until they are translated into the language of action within the caregiving dyad.

It is easy to imagine how these factors could influence the quality and quantity of specific interactive behaviors directed toward the infant during the first year of life. Nonetheless, the central point bears emphasizing, because clinicians and theorists often think, act, and write as if these influences acted directly or through some unspecified medium to affect the baby. We already know the medium. This neglect of the obvious role of the parent-infant interaction as the principal—at times the only—translating medium of external influences is curious. Some of the possible reasons for this deemphasis of the obvious are mentioned later in this chapter.[1]

Finally, the interaction plays a crucial role in determining the symptom or problem that brings the family to treatment. Most of the chief complaints of the parents (usually about the infant, e.g., problems of sleeping, eating, conduct, or attachment) or, on the mother's part, problems of feeling rejected or unloving, ultimately arise in the interactive setting. I do not mean that the cause of the problem necessarily lies in the interaction but that the primary symptom takes place within the context of the interaction

---

[1]The notion of the early centrality of the interaction is compatible, I believe, with current concepts about modes of influence, such as Sameroff's transactional model (Sameroff & Fiese, 1990).

and is evaluated in the terms of that context, because that is where the parents "live it." Even the presence of a physical handicap in the infant is only a partial exception, since the handicap is "lived" by all concerned in the daily interactions. Accordingly, therapies cannot afford to be interested in the entirety of the mother's representational world or in the full spectrum of cultural influences on the family. Rather, only those influences that bear significantly on the parent-infant interaction will be chosen for therapeutic focus. In other words, the scope of the therapeutic universe is ultimately defined by and brought back to the parent-infant interactions.

This centrality of the interaction within the clinical situation does not mean that it has to be the preferred subject matter for the therapeutic sessions or the privileged port of entry into the system. Some therapies make minimal use of the actual parent-infant interaction as clinical material. Others encourage it, structure it, and focus on it heavily during sessions. In either case, these interactions, as they occur in treatment and at home, remain the key element.

Identifying Clinically Important Events

We can start with the assumption that the clinically important events and moments are the very small, ordinary, daily, repetitive, nonverbal events that, objectively speaking, did happen. In fact, these may be the only kinds of human events that initially exist for the infant. In any case, they are the events into which the representations of the parents and infant get transformed and enacted so as to play their role in creating a clinical problem.

Let us examine the features of these events in more detail.

1. *The events are the subjective experience of "real" events.* Much psychoanalytic thinking suggests that psychic reality for the infant starts with and consists mostly of innate fantasies. Some therapists, such as Melanie Klein (Isaacs, 1952/1989), write as if these fantasies are primary in the sense that they will occur, if not in an interactive vacuum, with only a minimum of triggering from the interactive contact, which is viewed as almost nonspecific. Others, such as Wilfred Bion, suggest that infants have something like latent fantasies ("preconceptions"), which are innately organized and are experienced when they encounter an appropriate specific counterpart in real interactive life. I take the position that the infant has many strong, innately determined preferences and action tendencies that will greatly influence the very nature of his experience with the world as well as what part of the objective world he will have experience with.

The early interaction of infants and mothers has probably changed relatively little over millennia, compared with many other human interactions. This is exactly the kind of evolutionary stability that would favor the innate preprogramming of many of the perceptual aspects and motor patterns that make up these early interactions. The question is not whether much of this interaction is prewired—it certainly is—but whether it is necessary to postulate innate fantasies that exist prior to the experiences that the fantasies are waiting for or seeking. I would guess that the idea of innate or primary fantasies is not necessary, because, as we will see in chapter 5, the infant will so quickly form representations of those experiences that his nature leads him into. One can, of course, call this aspect of his nature "preconceptions," but these are not fantasies. Accordingly, except for the first few such experiences of an event, the infant will never be without some kind of experience-based representations that his preconceptions have led him to form. Still, it is the subjective aspects of his encounters with this selected world that will determine his representational world and then, secondarily, his fantasy life. In other words, interactive experience, innately guided, precedes fantasies, not the other way around. We will thus concern ourselves with interactive experiences in this chapter and derive fantasies from them later, in chapter 6. (When speaking of "real" interactive experience, I mean the subjective experience of being in objectively observable interactive events.)

2. *The events are microevents.* Parent-infant psychotherapies focus on the relatively small and short-lived events, such as what the mother does with her eyes and face at the moment when the infant's smile at her increases in amplitude. This descriptive level of events, which can be called microevents, can be contrasted with the larger macroevents that occupy most clinical theories: the mother's becoming depressed, the birth of a sibling, the emotional availability (or unavailability) of the mother, and so on. The point is that a macroevent such as mother's becoming depressed can have no possible meaning to the infant in that form. A maternal depression is a large concept made up of many smaller criteria that are present over a period of time. And there are different types of depressive interactions. The infant lives the depression in terms of the microevents that are its palpable manifestations.

In chapter 6, I will compare two points of view on the infant's experience of having a depressed mother: one in terms of macroevents as reconstructed by the adult who was once the infant of a depressed mother, the other in terms of the microevents that impact now on the infant who has a depressed mother. In brief, the macroevent view sees the maternal depression as a single traumatic macroevent—love lost at one blow. In the microevent view, the maternal depression is as knowable to the infant as many repetitive microevents, each of which is a different "way-of-being-with-mother."

Focusing on the descriptive level of the microevent is essential, because it is at that level where so much of the parent-infant interaction is played out. The nonverbal behaviors that make up a great part of this relationship are not communications about, nor comments upon, nor interpretations of the relationship; they *are* the relationship. They consist of microregulations of the level of affect and activation. To the extent that these interactions are purely social with no other goal in mind, they consist of the mutual microregulation of affect and activation. These mutual microregulations last split seconds, more rarely longer. They are the basic step of an interactive regulatory process. And, indeed, their split-second duration conforms to current notions in the neurosciences of the timing involved in most animal regulatory processes at the behavioral level and perhaps the physiological level.

3. *The events are ordinary, daily, and concrete.* Events are known to be clinically important by virtue of the changes they introduce into the weave of life. Even most traumas very rapidly become variations of the ordinary, daily, and concrete. In the life of the infant, they are recognized through changes in the patterns and quality of the main activities of eating, sleeping, playing, and so on—that is, in the activities that make up the fabric of life. Most often they are designated as traumatic long after the fact.

4. *The events are repetitive.* For the most part, it is the repetitiveness of events that makes them easily represented. Repeated microevents are assumed to be the basic building blocks of the representational world of both the infant and the parent. It is the experiencing-reexperiencing process that permits the formation of prototypes and generalized models (representations) of events. In this light also, it is to be expected that the changes or variations in eating, sleeping, or playing will tell the story. In the major motivational systems (or drives), these activities are repeated at regular intervals. Drives thus format life to facilitate learning.

Reading the Clinically Important Events

It is the banal, nonverbal, and diminutive nature of this interaction that holds some unexpected and unique features that perplex many clinicians who have not had considerable experience with infants and parent-infant relations. A full training in adult or even child psychotherapies does not necessarily prepare one for this clinical situation; in fact, it can sometimes be a hindrance.

Parent-infant therapies construct a first reading of the clinical story on the basis of the nonverbal actions and interactions that make up the microevents. The mother may of course vocalize—sing and say a great deal of sense and nonsense—but there need be no important verbal content in what is happening from either partner. The situation can be almost exclusively nonverbal.

The situation also need not be symbolic. In play therapies with older children, symbolic play may be utilized. The observer assumes that the play-actions are symbolic of an underlying psychodynamic text that could be told in words, usually not by the child but by the therapist. That is not the case in these earlier parent-infant interactions. There is not necessarily an underlying psychodynamic text in the usual sense of the term, at least certainly not for the infant. The actions do not symbolize anything. They *are* what it is about. The action patterns involved and their linked intuitive interpretations are greatly overdetermined by innate, phylogenetic considerations. We are at the level of intraspecific events best addressed by human ethology.

The first clinical reading of the interaction occurs at this level. Of relevance are such questions as, What is the physical distance between the partners? Is there an approach or a withdrawal, and at what speed? What is the orientation, or shift in orientation, of the pelvis and the shoulders? Is there a full orientation toward the other ("squared off")? Is there a turn toward or away from full orientation? What is the orientation of the head—that is, the facing position? Is there a shift of the head orientation of either partner toward or away from a direct vis-à-vis position? Is the shift away to the side? Is it with head tilted up or down? Where are the eyes looking? Is there mutual gaze? Is mutual gaze avoided with the eyes or with the head, or both? And there are the Darwinian facial expressions that accompany these actions and body positions, as well as the tone and volume of voice. There are also the anatomical places and patterns of mutual touching—for example, ventrum to ventrum, front to back, or head in the crook of the neck. For each and every one of these acts, we assume that the action is both motivated (usually out of awareness) on the part of the actor and unconsciously read on the part of the recipient.

What is read by the recipient (and by clinicians, as observers) are the motives that regulate the framework of engagement or relatedness: to get closer or farther away, to signal readiness for or avoidance of engagement, to initiate or terminate an engagement, to amplify or reduce the intensity of an ongoing engagement, to signal a positive or negative action tendency, to signal an affiliative or aggressive action tendency, and so on. These are basic human (and animal) motives at the level of an ethological reading. The infant is given both an innate general repertoire of these behaviors to perform and the mechanisms to decode their performance in others. Nonetheless, he must learn the cultural and familial variations on this universal human language.

This first clinical reading, at the level of motives and actions for regulating the engagement framework, provides the base and starting point of the clinician's observations. I call this level of interpretation the ethological reading. I was recently shown a videotape of a free play with a 4½-month-old seated in a baby seat. Immediately one was struck by the mother's position. She was very close to him, her face about 10 cm away from his. Her head position was full-facing. Her shoulders were squared off, so that she was fully oriented toward the baby. In addition, her arms were spread out to flank and enclose the baby. And from that position, she wove her head closer and back as she vocalized quite loudly. The infant, in response, showed repeated head movements away to the side. He frequently broke gaze, and his smiles alternated with a more sober, distressed expression. He emitted somewhat tense vocalizations that grew in amplitude.

An ethological reading assumes that the observed actions express motives to regulate the engagement. The mother is overregulating the interaction, showing an overreadiness to engage, forcing the initiation and maintenance of engagement, and mixing affiliative and aggressive signals. The infant is trying to escape, to protect and defend himself. In short, this is the description of intrusive, overcontrolling maternal behavior and the infant's response to it. But such a reading at the ethological level is not an individual psychological reading (although it is often mistakenly thought to be). It requires no knowledge of the past of either individual or of the dyad. No information is required about why that mother is conducting that kind of engagement regulation, or why she is doing it now. (See Corboz-Warnery et al., 1993; Fivaz-Depeursinge, 1987, 1991; for more details at this level, see also Stern, 1977.)

The second reading is an individual psychological one, in which the reading at the ethological level becomes individualized. Why this mother? Why this baby? Why that kind of engagement regulation? Why now? A full clinical reading requires the ethological gloss at the intraspecific level and a psychological gloss at the level of the individual and his past experience.

One gloss is not clinically (or otherwise) better or deeper than the other. They are at different levels of description, and they are complementary. The ethological level tells what happened, what actions and motives were in play. The psychological level tells, in light of the individual's past life history, why those particular actions and motives were in play at this time. It concerns the personal meanings attached to those actions and motives, which are beyond the more general intraspecific meanings. The cultural level mediates between the two.

The ethological level concerns the influence of an evolutionary past on the present. The psychological level concerns the influence of the personal, lived past on the present. The distinction between these two levels of readings, however, is not always so clear, especially when metapsychological theories of human behavior assume a genetic base for certain behaviors and fantasies.

Toward an Improved Reading at the Ethological Level

In spite of their overwhelming obviousness—or exactly because of it—these ethological level microevents are not so easy to see and describe as might be expected. It is paradoxical that in adult psychiatry, clinical psychology, and psychoanalysis, we are so well trained to look for and "see" the causes, explanations, and meanings behind overt behaviors (i.e., the individual psychological level) that we tend to become blind to what actually happened. Meaning supersedes description and eclipses it, especially for clinicians in training. (This is part of the evidence that action is seen in its motivational context.) I once hired a group of very good advanced psychiatric residents, untrained in infant psychiatry and not yet parents, some of whom were candidates in psychoanalysis, to help score parent-infant interactions. They were terrible at it. They were superb at seeing past the behavior to its meaning, but they could not code unelaborated descriptive events. A great deal of retraining was required for them to be as good as untrained, psychologically naive observers.

Psychiatrists are trained such that in order to see naively again, they must learn to hold clinical inferences in suspension. (Whether such inferences are right or not is irrelevant.) A certain amount of retraining is required, for several reasons:

1. Even when much of clinical interest is being said by the parent, from the infant's point of view the action is vocal, not verbal. The music and not the lyrics are being attended to. The observer must let pass by

some of the spoken information that is usually the basic source of clinical data. When watching television recordings of interactions, it is helpful either to turn off the sound or to have it just low enough so that the prosody but not the words can be discerned, at least for the first pass through the material. (This technique suggested itself to me when I was doing consultations with parents who spoke in a language I did not understand—an ideal situation for a first impression.)

2. The initial approach to the interaction requires a detailed description of what happened on a behavioral level. For instance, the baby suddenly broke the mutual gaze with his mother and turned his head rapidly away and down to the side. The mother then pulled back, wrinkled her nose, said "Yuuuk," and left the room. One could easily go right past the behavior to the higher level of explanation and say that the mother found the baby disgusting and rejected him. This is likely to be true, but it omits the descriptive key that her disgust and rejection were triggered by the infant's visually disengaging from her. Exactly that piece of information may be needed to understand clinically the entire sequence and even its precedents—for example, disgust was her response to feeling rejected. Explanations may accompany descriptions but cannot replace them. These behaviors carry species-specific meanings that are intuitively apparent and do not require a second explanatory, interpretative step.

3. Why-questions should be limited to why-now questions, much as in other clinical interviews. But here, the why-now refers to a small behavior: "Why did the mother pull back *then?*" or, preceding that, "Why did the infant look away *then?*" It is the sequence of why-now questions that starts to make evident the patterns of the interaction. By focusing on it one stays within and explores more deeply the descriptive stream.

4. The temporal parameters of this interactive world are different from those of adult psychiatry. As I have mentioned, it is a world in which events occur in split seconds. The time frame of observation, of the basic units of information, is usually shorter than what one is used to in traditional therapies. One has to come to trust one's on-the-spot visual impressions. There is a technique for heightening sensitivity that consists of evaluating someone by not looking at the person, then taking a quick but full glance and looking away again immediately. The evaluation is based on whatever was seen in that split second. Such sensitivity-raising techniques can be useful.

5. Clinical pattern recognition is based on patterns of movement rather than on propositional meanings—more like dance than like a written

text. In a sense, the first order of business is to discover the repeating patterns or sequences that form the backbone of the interaction. This requires the observer to have a mental set attuned to what will happen next, like that of a photographer seeking the "decisive moment" that is about to happen. With this mental set, one progressively identifies the repetitive elements that make up the patterned sequences. Generally speaking, it is easier and faster to identify the sequential patterns in more pathological interactions. They show more stereotypy and more dramatic ruptures or discontinuities that are easy to identify. They also usually show less variability. Nonpathological interactions are often so subtle, varied, and freely flowing from one theme or variation to the next that the flow appears almost seamless and pattern identification is difficult (see Beebe & Stern, 1977, and Stern, 1971, for examples).

Because of the importance of describing interactions and the difficulties in doing so, clinicians as well as researchers have taken to using video to aid in this task. Many therapies routinely use video replay as a fixed feature of the therapy, as we will see later in this chapter. Video viewing of interactions can also be highly useful in furthering the process of observing interactions as they happen, that is, without video.

One of the great advantages of video is the capacity for immediate replay. The viewer can not only see exactly what happened but, just as important, by repeating a sequence can quickly learn it "by heart." If one knows what will happen, one can view it differently. For instance, when watching a tennis match, one watches the ball and the action of the player who has the ball in his court. One wants to know what will happen immediately. If you know by heart what will happen, you can tear your attention away and do the opposite—that is, watch the actions of the player when the ball is not in his court. There one sees a different world of anticipation, responses, strategies. The same applies in the parent-infant interaction. The structure and the function of the interaction become clearer. Once this technique of observation has been learned with video, it can be applied to ongoing interactions. (In most interactions, the ball is in the court of the person who is talking or vocalizing or altering a nonverbal pattern.)

A second advantage of video is the freeze frame. It too can be used as a technique of learning to observe ongoing interactions. Thinking and seeing in freeze frames augment the sensitivity to the high point of an interaction, the moment around which the sequence turns.

In short, video and film analysis have taught clinicians much about being better observers. It is particularly helpful in the training or retraining they need to "see" at the level of microevents.

To observe the temporal aspects of the interaction—the responsivity and contingency and fine regulation—it is often necessary to forget about exactly what the interactants are doing (for the moment, at least) and focus on the timing. The focus of attention is aimed somewhere between the two partners, so that the behaviors of both can be seen equally in one's peripheral vision, which is more sensitive to motion.

What are the temporal criteria of contingency for the infant? For infants during the first year of life, three seconds is the rule of thumb for one behavior to be considered responsive to or contingent upon a preceding behavior. And a quarter of a second (i.e., approximately minimum reaction time) is the inner limit. Three seconds is, in fact, rather long after several months of age. And as three seconds approaches, one receives the impression (the baby will come to do so as well) that some intervening processes such as reflection, decision, inhibition, or overcoming inhibition have occurred to delay the response behavior.

It is first necessary to establish if the parent's behavior is responsive to that of the baby. Only then is it easy to discern whether it is positively or negatively contingent. For instance, each time the baby smiles, the mother could, three quarters of a second later, smile back or turn away. These actions are equally "responsive"; it takes the same sensitivity to be negatively contingent as to be positively contingent—a clinically crucial point.

This kind of interactive process evaluation must be undertaken for each of the main activities between parent and infant: regulation of arousal and activation, regulation of affect quality and level, physiological regulation, teaching, and so on. This reevaluation is necessary because sensitivity, responsivity, and contingency can be activity-specific.

All this sounds onerous, and for the purposes of quantitative research it is, but clinically these evaluations are made globally and rapidly. An experienced observer could suggest after one short viewing that a certain mother was oversensitive and overresponsive to the physiological needs and demands of the infant but relatively unresponsive to social-affective demands. Knowing the workings of the interaction processes involved can aid observational acumen.

Clinical Windows into the Parent-Infant Interaction

So far, I have discussed how to look, but not when to look for what. Here again there are features unique to the parent-infant relationship. The cardinal clinical issues that one is familiar with in adulthood are found here in different forms, often not immediately recognizable.

What follows is based on the notion that the basic clinically relevant issues such as trust, attachment, dependence, independence, control, autonomy, mastery, individuation, and self-regulation are life course issues. They are not issues that are age- or phase-specific. No one early period of life is specially devoted to the indelible writing of a definitive version of any of these issues. That is to say, there are no critical or sensitive periods in early life concerned with the irreversible consolidation of these clinical issues. Rather, they are being worked on all the time.

Nonetheless the manner in which they get worked on and the forms these issues take change across developmental epochs. The battleground constantly shifts, but the war may stay the same. This point of view has been argued elsewhere (Stern, 1985). And the basic idea has been put forward and used clinically by T. B. Brazelton in a manner adjusted for the clinical realities of behavioral pediatrics (1992, 1994). It is the same general view of development that permits one to think in terms of touchpoints or clinical windows.

The reason why the "battleground"—that is, the form, time, place, and local conditions—always changes is that development is always progressing but in discontinuous, quantitative leaps followed by periods of relative consolidation of the new acquisitions. The timing of these discontinuities is fairly well agreed upon, because at these nodal points of change almost all aspects of the infant's functioning change: motor, affective, cognitive, social, and so on (Emde & Harmon, 1984). From whatever perspective one views the infant, one finds a major change at these points. These leaps, during the first 2 years, occur at about 2–3 months, about 5–6 months, about 8–12 months, and about 18 months. As each leap brings into place new social, affective, motor, and cognitive capacities, the interaction with the parent is reorganized. What that means clinically is that the life course issues, such as independence or trust, will now be negotiated differently and in the new terms of the capacities for relatedness that the infant has just acquired. With each developmental leap, the lifelong grappling with such issues as independence and attachment simply continues but under a new form that may only disguise the unchanged function.

To deal with these age-related changes in form, it is helpful to know when and how the infant's capacities for relatedness change and what will be the new interactive battlefield. Each advance in interactive competence provides the therapist with a different "clinical window" to view the progress of the major life course issues.

The progression of clinical windows can be summarized as follows:

0–2½ months: During the first weeks, feeding and/or putting to sleep (including a nap) and episodes of crying and soothing are the events that constitute this first clinical window. The major interactive tasks at this age concern the regulation of the infant's feeding, sleep-wake, and activity cycles, and the majority of social exchanges occur around and within these activities. More specifically, social and affective exchanges—the parental smiles and baby talk—are used largely to cue and to regulate these events, as well as for themselves (Sander, 1962, 1964). It is the regulation and repair of these activities that is of clinical interest. For instance, when feeding starts and the infant is still avidly hungry, does the mother know to stay behaviorally quiet and let him proceed at a full unimpeded gallop? When the baby's hunger is partially satisfied and he needs a certain amount of parallel stimulation to keep a productive sucking rhythm going, does the mother know how to jiggle the bottle, play with and stroke the baby's hand, bounce him a little in her arms, say something, to arouse him just enough to start sucking again but not enough to startle and throw him off? When the baby gives signs of satiety, does the mother read them, and how does she respond? Can she orchestrate the baby's level of arousal and activity by using cues from him? It is in the conduct of these activities that one observes clinical issues of parental or infant responsivity, sensitivity, temperamental fit, overcontrol, undercontrol, bizarreness, and so on.

Because the regulatory process normally breaks down frequently, much crying by the baby and many attempts to rectify the situation by the parent are inevitable during this early life period. The repair of crying, then, is an important part of this clinical window. Charles Zeanah (personal communication, 1994) finds that crying is overwhelmingly the main complaint motivating parents to seek help in a clinic setting for infants under 3 months of age.

If home visits are made, the observation of an entire wake-to-wake cycle of 4 hours or so is very rewarding in clinical impressions. Practically, however, a considerably shorter office visit can achieve much if it includes a feeding and perhaps a putting to sleep thereafter. With a certain amount of planning and flexibility this can be arranged.

2½–5½ months: Face-to-face social interaction without toys or other objects provides the next clinical window (see Beebe & Stern, 1977; Stern, 1977, 1985; Tronick & Cohn, 1989). The infant is now, both by design and by default, perfectly adjusted to show his full social and affective capacities (and elicit the parental counterpart) in face-to-face play.

I say by design because the infant's innate preferences for the human face, voice, touch, and movement come strongly into play at this time. There is nothing in the world that can compete with these stimuli for attracting and holding the baby's attention. At this age his nervous system is designed for the situation of face-to-face play. Moreover the social and affective behaviors used to regulate the face-to-face interaction—that is, control of his gaze, responsive smiling, and vocalizing—become mature. Because these infant behaviors are so precocious, a face-to-face interaction at these early ages is an interaction between two people (parent and infant) with almost equal control and will to contribute to the initiation, maintenance, modulation, termination, or avoidance of the face-to-face engagement. A mutual regulation of the social interaction has begun.

The face-to-face interaction is also the preferred clinical window at these ages by default. What else can the baby do? His hand-eye and hand-to-hand coordination is not yet good enough for him to be interested in the world of inanimate objects or to reach for or manipulate them. He cannot get up and crawl or walk away. By his nature he is a kind of prisoner to the face-to-face situation, for better or worse.

At the same time, feeding and sleeping regulation may by now have become relatively routine. The action and passion have now passed to face-to-face play, and it is here that one can best see the same clinical issues at play that one observed during feeding several months before. For instance, if the mother was overcontrolling (e.g., intrusive) during the feeding, she will now overregulate the face-to-face interaction. It may be she who initiates most of the face-to-face dialogues. She will modulate the intensity of the interaction when she decides it has climbed too high or fallen too low. It is she who will decide when an episode of play is to be terminated; if the baby averts his gaze to close out an episode of mutual gaze, she may decide not to respect that act and instead chase after him to reestablish a mutual gaze so that she can then be the one to end it (Beebe & Stern, 1977).

It should now be clear what I mean by the continuity of issues (e.g., maternal overcontrol) in the face of the discontinuity of form (feeding versus face-to-face play). One observes the negotiation of the same issues, but at each developmental leap the negotiation takes on a new guise. It is this reality that makes the sequence of changing clinical windows clinically useful, both for seeing the common thread and for dealing with it therapeutically.

5½–9 months: During the next period, joint object play—that is, parent and baby playing together with some inanimate object—becomes the activity that provides the clinical window. The child has now acquired adequate hand-eye and hand-to-hand coordination and with it an avid curiosity about the inanimate world, so object play is where the clinical action is hottest. The observation of how the parent and infant conduct the direction, timing, focus, elaboration, scaffolding, change in subject, and disengagement of such play now reveals the same clinical story that one could glimpse several months before in face-to-face play.

Intrusiveness, for example, now takes on a new form in this new terrain; it is seen in how the mother overcontrives and overcontrols the infant's object play. For instance, while the child is sufficiently engaged with one toy, the mother decides that another toy is more interesting (that could mean more stimulating, more educational, or more pleasing to her), so she takes the first one away and offers the second. The infant accepts and explores this one, then loses interest and looks about for a third toy. Mother, however, feels that he has not spent enough time with this second toy and shows him yet a new aspect of the toy that he had not noticed. She insists on his not only noticing but being fascinated by this new aspect and in so doing fails to pick up his signals of boredom. (I have described the pattern by focusing on the mother's contribution and not the infant's to such a pattern, which he accepts and supports with his behavior.)

This overregulated negotiation about toy play is essentially the same as the overregulation seen in the face-to-face interaction several months before. It is played out in who initiates what, who terminates what, and when. But now play with objects is where the relationship gets lived and where the overdetermined patterns are revealed clinically. (There can also be patterns of underregulation as well, where the mother does not participate enough to scaffold the baby's initiations.)

8–12 months: There are two major developmental events that provide convenient and telling clinical windows during the period from 8 to 12 months. The first involves attachment. Beginning toward the end of the first year, the infant starts to manifest in a very clear and readily observable fashion the behaviors characteristic of attachment and separation from the primary caregiver. This process is accelerated by the infant's growing capacity to move away from and return to the mother (crawling, then walking). The patterns of attachment established by parent and infant are proving to be one of the best predictors of the quality of the parent-infant relationship. The clinical view into the relationship provided by patterns of attachment seems to apply to a large array of potential clinical problems and not just those related to the diagnosis of "problems of attachment" (Bretherton & Waters, 1985).

Watching how both parent and infant negotiate the comings and goings, the moving away and returning that are inevitable at this age, provides the raw data. It is not necessary in a purely clinical setting to establish the rigorous conditions of the "strange situation" demanded of research on attachment (Ainsworth et al., 1978). The idea is to get a clinical glimpse that may prove therapeutically useful, but not to establish any form of clinical diagnosis or research typing. Zeanah et al. suggest behaviors other than separation/reunion behaviors as the basis for assessing the nature of attachment—for example, showing affection, seeking comfort, reliance for help, and cooperation (Zeanah, Mammen, & Lieberman, 1993).

The second clinical window involves the advent of intersubjectivity (Astington, Harris, & Olson, 1988; Premack & Woodruff, 1978; Stern, 1985; Trevarthen, 1980, 1982). In brief, the infant comes to realize that his mother can have "things-in-mind," that is, contents of mind, such as attention to something, an intention, or an effect; that he, too, has things in mind; and that the contents of his mind and of his mother's mind can be the same or different. And if they are not the same, they can be brought into alignment. Several manifestations suggesting the presence of intersubjectivity can be regularly observed at this age, such as social referencing (Emde & Sorce, 1983; Klinnert, Campos, Sorce, Emde, & Svejda, 1983), affect attunement (Stern, 1985; Stern, Hofer, Haft, & Dore, 1984), joint attention getting (Collis & Schaffer, 1979) and reading of the other's intentions (Trevarthen, 1979), and taking the intentional stance (Gergely, Nàdasdy-Gergely, & Birò, in press). What is at stake here is the negotiation between parent and infant of what will constitute the shareable universe of mental phenomena: what can be public, what must remain private, what happened but is not to be referred to between people, and what is shareable. Viewed this way, the negotiation of intersubjectivity is a fascinating and rich observational perspective on the parent-infant relationship (for a further discussion, see Stern, 1985).

To continue with our example, maternal overregulation, at this life phase, would be manifest in the mother in various ways. One could see the mother establish the limits of exploration and the physical distance between her and the child satisfying her own criteria rather than the child's attachment needs. In the domain of intersubjectivity, one could see a parent establish very definitely which of the child's emotional experiences will be responded to as legitimate and shareable, and which will not. If, for instance, the infant feels only moderately excited and enthusiastic about something that has just happened but the overcontrolling mother feels that the event is—or ought to be seen as—far more exciting, she may make a modifying attunement upwards to show the level of excitement or enthusiasm that she is after. In order to share fully the same experience, the infant may be forced to manifest a "false" reaction. At an intersubjective level, the mother is being insufficiently sensitive to the infant's indications of what he or she would like to share.

18–24 months: During the second year, two other developmental leaps offer good clinical windows. First, there is the advent of language. Clinically, language learning is something like learning to play with objects. Both will happen anyway, even with thin parental input. Still, what one generally sees is a rich interaction where the parent helps, scaffolds, and elaborates in response to the infant's sensitivities, desires, and capacities. In a sense there is a clinically revealing triad established between the infant, the parent, and the word with its meaning. Just as one clinically watched this kind of triad at 6 months with real objects, now one watches it with "sound objects," that is, words (Berthoud-Papandropoulou & Veneziano, 1989). Once again, we see similar interpersonal issues (over-control, undercontrol, and so on) being negotiated differently at different ages.

The second developmental change ushered in at this age is the increase in mobility and physical capacity that leads to the need for limit-setting. The infant now has the ability to hurt himself and to do considerable damage. Also, it is at this age that society asks parents to begin the process of socialization in earnest. Often enough, the issue of limit-setting is presented by the parents as one of the chief complaints. Setting limits is, most often, not a process of establishing and enforcing rules; it involves negotiating them. Most of the time, the parent and infant are working in a grey area. Infants and children are uncannily creative in finding, or leading parents into, grey areas. And it is there that the negotiations that reveal the structure and functioning of the relationship are to be found. The manner in which the limits get set tells as much of the clinical story as what the limits are.

These, then, are some of the most commonly available and easily used clinical windows that answer the question, Where does one look in the parent-infant interaction, and when, to get a clinical sense of the relationship? Elsewhere I have attempted in a more popular fashion to give a sense of what it may be like for the infant to live these clinical windows, that is, a point of view from the baby's subjective experience (Stern, 1990).

The central point is that most of the basic clinical issues are continuous life-course issues, but the form in which these issues are negotiated is discontinuous, changing with each major qualitative leap in development. The developmental leaps provide the infant with new behaviors and means for conducting the same old issues. At each developmental leap, therefore, there are new clinical windows through which the basic issues can best be seen. This information is also valuable to the researcher devising observation strategies at the different ages. The notion of developmental changes in the forms for negotiating the same clinical issues will reappear again in chapter 10, as it has implications for the processes of generalizing or "working through" in the treatment.

Two final points must be added. First, the list of clinical windows suggested here is not meant to be exhaustive. Others, with different particular interests and perspectives, can be readily added. Since there are such major changes in the infant—and accordingly in the interaction—at each developmental leap, it is to be expected that these changes can be used from different vantage points (see, e.g., Brazelton; 1992, 1994; Greenspan, Lourie, & Nover, 1979; Mahler, Pine, & Bergman, 1975; Sander, 1964). Also, when a new clinical window becomes available, the previous ones do not disappear and become lost to use. Each manner of interacting that forms the basis of a clinical window provides the base upon which the subsequent manner of interaction is built. For instance, effective parent-infant play with an inanimate object relies heavily on constant reframing and contextualizing with bouts of face-to-face interaction. And later, intersubjective relatedness depends in large part on a shared base of having played together with inanimate objects.

The clinical window helps direct clinical observations. It is not intended as an exhaustive or even rigorous classification from the point of view of developmental psychology, but rather as a clinical guide for understanding the parent-infant interaction.

Some Theoretical Issues

We can now return to some of the implications of the reality that action must occupy a central position in viewing relationships with a preverbal infant. This requirement is sometimes interpreted as a reason for describing (or dismissing) the parent-infant interaction as belonging more properly to ethology or behavioral psychology, rather than to the more psychodynamic psychologies. My disagreement with this view requires a larger discussion.

A distinction must first be made about whether we are putting action (and interaction) at the theoretical center or the technical center of the therapeutic approach. Behavioral, systemic, psychoanalytic, and cognitive approaches differ in the technical attention they give to overt acts, as opposed to thoughts about such acts. This difference is in large part one of technique. In most behavioral and some systemic approaches, the field of clinical vision is initially limited to actions and interaction, that is, overt behavior. In technically "pure" traditional psychoanalytic approaches, the field of vision admits everything but action. Action is eliminated by the nature of the analytic setting, thus by technique; in fact, it is prohibited as "acting out." And in the place of action, one sees and works with the thoughts, feelings, fantasies, and so on, that emerge when direct, immediate action cannot take place. These mental derivations then become the exclusive subject matter of the analysis (Freud, 1938/1940, 1912/19, 1915a/19). Similarly, cognitive approaches concern the mental sets surrounding acts.

At a more theoretical level, beneath these aspects of technique, the centrality of action is implicit in all these approaches. Freud was very clear that unmodified motivated actions such as "specific action" (1895/1950) were indissolubly part of the drive. In fact, a specific action is always the local goal of a drive; energy discharge is the general, nonspecific goal. Thoughts, representations, and memories were thought to result from the inhibition of specific actions and thus were secondary derivations. In this sense, the extreme behaviorists and the classical Freudian positions are in agreement that the act, whether clinically addressed or not, is the basic point of departure for understanding motivated behavior. The fact that behaviorists plus some system therapists work largely with overt behavior and psychoanalysts work largely with the mental derivations of inhibited overt behavior tends to obscure this basic point of agreement about the centrality of the act.

A second important theoretical issue is involved. There exists a strong intellectual current against placing action at the center in understanding human behavior. As Eugene Gendlin states the problem, "Many people conclude that anything human *depends entirely* on language, concepts and history. Nothing of the human animal seems to remain. As Foucault (1977) puts it: our erstwhile animal bodies were 'utterly destroyed' by history. History and language seem utterly to determine what we will perceive, what we will distinguish as touched, seen or heard" (Gendlin, 1992, pp. 341–342).

Even actions committed by a human are assumed to have cultural concepts and language implicitly behind or within them. This may be increasingly true as development proceeds, but it is only partially so at the ages that interest us.

Psychoanalysis, leaning on the hermeneutic tradition, has developed its own version of this language- and culture-based position. Many modern strains of psychoanalysis privilege the narration or interpretation that stands behind or over an act, and that presumably defines it and gives it its psychic reality, rather than the act itself. This preference for the thought that surrounds acts is systematized in the psychoanalytic technique. It is the same perspective adopted by many psychodynamic approaches that give cardinal importance to the notion of reconstruction, the idea that what one experiences is not determined by the actions and interactions that make up the lived event, but rather by the later mental reconstruction of what happened. That is what becomes the lived experience. The reconstructed event (after the fact) becomes not only the "real" event but the only event. Action and interaction are not simply pushed out of the center but relegated beyond the pale. Chapter 5 contains a further discussion of this point.

In ethology and behavioral psychology, the opposite tendency previously reigned, and many considered the mental representation of actions off limits. Currently, however, the two extremes are approaching one another. Psychoanalysis is moving from the base of thought to admit action, and ethology and behavioral psychology are moving from the base of action to admit representation.

Thus the parent-infant interaction is a key element of the clinical system. It acts as a bridge between the other elements and is the major arena in which the symptoms and problems that motivate the consultation are formed. The clinically relevant parts of the interaction are considered to be the microregulatory events that make up the interaction. The clinical observation of the interaction is therefore somewhat different from most clinical endeavors. Some of the practical and theoretical aspects of this unique situation have been discussed, and they will reappear frequently as we proceed.

CHAPTER 5

The Nature and Formation of the Infant's Representations

W E CAN now turn to the infant's side of the relationship, or at least that part of it that exists in his mind. How does an infant represent the subjective experience of being in a relationship? (How does an adult, for that matter?) This remains one of the more intriguing questions that we left hanging from chapter 2, where it might have seemed easier to pursue such an inquiry with the parent's representations. When thinking about infants, we are far less sure what such representations are and how they get there. We are forced to reconsider the question from its very foundation.

The infant's representations are one of the main elements of the clinical situation, for a simple reason. Even if we could intervene clinically in a troubled relationship and successfully alter what the parents do and how they interpret events, so long as the infant's representations are not changed, he will act as he did before the alteration in his parents, insofar as that is still possible. The therapeutic effect would be partial and would probably not last long. After all, the infant's representations are his guide to what he expects, how he will act, perceive, feel, and interpret in the relationship with his parents. It is with this in mind that the infant's representational world must be explored.

Parts of this chapter have appeared in an earlier, less developed form (Stern, 1994b).

In this chapter I will speculate on the nature and formation of the infant's representations. I have made a previous imaginative attempt to depict the infant's representational world (Stern, 1990). Here, speculation will be more limited to available data and guided by theoretical concerns and conceptual lacks. This discussion may at times appear to wander from our immediate clinical concerns. It is intended, however, to prepare for the following chapter, which concerns the direct clinical application of the concepts and terms developed here.

Key Features of the Infant's Representations[1]

We are interested in the infant's subjective experience of being in a relationship. Accordingly, we must stay close to the baby's subjective point of view, even if we can only imagine it.

The representations we are interested in are different in nature from those of inanimate events in the physical world that the infant experiences, where the process of representing has been better studied. There are several important differences between the representations of inanimate physical happenings and those of subjective interpersonal happenings. For inanimate physical happenings, the mental events in a representation are thought to be isomorphic with the real events; they are simply performed virtually on an internal stage. For instance, Piaget's schemas concern objects and actions that can be performed concretely in external reality or mentally in internal reality. Similarly, some of the recent, more successful attempts to understand the infant's representation of human events have also chosen objective events such as going to a restaurant or a birthday party to be represented isomorphically (e.g., Mandler, 1979, 1983; Nelson, 1986; Nelson & Greundel, 1981). These events generally are affectively neutral. For subjective interpersonal happenings, however, the mental events are usually not isomorphic with events in external reality. Furthermore, such events are affectively charged and unfold in time with irreversibility.

Second, we will be concerned with recurring experiences, namely the ordinary daily interactions between the baby and his parents as well as the

---

[1]I shall use the term *representation* in spite of the general practice in developmental psychology of respecting the Piagetian distinctions between schemas and representations, between savoir faire and knowledge (1952, 1954). I do this for two reasons. First, the clinical literature generally does not bother with this distinction. And more importantly, the distinction itself, while of great value, is coming under new scrutiny with respect to infancy, especially as it regards interpersonal and affective events. In addition, the notion of representations as procedures or processes for reexperiencing, rather than as mental products and structures, leaves this distinction unclear.

less frequently recurring. The routine daily events are those that cluster around the vital life activities, such as eating, sleeping, and playing.[2] Thus while ordinary, they are of cardinal physical and psychic importance. These are the experiences of clinical interest that we are likely to encounter later when an adult talks of his or her childhood (e.g., what it felt like to do something with father). The feature of repeated exposure to these experiences is very important, because it is from the repetition that the infant can gradually construct a representation that is a generalized or prototypic happening.

This emphasis on interactive experience is key and marks a difference between the viewpoint adopted here and others. It is my assumption that these representations are constructed from interactive experience with someone. In that sense, they are not about objects (human or other), nor about images, nor about knowledge. They are about interactive experience. Fantasies and imaginary elaborations and additions are seen as later reworkings.

Third, these representations are not formed from external events or persons that have been internalized. They are not put inside from the outside. They are constructed from the inside, from the self-experience of being with another. Nothing is taken in. For instance, even if the infant is imitating another and acts and feels like that person at that moment, he will start to form a representation of how he feels, *within himself*, while being with the other in that way—for example, an identification. (See also Sandler, 1987.)

Fourth, the representation of the experience of participating in these human interactions must include many different elements: sensations, perceptions, affects, actions, thoughts, motivations, contextual elements, and so on. After all, these representations must be able to contain all the elements that occur and can be registered in the lived experience and that may be parts of a recalled memory of being-with-another. However we may conceive of these representations, they must have the complexity to accommodate all these elements.

Fifth, the form of representation must on the one hand allow for the coordinated and integrated existence of all these elements and on the other hand permit each element (e.g., the affect or the motor act) to be represented independently from all the other elements. It is common experience as well as an important clinical fact that one can experience any one of these elements floating freely or acting independently from the rest (e.g., as free-floating affect, disembedded perceptions, or isolated motor memories).

Finally, these representations are nonverbal. They are less concerned with knowledge and more with doing and being.

---

[2] In psychoanalytic terms, they are the drive-related activities.

In sum, we will need a representation of the subjective aspect of engaging in repeating interpersonal experiences in which all the basic elements of experience (actions, affects, and so on) can be represented both together and, at the same time, separately. We will call this representation a "schema-of-being-with-another."

Ways of Representing Experience

What fundamental formats for representing already exist to account for each of the basic elements of an experience as well as to tie them together? Taking each element separately, we have perceptual schemas (e.g., visual images) and we have conceptual schemas (e.g., symbols and words). Historically, these two kinds of schemas have long been accepted in psychology and psychoanalysis as different fundamental ways of representing experience. Piaget introduced the sensorimotor schema, which added motor acts and their coordination with sensory experiences as yet another fundamental way of representing experience. More recently, another basic form of human representation available to children has been added, namely, an invariant sequence of events that is represented as a single script or scenario or event representation (Mandler, 1979, 1983, 1988, 1992; Nelson, 1986; Nelson & Gruendel, 1981; Shank, 1982; Shank & Abelson, 1977). This gives us at least four separate and different kinds of basic representational formats to work with in creating something like a schema-of-being-with-another: percepts, concepts, sensorimotor operations, and event sequences. (The last two formats also tie together some of the elements of experience.)

Any one of these alone is inadequate to our task, and even all of them taken together would not produce enough of clinical interest. They are sufficient for explaining motor acts, event knowledge, and so on—that is, they are good for explaining what they were created to explain. But as concerns person-related subjective experience, at least two other forms of representation are needed: a basic format for representing affects and a format for representing the whole experience as a meaningful happening. I will take up each of these in turn.

Affect-Schemas in the Form of "Temporal Feeling Shapes"

There are two basic questions concerning affects: How might affects be represented alone (if indeed that happens), and how are affects linked to or attached to actions or perceptions or thoughts or memories.[3] Because of the phenomenon of free-floating affects—that is, affects that appear to be unattached or detached from thoughts, motives, or perceptions—it may be necessary to theorize a form of representing affects that is independent from cognition, perception, motor action, and so on. On the other hand, there is a tendency to view affects as linked to other mental events in their representations—for example, to cognition or event knowledge (Bretherton, 1984) or to motivation and adaptive goals (Trevarthen, 1993). In either case, it is rarely specified what might be the nature of such representations.

What we are after here is the subjective quality and quantity of feeling that accompanies experience. From the subjective perspective, the word *feeling* may be better than *affect,* precisely because it is vaguer. *Feeling* will be used here to refer to the subjective, feeling aspect of any and perhaps all experience. (*Affect* usually refers to both the subjective and objective aspects of only certain innately organized experiences, the Darwinian ones.) Used in this wider sense, feeling will include the subjective aspect of not only the discrete Darwinian emotions but those experiences that involve cognition as well as hedonic evaluation to produce a feeling. It will also include those experiences that are considered largely cognitive or perceptual or motor, to the extent that they too have a subjective, feeling aspect. The flow of thoughts or of perceptions or of motor patterns also creates feelings without any direct or simple relationship to classical emotions. These would include what I have called *vitality affects* (Stern, 1985). In other words, I want to withdraw the word *feeling* from the argument about the extent to which emotional experience is secondary to cognition. The existence of feeling then will be reserved for the subjective experience without consideration of the mechanisms of causation that are thought to produce it (which may not be subjectively experienced anyway). At the present time, when some are questioning to what extent distinct affects do indeed exist and there are theories that view affect as the feeling that results from a series of evaluations of such aspects as novelty and hedonics (Scherer, 1984, 1986, 1993), the advantages of an umbrella word, grounded in subjectivity, are appealing.

Let us first try to imagine how a feeling that is floating free might be represented, even if it is never fully free of other mental phenomena. What might its form or structure be like? Music suggests one possible answer. What music evokes is feelings more than affects, feelings that are "pure"

[3]Many different metaphors have been used to describe how affects may be attached to experience or memory. For instance, Freud suggested that affect is spread over the memory-traces of ideas somewhat as an electric charge is spread over the surface of a body (1894).

and abstract because they are "released from entanglements with contingency" (Langer, 1967, p. 88), that is, everyday specific external reality. And certainly the most essential aspect of music in producing this effect is the experience of time and the structuring of subjective time. I believe that it is the same for other feelings, that they too structure the subjective experience of time and that the subjective changes in time may provide the key to how affective experiences are represented.

It is important to remember that when experiencing affects, as when experiencing music, one is "in time," in the flow of time. It is a temporal experience, in which the changes unfolding in the present create the experience. Unfortunately, most often when we talk about affects we forget that they are experienced only in time, and we treat them like other mental phenomena that can be viewed as static events outside of time. One cannot take a short temporal slice, like a photograph does, of a musical phrase nor of a feeling, without destroying the whole. Yet we act as if experience had no temporal extension, or we consider that the temporal aspect is adequately covered by the sequencing of events, but the events, in themselves, are not considered in temporal terms. It is perhaps for these reasons that we have largely overlooked the idea that temporal contours provide the backbone that permits affective experiences to be represented. (The "in time" aspect of affect has indeed been addressed by others [e.g., Clynes, 1978; Langer, 1967; Stern, 1985; Tompkins, 1962, 1963], but these studies have penetrated insufficiently into the general domain of affect research.)

More specifically, whenever a motive is enacted (whether initiated internally or externally, as in drinking when thirsty or receiving and adjusting to bad news), there is necessarily a shift in pleasure, arousal, level of motivation or goal achievement, and so on, that accompanies the enactment. These shifts unfold in time and each describe a temporal contour. The temporal contours, although neurophysiologically separate, act in concert and seem to be subjectively experienced as one single complex feeling, which is a combination (an "emergent property") of the individual temporal contours of hedonics, arousal, and motivation. This is the *temporal feeling shape*, which I will call the *feeling shape*, for short. The feeling shape will also include the particular quality of feeling that gets temporally contoured. And that will depend on which affects and motivations are involved.

To examine further the feeling shape and what is meant by the subjective structuring of time, we can start with a simple example of a regular beat that is anticipated. Let us first take an example in music, where there are no contingencies of reality. In objective time a beat can be schematized as:

In subjective time, the same beat can be schematized in terms of the shifts in arousal, expectation, and perhaps pleasure as:

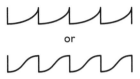

where each separate wave crest and trough is a temporal feeling shape and the series of these form a composite feeling shape in which the smaller ones are nested.

Switching from music to the parent-infant interaction, a good example is provided by one of the universal forms of a suspense game, "I'm gonna getcha." In this game we find a set of parental behaviors that repeatedly lead up to a climax. The parent, often the father, says, "I'm gonna getcha," while moving his face closer and walking his fingers up the baby's belly step by step. He pauses and starts over. He says it again with even more vocal drama, stretching the suspense by progressively retarding the beat, until after the last pause he finally says "Gotcha!" at an unexpected moment and tickles the baby under the chin. The baby then explodes with laughter. In this case the baby's affective experience is the subjective contour of his cresting waves and troughs of excitement, suspense, and pleasure. A kind of meaning in the form of a feeling shape has been added to the pure temporal beat.

The two above examples concern a beat that repeats. That need not be the case. There must, however, be a beginning and end to the period that will be subjectively structured in time. The end point can be intrinsic to the event. For instance, imagine a hungry baby, crying in the morning for his mother to come in and feed him. We will begin the first period (and feeling shape) at the moment the mother enters the baby's room and stop when the immediate goal-state is achieved of being positioned at the breast, sucking, drinking milk, with an initial reduction in hunger. The second period (and feeling shape) begins when the edge is off his hunger and he continues to suck until he is contented enough to stop.

We will call each of these periods an envelope, because it holds a discrete feeling shape and bounds the unfolding of a motive. In fact, it is a form of prestory, in the sense that it encompasses the enactment of a local motive with its attendant affects. It will thus be called a *protonarrative enve-lope.* For the moment we are concerned only with the temporal contouring of feelings during one of these periods or envelopes.

We will follow the time contour of only five of the possible invariant elements. (Invariant because they are always part of this event.) These are schematized in figure 5.1.

FIGURE 5.1

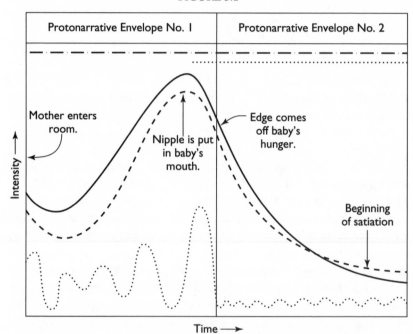

A Schematic of Five Invariants During a Sequence of Two
"Protonarrative Envelopes"

(—) The subjective sensation of hunger. In protonarrative envelope (PNE) 1, starting from a high level, subjective hunger should decrease a bit upon the sight of the mother. This abatement is transitory and the sensation of hunger may rise as the feeding approaches. Once the nipple is in the baby's mouth and sucking begins, the hunger will probably remain intense at first and then drop off.

(- - - - -) Negative affect. This contour should adhere fairly closely to the sensation of hunger. It may be more sensitive to the psychological effect of seeing the mother and to the nipple in the mouth, even before much milk intake.

(— . — .) Visual perception of mother. The infant will gaze at and visually pursue the mother throughout PNE1. In PNE2, he is likely to remain looking at her for this first phase.

(· · · ·) Tactile contact with mother. Variable in PNE1. Constant in PNE2.

(· · · ·) The baby's arm and leg movements. These would consist of large, jerky ballistic movements till mother appeared in PNE1. They then would quiet somewhat at the sight of her but would resume with progressive amplitude until the sucking began. At that point, the baby's motor action would be dominated by the rapid frequency, lower ampli-tude sucking movement.

The resultant feeling shapes of these events would be roughly as shown in figure 5.2.

FIGURE 5.2

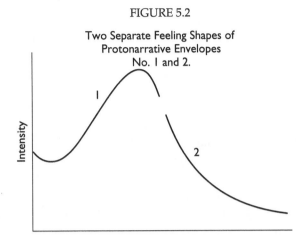

Two Separate Feeling Shapes of
Protonarrative Envelopes
No. I and 2.

There are two quite different temporal patterns of elements in these two affective sweeps. Each is dominated by a different immediate goal (sucking and drinking versus contentment). Each is a different feeling shape: mainly progression and acceleration leading to a crescendo in the first and deceleration and fading in the second. Discriminating them as two different global units of subjective experience seems within the infant's capacities, as we will see later in this chapter.

This example illustrates the notion that the temporal shape provides the structural frame on which the feeling takes its form and can be represented. The temporal feeling shape is a sweep or unit of affective experience that can be nested in larger (i.e., longer or more complex) feeling shapes. The temporal feeling shape can thus be viewed as a plausible representational format for schematizing affective experience.

The idea of describing affect experience in terms of temporal contours is not new. Silvan Tomkins (1962, 1963) linked specific intensity and time contours of neural firing to specific discrete affects. For instance, a rapid rise time of activation and stimulation resulted in fear, and a less rapid rise time, in surprise. Manfred Clynes (1978) linked certain intensity and time contours of activation to characteristic emotional states, such as love. I am not linking a feeling shape to any discrete affect; rather, I am suggesting that particular experiences, such as being hungry or waiting for the bottle, have their own individual, characteristic temporal feeling shapes. This description is closer to that of Niko Frijda and his colleagues (Frijda, Mesquita, Sonnemans, & Van Goozen, 1991), who observe in adults that specific emotional experiences are felt as having a duration and intensity contour. It is interesting that their contours are minutes and hours long. Those that I am postulating are more in the range of seconds, because the events that concern us here are mostly the microregulations that direct and correct the course of the larger sweeps of motivation and affect.

But can infants identify and discriminate feeling shapes? The relative neglect of the temporal aspects of experience, especially in infants, is surprising in light of the ample evidence that exquisite timing abilities are in place very early in life. Many experimental studies suggest, explicitly or implicitly, that infants are sensitive to the temporal features of both speech and nonspeech sounds (Beebe, Jaffe, Feldstein, Mays, & Alson, 1985; Bertoncini, Bijeljac-Babic, Blumstein, & Mehler, 1987; Bertoncini, Bijeljac-Babic, Jusczyk, Kennedy, & Mehler, 1988; Clarkson, Clifton, Swain, & Perris, 1989; Clarkson, Swain, Clifton, & Cohen, 1991; Jaffe, Feldstein, Beebe, Crown, & Jasnow, 1994; Kaye, 1992; Spence, 1992; Swain, 1992; Zelazo, Brody, & Chaika, 1984). It is also suggested that infants by 3 months of age can imitate, in their own vocalizations, musical elements of what they hear (Papousêk & Papousêk, 1981). Even simple games played by mothers and young infants demand a precise evaluation of short periods of time on the infant's part (see Stern, 1977, 1985). Recent work and reviews by David Lewkowicz document the experimental evidence supporting the notion of the infant as having precocious and often exquisite abilities to discriminate different features of time such as duration and rhythm and even to make cross-modal matches of temporal features (Lewkowicz, 1989, 1992). The feeling shape as a format for representing affective experience thus seems to be within the grasp of infants.

The Protonarrative Envelope

So far, we have five different basic formats for representing the infant's subjective interactive experience: schemas of perceptions, of concepts, of sensorimotor events, of event sequences, and of affects (temporal feeling shapes). It is assumed that these different schemas of a repeated interaction will form simultaneously and in parallel. Each will exist independently (probably in a different part of the brain or at least in a different neural network) but remain connected with each of the others. A question then arises of how these five separate representational formats are reassembled or reactivated so as to serve as a record (memorial or representational) of experiences that were, when lived, rich, complex, and ordered and that contained information that resides in each of the formats. Recently, the cognitive sciences have evolved new notions to solve the problem of coordinating the diverse schemas into a single coherent experience. The idea of *emergent properties of mind* is a way of describing how the mind makes sense of or renders coherent an experience made up of many simultaneously occurring, partially independent parts (Céllerier, 1992; Churchland, 1984; Dennett, 1991; Edelman, 1989; Maturana & Varela, 1979; Rumelhart, McClelland, & PDP Research Group, 1986). An emergent property is an organization that is in the process of coming into being or that has just taken form. In this view, the mind appears to process in parallel and in partial independence a large number of simultaneous mental happenings that occur during any interpersonal interaction. Motivational shifts, visual images, affect shifts, sensations, motor actions, ideas, states of arousal, language, place and space, time, and so on, are all processed simultaneously in parallel throughout all centers in the mind as well as in specialized areas devoted to processing each (*parallel distributed processing,* or PDP). It is in this manner also that the five fundamental formats mentioned so far are treated. The parallel processing of each schema is carried out with lower-level, local, mental operations that are unconscious. The result is a sort of mental pandemonium consisting of the mental action in multiple centers—many characters in search of an author. This is the normal state of things. And from the interplay, coordination, and integration of these lower-level processes, a more global mental event emerges: an emergent property of the mind, which has coherence and sense in the context in which it emerges. That is to say, the diverse events and feelings are tied together as necessary elements of a single unified happening that, at one of its higher levels, assumes a meaning.

The problem with this and other such solutions is how the meaning, even a very primitive one, slips in or gets assigned or is constructed from the pieces. There is a way out of this dilemma, and that is to assume that there is yet another fundamental way of representing human events, a sixth schema made up of "acts of meaning," as Bruner and others have argued (see Bruner, 1990). The basic idea is that certain interactive human events are directly perceived and apprehended right away in terms of meanings, even primitive ones. These meanings do not have to be constructed from diverse pieces but emerge from a global intuitive parsing of experience. Colwyn Trevarthen has long argued for a version of this basic form of apprehending human motives by young infants (1980, 1982).

More recent developmental research is beginning to suggest that the infant is intuitively endowed with some kind of representational system that can apprehend the intentional states of agents (e.g., Gergely, Nàdasdy-Gergely, & Birò, in press; Leslie, 1987, 1988; Leslie & Happé, 1989; Mandler, 1992; Premack, 1990). The notion is growing (but far from proven) that the infant may be able to take an "intentional stance" (Dennett, 1987) quite early and thus be capable of interpreting goal-directed, motivated human behavior in an intuitive and primitive fashion.

There is a representational format ready at hand to render meaning in the sense intended here, and that is the narrative-like mode of thought that concerns motivated, goal-oriented behavior. The schema (the sixth schema) that I suggest to render a meaning in infants is what I have called a *protonarrative envelope*.

The concept of the protonarrative envelope is based on the notion that goal-directed motivation is central to an understanding of clinically relevant (or any) human behavior, especially its subjective aspects. This centrality is pervasive in the theories that inform us. Goal-directedness is at the core of Freud's notions of drive, unconscious fantasy, and purposive ideas. It is interesting in this regard that Darwin in his notebooks mused that motives are the basic unit of the universe in that they are the functional units of evolution. From a different perspective, students of event knowledge and narrative structure have found motives and goal orientation indispensable aspects. Similarly, students of affects (Scherer, 1986; Steimer-Krause, 1992), of motor action (von Cranach, Kalbermatten, Indermühle, & Gugler, 1982), of cybernetics (Céllerier, 1976), of earliest language production (Bloom, 1973; Brown, 1973), of ethology (Hinde, 1982), and others all place goal-directedness at the core of their explanatory concepts.

The range of motives and goals that may take a central role includes external and internal states of object-relatedness (e.g., attachment and security), affect states, and states of self-esteem and safety, as well as physiological need satisfaction and consummatory acts (Emde, 1988; Lichtenberg, 1989; Sandler, 1985; Sandler & Sandler, in press). Also, attempts to reestablish a state of equilibrium when it has been perturbed must be added, as these are frequently the subject of affect research.

When the motive or desire is enacted in an interpersonal situation, it creates, subjectively, a narrative-like structure. As the motivated event moves in time toward its goal, it generates a dramatic line of tension, which is an essential temporal feature of the narrative-like structure (Labov, 1972), as well as a narrative-like mode of perception. This line of tension is created by the temporal unfolding of events, from a phase of action that complicates the plot, through a phase of crisis (the dramatic high point), to a phase of resolution. In this goal-directed movement, other events of the experience are also perceived in the light of the progression toward the end state. The result is the subjective formation of the other main elements of a narrative-like structure, namely a protoplot with an agent, an action, an instrumentality, a goal, and a context (Burke, 1945). In brief, goal-directed movement leaves in its immediate wake the tendency to experience events in terms of dramatic temporal lines and plots. These provide coherence and boundary features to the moment. Jerome Bruner (1990) points out that this narrative unit is a basic unit for comprehending human behavior in most folk psychologies and for children. Narrative-like structures can be seen as the inevitable counterparts of motivated, goal-directed behavior, and their comprehension should appear long before the ability to produce these structures verbally.

The protonarrative envelope is thus a time envelope as well as an event envelope. The elements of plot get temporally distributed on a line of dramatic tension. And the dramatic line of tension is invariably synchronous with the temporal feeling shape. This is natural, since the motive-goal tension is played out in terms of temporal shifts in arousal, pleasure, motivational strength, and goal attainment. In a sense, the perceived plot is superimposed or rather dispersed along the temporal feeling shape, which then acts as the line of tension to carry the narrative.

This notion that the temporal feeling shape provides the narrative line of tension is key, because it links the affect schema with the narrative schema. It is in this sense that affect—in the form of feeling shapes—plays a special role in coordinating and organizing memory and experience, as others have long suggested (e.g., Emde, 1980, 1983a; Emde, Biringen, Clyman, & Oppenheim, 1991; Freud, 1915b). This coordination between the feeling shape and protonarrative envelope can be visualized in a redrawing of the situation of the hungry infant. The temporal feeling shape labeled 1 in figure 5.2 will serve as the dramatic line of tension along which the plot unfolds. The two, plot structure and temporal contour of dramatic tension, that is, the feeling shape put together, are shown as figure 5.3.

Can an infant apprehend a protonarrative envelope, and when? It is called "proto-" because I suggest that it exists well before the capacity to tell narratives. I am assuming that the ability—in fact the necessity—to see the human interactive world in terms of narrative-like events and their motives, goals, and so on, is achieved very early. This is thus yet another case of comprehension preceding production by a long stretch.

Regarding when the infant might be able to identify the separate features of the protonarrative-like structure, I have suggested above that infants may be able to identify temporal feeling shapes, which is tanta-

FIGURE 5.3

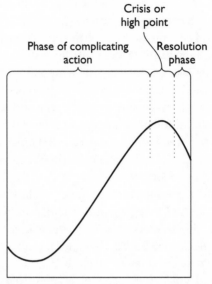

The phases of the plot superimposed upon the temporal feeling shape, which then serves as the dramatic line of tension.

mount to identifying the line of dramatic tension. Concerning the elements of a protoplot, when might the infant be able to apprehend them?

I will begin with the elements of the plot. By 3–4 months of age, if not before, the infant has sufficient capacities to differentiate self from other. Part of this differentiation rests on his ability to recognize his own agency, being the author of intended actions (see Stern, 1985, for detailed argument). At the same time, he starts to have an appreciation of primitive forms of causality, and his behavior is clearly goal-oriented. We even speak of "instrumental crying" at 3 months, as well as other instrumental behaviors, such as smiling. In a sense, then, well before the end of the first half of the first year, the infant has a primitive sense of agency, object, goal, and instrumentality. These abilities may well be demonstrable only for specific tasks—that is, those for which apprehending human goals and motives may be highly adaptive. (But we are getting used to this kind of task specificity [e.g., Spelke, 1994].)

Context, the where and when of the plot, remains to be discussed. Here the work of Carolyn Rovee-Collier and her colleagues (Rovee-Collier & Fagen, 1981) shows that by 3 months, infants have a great sensitivity to special surroundings (the "where"). Less work on the "when" in infancy is available. Colwyn Trevarthen has long held that beginning in the first months of life, infants share with the mother "primary motives," which imply an abbreviated protoplot (1980, 1982). These are evident in what he calls protoconversation (Trevarthen, 1989). These ideas are quite compatible with the point of view being developed here and have at various points stimulated and inspired it.

In sum, I am suggesting that the infant, very early on, has the capacities to schematize interactive events in a primitive form of narrative-like mode of thought and perception that I call a protonarrative envelope.

A Network of the Six Schemas:
A "Schema-of-Being-with-Another-in-a-Certain-Way"

We now have six schemas in which different parts of the subjective interactive experience are registered. (The protonarrative envelope is the most global and could be conceived of as playing a larger role as a guideline for the recomposition of the experience.) After repeated experiences of many moments of the general class of being-with-another-in-a-certain-way (e.g., being hungry and waiting to be fed), each of the basic schema formats of that class of moments-of-being-with will form—that is sensorimotor, perceptual, and conceptual schemas; feeling shapes; scripts; and the global protonarrative envelope. Together they form a network of schemas. The term *schema-of-being-with* refers to all the above schemas, the entire network of schemas that represent the different aspects of a repeated interpersonal experience.

The network of schemas, then, *is* the form in which the lived experience is represented. The different components of the lived experience are represented in the six different basic formats. And many components are represented multiply and simultaneously in different formats. For instance, in order to render event sequences, an experience must be divided into distinct units ordered in time. In order to render the affect, the same experience must be represented in an analogous form to preserve the temporal feeling shape. Thus the network of schemas-of-being-with is rich and diverse and with multiple codings.

We assume that each of the separate and parallel schemas making up the network forms in the manner now well described—that is, by the identification of invariant elements and the construction of prototypes and categories on the basis of constellations of invariant elements (Rosch & Floyd,

1978; Strauss, 1979; see also Stern, 1985, for such prototypes involving interpersonal interactions).[4]

Fantasies, Memories, and Autobiographical Narratives

We can now proceed to the question of where fantasies, certain memories, and autobiographical narratives come from—that is, what serves as their reference material. We will assume that the network of schemas-of-being-with is, in fact, the only reference for elaborating fantasies, memories, narratives, and "emergent moments." (Where else could they come from if they are not innate?) To accomplish that role, the network of schemas must be of a flexible and general form from which diverse mental phenomena can be constructed. The multiple system of schematization described in this chapter provides just such a flexible system. We now need a process that can use this flexible system. I call this process *refiguration*, borrowing the term proposed by Ricoeur (1983–1985) for the process of going from history to narration, from fixed serial order to arranged reorderings, from one pattern of emphasis and stress to a new pattern, from objective events in real time to imaginary events in virtual time.

Refiguration, as I am using the term, is the process whereby attention can move back and forth freely between the various schematic formats. The patterns of shifting attention create virtual sequences, virtual overlaps, or virtual co-occurrences, or various combinations of these. Attention can also be directed to two formats at the same time, one held in central attention and the other in peripheral attention, in a foreground-background relationship that can be reversed. The possibilities for montage are vast, almost unlimited.

The process can be illustrated with a familiar example. Imagine fantasizing your favorite sexual event. The mind can wander over the network of schemas of the event. It can visit each part at whatever speed (lingering in time) it wishes. It can revisit certain parts. It can start over. It can rush to the end and then fill in the middle. It can hold the high point in the fore-

---

[4]The schema-of-being-with is analogous to what I have previously called a RIG, the Representation of an Interaction that has become Generalized (Stern, 1985). The difference between the two is that the schema-of-being-with is conceptualized from an assumed subjective point of view of the infant in the interaction, while the RIG is identified mainly from the adult's objective point of view, observing the interaction from the outside.

ground and replay another portion at the same time in the background, and so on. In short, it can create the montage that is most satisfying or functional. The fantasy, then, is one possible virtual experience that results from refiguring the network of schemas.

The exact form of the fantasy is mostly determined by the immediate present context. That context would include, at a minimum, the reason (motive) for evoking the fantasy and the functional use to which the fantasy will be put, though it may account for much more. What is the difference between a fantasy, a generalized memory, and the script that emerges in preparation for telling a narrative? Are they not all refigurings of lived experience as represented in the network of schemas? The basic difference between these three mental phenomena may only be the function required of the refiguration by the demands of the immediate present context, each function having a different format.

This is a different view from one that postulates primary infantile fantasies. It sees memories, fantasies, and narrations as all coming, secondarily, from the same cumulative interactive experience but emerging (being refigured) under different demand conditions.

The Natural Selection of Schemas and Networks

Gerald Edelman (1987) suggests that the neural networks within each individual brain compete with one another, with the most functional networks surviving on an ontogenetic scale. Guy Céllerier (1992) has offered a similar proposal, in which the units vying for natural selection within the individual are schemas; the more adaptive ones are selected and given more active time and control over behavior. Ester Thelen (1990) provides a concrete illustration in the evolution of the infant's schemes of reaching. When infants first start to reach, there is great variability among them as well as a wide range of reaching patterns (and reaching schemes) within each child. Over the next months, a competition between reaching schemes (and the resultant motor patterns) takes place within each child, with the most functional winning out.

In a similar fashion, several schemas-of-being-with are probably constructed for the same repeated experiences and are subject to natural selection during the infant's development. This point is important to emphasize for several reasons. How does the infant know what invariants to use in chunking the flow of experiences into moments-of-being-with or which ones to privilege in constructing his schemas? How does he know which portions of the emergent moment to select to become part of the schema? How does he know how many different parallel and multiple forms of encoding make up the most useful network of schemas? He doesn't. Through trial and error and progressive approximation, he arrives at a form that is most functional for adaptation to ongoing events and for the refiguration of the network of schemas into fantasies, memories, and (later) narratives, each with functional values for adaptation.

The Problem of the Present Moment

What do the schemas-of-being-with represent? After all, schemas are about something. They have a referent, which is an experience that was lived—in our case, putting into action a motive with a goal. But one lives events only in the present. Can anything in the tight confines of the strict present moment be sufficiently coherent or organized that it can be represented? Some schools of thought assume that an experience in the present—that is, at the moment of living—is never organized into a recognizable coherent entity until after the fact, when what happened during the moment is constructed or reconstructed, especially by language. (The *après-coup* of psychoanalysis is such a construction.) There is, in a sense, an after-event but no event. Infants, of course, do not have language to perform this post facto organization, or more accurately, creation. Some thus conclude that infants do not have coherent experiences, only passing experiences that disappear once lived. Yet this cannot be the case, since infants do represent their experiences and appear, convincingly, to utilize those representations in their everyday behavior.

We are forced, then, to imagine a present experience that has enough temporal extension and coherence to be represented. Let us imagine a unit of time-present, an emergent moment of ordered interpersonal experience. This emergent moment is a subjective chunk of experience that is constructed by the mind as it is being lived. One experiences oneself as being "in" a moment. It organizes the diverse simultaneous happenings that are registered during a motivated event. In this sense, the moment is an emergent property of mind, which was described earlier, in chapter 2, and will be called an *emergent moment*. It will be our referent event for representation. (Remember, we cannot use an object—out there in the real world—as our referent.)

How long is an emergent moment? It cannot be the passing instant of the moving interface between the past and future. It must have some extension. Once again, an appeal to music may be helpful. Musicologists have been led to conceive of the present moment as a stretch of time in which the form of "what is happening now" can be grasped. The limits of this present are the immediate past (within short-term memory) and the immediately anticipatable future. These define the "horizon of the present." And we view these horizons while riding on a "crest of the present," a moving instant, between the horizons behind and ahead, where the present is most subjectively "dense" (see Darbellay who has provided these terms, 1992). During the emergent moment, which is just such a stretch of the present, a draft of what is happening is seized and created—that is, it emerges. There are, of course, plenty of markers in the interactional flow (just as there are in music) that help the process of parsing and creating meaningful units, such as a gesture or a change in posture that has a beginning and a predictable endpoint or a vocal unit with a predictable sound contour (e.g., Weinberg & Tronick, 1994). The highly marked nature of our interactive behavior thus provides the creative process of making a subjective moment emerge.

It is these emergent moments that become represented in the schemas-of-being-with. It is in this sense that representations are founded on interactive experiences that have been subjectively lived.

A Model of the Infant's Representations

We now have all the elements in place for a model of how the infant might form clinically relevant representations. During an object-related interaction, the infant has a subjective experience composed of unorganized data from his senses. At the time of the experience, some form of coherence arises as an emergent property of mind during an emergent moment. Separate aspects of the experience seized during the emergent moment are schematized separately and in parallel in the six schema formats that have been mentioned. This network of schemas serves as the schema-of-being-with, which then feeds back to influence subsequent emergent moments. This network schema-of-being-with can also be refigured to make fantasies or memories or (later) narratives. Figure 5.4 schematizes these relationships.

With this model in place, we can look in the next chapter at some infant schemas-of-being-with that are of clear clinical relevance. Before we do that, however, it is important to apply these concepts of schemas-of-being-with to the representational world of the parents as well. In

FIGURE 5.4

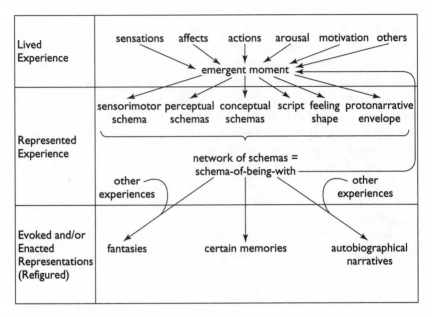

chapters 2 and 3 on the parents' representations, I made reference to groupings such as "the mother's network of schemas about the infant" or about herself-as-a-mother or about her own mother. We can reread these groupings in terms of networks of schemas-of-being-with as developed in this chapter.

CHAPTER 6

The Infant's Representations Viewed Clinically

EMERGENT MOMENTS and schemas-of-ways-of-being-with are units that encompass any form of patterned subjective experience involving interpersonal happenings. With these basic units of subjective experience fully assembled, we can now apply them to several clinical situations, to put some clinical flesh on the conceptual skeleton described in the last chapter. The examples that follow are intended to be illustrative but in no way exhaustive.

Being with a Depressed Mother

I will start with the "dead mother complex," a particular situation associated with maternal depression, as described by André Green (1983/1986). In this situation, the mother is physically present but psychically and emotionally absent, because she can no longer remain engaged with or emotionally invested in her child. This example is chosen for several reasons. Green's description is widely recognized as a superb analysis of a clinical situation that is both frequently encountered and of theoretical interest. It includes interactive events presumed to happen between an infant and a mother, as well as intrapsychic events. It provides a picture of adult reconstructive modifications of the original infantile representations. And perhaps most important, it describes in detail the task of reconstructing the developmental situation, according remarkably well with what one sees when observing these potential cases prospectively. Because there is agreement, in the main, about the phenomena present when the situation is viewed prospectively or as reconstructed, we can look at essentially the same phenomena from a different perspective, from which they look quite different.

In the past years, observers have explored more and more the interactions between infants and depressed mothers (e.g., Emde, 1983b; Field, 1987; Lewis & Miller, 1990; Murray, 1988, 1992; Osofsky et al., 1990; Weinberg & Tronick, 1995). What follows is informed and inspired by this work, to which I have added some of my own clinical observations.

All maternal depressions, including those postpartum, are not the same. Of the several types of maternal depression, the descriptions below concern mainly the type that is characterized more by psychomotor retardation, sadness, and internal preoccupation than by agitation and anxiety. When mothers get depressed, there is not quite the "brutal change" and "love lost at one blow" that adult patients may reconstruct and describe as a single clear traumatic event. Rather there is a progressive process of disengagement, usually partial disengagement. Instead of one traumatic subjective experience, there are at least four different chronic or repetitive subjective experiences—leading to four separate schemas-of-being-with—that together start to make up part of the infant's representational world from the onset of the mother's psychic disappearance in the context of her physical presence.

THE INFANT'S EXPERIENCE OF REPEATED "MICRODEPRESSION"

Compared with the infant's expectations and wishes, the mother's face is flat and expressionless. (I am assuming that the mother has become depressed recently enough that the infant has a set of schemas of her normal behavior with which to compare her present, depressed behavior.) She breaks eye contact and does not seek to reestablish it. Her contingent responsiveness is less, and her animation and tonicity disappear. Along with these invariants coming from mother, there are the resonant invariants evoked in the infant: the flight of his animation, a deflation of his posture, a fall in positive affect and facial expressivity, a decrease in activation, and so on. In sum, the experience is descriptively one of "microdepression."

What gives these moments their special character is that they are triggered by a desire to be-with-the-mother. After the infant has failed in his attempts to invite and solicit the mother to come to life, to be there emotionally, to play, it appears that he tries to be with her by way of identification and imitation. (It is becoming more clear that the infant's microdepressions are the result not only of lack of responsive stimulation from the mother, which is nonspecific, but also of imitative or contagious processes, which are highly specific.) The invariants of this attempt at identification consist of such elements as increased imitation, greater intersubjectivity, and diminution of self agency. Accordingly, when the infant—for whatever reason—is motivated to seek interactive or psychic intimacy with his mother via imitation, identification, and intersubjectivity, he will concomitantly experience a fall in positive affect, an increase in psychomotor retardation, and so on—in sum, a microdepression. The two phenomena—trying to be with via identification and imitation and the experience of depression—become linked in a single moment of subjective experience. This combination of the two phenomena is a recurrent way-of-being-with-mother, which is identifiable and becomes represented as a regular part of his subjective experience; that is, it is assembled in a schema. Clinical evidence that corroborates these descriptions has been observed by Joy Osofsky (personal communication, 1993). This clinical emergent moment can be schematized, just as was done for the hungry infant. The temporal unfolding of such a moment is shown in abbreviated schematic form in figure 6.1.[1]

FIGURE 6.1

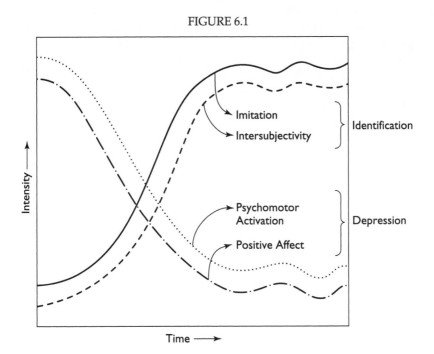

With certain adult patients, one often observes abrupt and usually short-lived plunges in positive affect—that is, microdepressions—that do not have an obvious external trigger. Clinical inquiry reveals that at the moment of the abrupt hedonic fall there has been the memory, the fantasy, or the current experience of attempting to identify with someone.

One way to think about such a situation clinically is to realize that microdepressions and desires or attempts to identify are associated. This could imply that the two parts being associated come from different "places" originally and that the dynamic reason behind the association may be clinically interesting. From the point of view of schemas-of-being-with, however, the desire to identify and the microdepressive state have not been associated in the usual sense; they belong together, from the beginning, indivisibly, because they were components of a single coherent unit of interpersonal experience, that is, of repeated emergent-moments-of-being-with that became represented. One then does not seek the reasons for the association; one seeks to discover more about the original events that fused the two components into one subjective experience. In some cases the two approaches will arrive at the same end point in the same amount of time, but in other cases they will not. For instance, one could seek after and find a whole set of reasons belonging to other experiences in life to explain why the feelings of depression and wanting to be with or like someone go together.

THE INFANT'S EXPERIENCE OF BEING A REANIMATOR

Faced with the situation of a resonant microdepression, the infant invariably tries to get the mother to come back to life. At this stage, this is a coping mechanism, not a defense. He turns to face her and establish mutual eye contact. He raises his eyebrows and opens wide his eyes and mouth in invitation to interaction. He vocalizes, smiles, gestures, and is often very creative with humor and invention. When none of this works, he turns his head away for a moment and then turns back to try again. This pattern of trying to recapture and reanimate the mother (and the self) is regularly seen with maternal depression and also in the experimental situation called the "still face," which was developed to study what infants do under just these conditions (Tronick, Als, Adamson, Wise, & Brazelton, 1978).

The important point about this envelope of infant behaviors is that it sometimes works and the mother is reanimated, even though depressed. It works because maternal depression is not total and not constant. Mothers differ in their availability to be reanimated from day to day or from hour to hour. Most depressed mothers are very distressed by their relative unavailability for their infant and often fight harder against that than against any other feature of their depression, and with variable success. One might think that if the infant's attempts at reanimation are rarely successful, he will gradually extinguish his efforts. And indeed, some infants do, at least with their mothers. But many do not. (Variable, infrequent reinforcement is a good way to maintain a behavior, not to extinguish it.) And for those who do not, the experience as potential reanimator continues to be a second way-of-being-with-mother under these conditions.

This way-of-being-with can be readily seen as one root for the infant's later development as a charmer, a "sparkle plenty," or a life-giver. Part of the emergent moment and schema will include the gratification of having succeeded in the task of reanimation. The infant receives the rewards of having succeeded as well as the benefits of the goal itself. The situation is (to exaggerate) almost addictive. It is little wonder that if such a schema becomes important in daily functioning, it may later play a not insignificant role in object-choice. For instance, only people in need of frequently reapplied efforts of reanimation in life will be seen and considered as potential partners.

THE EXPERIENCE OF "MOTHER AS A BACKGROUND CONTEXT IN SEEKING STIMULATION ELSEWHERE"

If, however, the infant experiences repeated failures at reanimation, he will turn away to seek a more appropriate level of stimulation and world-interest. Here, there are such invariants as the solo search for stimulation, a certain level of autoregulated vigilance and activation, and an amplification of curiosity, all occurring in the invariant physical presence of mother but only as an element of the background. That is to say that the external search for stimulation implies the mother's presence somewhere in the background. This is yet a third way-of-being-with-mother. It is a paradoxical way-of-being-with in that it makes it possible for solo acts of curiosity and searching for external stimulation to serve also as acts of attachment. This is so because the presence of another (even though in the background) is invoked by such seemingly unsocial activities. What looks like an independent solo action can serve a hidden attachment function.

THE EXPERIENCE OF AN INAUTHENTIC MOTHER AND SELF

Depressed mothers often try very hard. They know, only too well, that they are insufficiently there for their child and not providing enough stimulation. They tend to overcompensate in bursts. They make a huge effort, reaching into their repertoire and going through the right steps, but without the feeling. The result is a certain inauthenticity, revealed in failures of fine-tuning and minor discrepancies of behavioral coordination. I believe that infants can discriminate a forced flow from an easy flow (because of their excellent time-discrimination abilities), but they are so eager for a more enlivened interaction that they accept the minor violations and adjust their own behavior accordingly. The result—to overstate the case— is a false interaction between a false mother and a false self. The behavior is forced, the feeling is off, but the desire is very real. And it is better than nothing. This is a fourth way-of-being-with-mother, a fourth schema.

These four schemas-of-being-with are likely to be present in all cases of the "dead mother complex." They do not exhaust the possibilities, however. For example, another very likely schema, seen clinically, concerns a feeling of imminent disaster (loss or abandonment) but under circumstances where the baby cannot predict if it will happen (i.e., if the mother will be psychically available). Such a schema-of-being-with could, with developmental elaborations, evolve into a variety of anxiety phenomena. Other case-specific schemas are to be expected.

The interaction with the "dead mother" shuttles back and forth among these four or more schemas-of-being-with for months, usually for the duration of the acute phase of the depression. Which of the four will have relative predominance is variable. Some mothers, for instance, cannot love well but can get themselves up to stimulate the infant. These infants have less need for autostimulation or stimulation elsewhere, but the acceptable (but not optimal) stimulation they receive is without a sufficient dose of loving. Other mothers can continue to love their infant—perhaps the only person they can still love—and it shows. But they cannot get themselves up to adequate levels of stimulation. In this case the split between exciting sensations and love tilts the other way. Yet other mothers can be reanimated enough of the time by their infant that the infant becomes something of an antidepressant, a creative signal-reader and performer.

What is remarkable is that the reconstruction from adult patients in Green's account includes most of the same elements that appear in the above observational-prospective account. (It adds others, of course. The prospective account can say nothing about reconstructions after the fact.) Where the two accounts mainly differ is in what are assumed to be the initial pathogenic conditions. The reconstructed account posits a single, abrupt traumatic event, which focuses on the mother's withdrawal of cathexis. The other elements are then added later on in the course of progressive reconstructions and defensive elaborations, which fill out the evolution of the clinical picture as development proceeds through its different stages.

The observational-prospective account, by contrast, posits an initial condition consisting of four or more different, related ways-of-being-with-mother, which are represented in four different schemas. These are not conceived of as reconstructions or defensive elaborations. Rather, they are four parallel subjective experiences that make up the original pathogenic terrain. All four are the starting conditions on which later reconstructions will be based. In this view, the initial conditions are richer and more elaborated. The trauma has been somewhat demystified and transformed into the everyday ordinary. This perspective requires less reconstructive work after the fact, since there is more to start with, to build upon. (This viewpoint is essentially the same as what has been called the *continuous construction model* [Zeanah, Anders, Seifer, & Stern, 1989].)

The reconstructive perspective, on the other hand, assumes a sharper and simpler beginning, which requires more and richer reconstructive work later on. It is not surprising that the reconstructive approach finds the lion's share of the action in progressive reconstructions after the historical fact, while the observational approach finds more of the action in the observable initial conditions created at the moment of origin.

Each of these two complementary perspectives is potentially enriching to the other, and together they provide the triangulation necessary to understand better the nature of the evolution of reconstructions. It is in this sense that the notion of the schema-of-being-with and its related fantasies can be of clinical utility in a specific case. Hypothesizing these subjective units permits the identification and conceptualization of early experiences that may be the origins of later elaborated pathology and may thus inform the reconstructive process.

Patterns of Attachment: Being with Mother During a Reunion

The behaviors seen at reunion after a brief separation of mother from child provide us with another example. This, of course, is the classical situation from which patterns of attachment are established in research terms (Ainsworth et al., 1978) and the prototypic situation upon which the idea of a "working model" (a representation) of attachment is based (Bowlby, 1969, 1973, 1980). In a "secure" type of pattern the distressed separated infant moves toward the returning mother with gestures to be picked up or to be held and to hold and to establish visual or vocal as well as tactile contact.

And as all of that happens, the infant's distress leaves and he relatively quickly refinds his joy in life and pursues it on his own. It is easy to image what kind of feeling shape is involved here and what other behaviors are orchestrated with it.

Instead, let us take the example of an "avoidant" pattern as our specific example. Here, the infant may act as if he hardly noticed the mother's return. He makes no effort to reunite with her physically, nor does she with him, for the most part. It is not that he really didn't notice. Current thinking suggests that he notices it very well, that he is vigilant and under considerable stress (as measured by hormonal responses [Grossmann & Grossmann, 1991] or by physiological responses [Sroufe & Waters, 1977]) and, in fact, is acting to avoid placing an attachment demand upon a parent who would not tolerate it and who might react by creating greater distance between them or with aversive behavior.

We have a behavioral picture of nothing happening on the outside (i.e., the absence of a response) and presumably much going on inside. This is a situation for which a subjective moment-of-being-with becomes an almost necessary concept. One can only guess at the feeling shape it engenders. For instance, suppose that the child's desire for a "normal" (type B) resolution of the separation remains, even though it is rarely or never used, because it is so favored on psychobiological evolutionary grounds. If that is true, one must imagine the child exerting an active inhibition of type B behavior.

Let us first establish the boundaries of the moment-of-being-with. The mother walks back into the room. That is the beginning. She moves generally in the child's direction, but not exactly toward him or to him (after all, she is an "avoidant mother"). Nothing, for the most part, happens between them (except, perhaps, subtle negative cues by the mother), but the possibility that something (bad) could happen is all too present. The end of this moment, this apparent nonhappening, becomes apparent in one or both of two ways. First, enough time goes by with nothing aversive happening that the participants have safely slipped unmarked into a different interpersonal topic. Or, after enough time, one or the other introduces a new and different topic, unrelated to reunion, such as the wonders of a new toy or activity, thus terminating the reunion moment without ever having dealt with it. In either case there is a contour of tension started by the mother's reentry into the room and terminated either by slipping away gradually with the uneventful passage of seconds or more abruptly thanks to a relieving redirecting signal. (It is reasonable to suppose that there is a considerable level of tension and neither a lack of interest nor a pervasive insouciance on the child's part, because the above-mentioned studies indicate that these children are quite stressed.)

Within the postulated contour of tension, then, one could expect a camouflaged awareness of time passage and proxemic changes between the partners, the avoidance or inhibition of all positive attachment behaviors, the threat of an untoward parental response, and so on—taken all together, an anxiety-filled waiting-and-not-acting time until a dangerous moment has passed. Such moments have a particular feeling shape and should be relatively easy to schematize. In their multiple variations, they are a well-known part of children's games, dreams, and everyday social life. Each of us has a personally well-known prototype and common variations that constitute a family of ways-of-being-with-another (e.g., how formally meeting a stranger is experienced). Once again, it is hoped that thinking about such situations in terms of moments-of-being-with and schemas-of-being-with will help in clinical inquiry as well as in developing and focusing research questions.

Some Other Examples of
Moments- and Schemas-of-Being-With

The main purpose of this section is to see how wide a range of experiences can be handled by the concepts of moments- and schemas-of-being-with. We have already applied these concepts to the clinical situations presented by maternal depression and certain attachment phenomena. Recall that the notion of these moments and schemas was urged into existence by the need to take more fully into account the unique aspect of individual experience. Our theories point the way to the important general forms of experience, but it is the specific variations on these general forms that makes up actual lived experience and ultimately our private representational world. We need a structure to think about an individual's unique personal version of experience—how it is formed and what it is like. After all, that is what clinical work is all about.

The schema-of-being-with is conceived as a unit of intermediate size, in between larger and more general units such as working models or person representations or role relationship models and the small acts of actual behavior requiring local knowledge of the other. They are viewed as the units through which these larger representational units take on form so that they can be enacted in behavior in specific contexts. They add the specificity and individuality that are the conditions that real life imposes. The examples that follow are selected to explore further the value and range of these concepts.

The first example comes from clinical experience with high-functioning

autistic children. For this material, I will rely heavily on the work of
Frances Tustin (1984, 1990) as well as of others deeply familiar with subjective phenomena in cases of autism (e.g., Aulangier, 1985; Houzel, 1985).
Tustin refers to an interesting subjective phenomenon in autistic children
that she calls *autistic sensation shapes* (1990). These are repeated, stereo-
typed, autogenerated, usually tactile or kinesthetic activities such as
stroking, rubbing, rocking, and feeling the edges of objects. These activities are experienced as soothing or tranquilizing and are assumed to divert
attention away from the outside world, and in so doing they are viewed as
defensive. These experiences are similar to what Winnicott has called *subjective shapes.*

There are several aspects of such experiences that are of interest and relevance to our larger discussion. It is clear that these experiences have a
temporal feeling shape; that is, each repetition of the activity creates a tension contour with a feeling quality. In addition, in Tustin's view, these
activities, even though largely automatic and stereotypic, imply a context
(interpersonal overstimulation) and a goal state (avoidance of an awareness of separateness). They force a reconsideration of the notion of
moments-of-being-with by asking, Are there not also "moments-of-being-
with-the-self-in-a-certain-way"? And if there are such moments, as we can
all attest, must they be viewed in an interpersonal context? Tustin's sensation shapes are clearly, in their origin, interpersonal in the inverse sense
that the main motive for their appearance is the need to escape interpersonal contact. I would add that these experiences structure subjective time,
much as music can. Such structuring not only organizes but heightens the
sense of existing.

Most normal adults I have talked to describe characteristic moments-of-
being-with-themselves that occupy an important place in their subjective
life, often a stable point of frequent return. For instance, a friend describes
a state of mentally floating, alone. During such moments she lets her mental activities proceed on their own, specifically without paying particular
attention to any one mental event (thought, feeling, perception) that bub-
bles up. None are allowed into a central conscious mental workspace,
which is kept empty. Such moments are experienced as free mental
ambling, quietly pleasurable, refreshing, and often productive, because
when she breaks the moment and "returns," she often does so with solutions to problems and questions that were pressing just before.

I would call such a moment a way-of-being-with-the-self or, more accurately, a way-of-part-of-the-self's-being-with-another-part-of-the-self. I assume
that it is a way of distantly experiencing one's own parallel distributed
processing, one's mental pandemonium, without interfering with its on-

going work—and without insisting on a premature closure, in the form of an unripe intuitive product. It is interpersonal in a double sense. It is a moment defined by keeping at bay the intrusions from both one's own conscious, observing ego or that of anyone else. In that sense it is a negative-way-of-being-with-someone not totally unlike the autistic sensation shapes of Tustin, except that it is a semivoluntary, constructive, and adaptive mental activity. Second, it is "inter" personal in that it is a way for part of the self to be with another part of the self.

I am arguing that the notion of being-with can be interpreted widely so that different ways of being with the self—or various parts of the self—can be included. This seems to be a useful extension in the sense that these moments- and schemas-of-being-with-the-self have the same general structure as the others, that is, the moments- and schemas-of-being-with-others. They use the same kinds of invariants, get built around feeling shapes, acquire narrative-like structure, and have interpersonal motives and functions.

How about being alone, where nothing is happening? I would argue that something is always happening. Consider, for instance, letting a quiet moment with yourself prolong itself. This moment would have a reduced plot, but one all the same, that involves the maintenance of a state of equilibrium, of an unwavering status quo, a high point distributed almost equally throughout. That is also a feeling shape.

Experiences of anxiety provide another instructive example that may challenge our description of how these moments and schemas are structured. Some have maintained that the experience of anxiety, by its very nature, cannot be structured and represented. H. S. Sullivan takes such a position in often stating that anxiety is something like a blow on the head; it disorganizes ongoing experience, thus preventing it from being structured (1953). This idea raises the question of whether or how there can be structured schemas involving anxiety. Do all such experiences simply leave holes in the structure of experience, or of memory, or of representational networks?

I would argue that anxiety does not leave holes but, like other experiences, is represented. It is yet another different moment and another special way-of-being-with, with its own invariant elements. Most anxiety bouts occur in particular contexts that contain solid invariants. There is the characteristic feeling shape of extremely high, almost intolerable, negatively toned tension or activation that remains unabated a subjectively long time. And when it does go away, it ebbs. The episode implies a narrative structure that has the perhaps unique and memorable features of the inability to find a means for resolution or escape and the failure of goal achievement. Repeated bouts of anxiety, be they direct or contagious with a parent, also lend themselves to schema formation as a particular experience of a way-of-being-with.

The final point I wish to make here returns to the idea of moments-and-schemas-of-being-with as all-purpose structures for thinking about unique private worlds and their formation. In observing parent-infant interaction or in listening to patients, the clinician cannot learn from theories exactly where the action is, or was. For that, a way of schematizing and representing subjective experience is required that can deal with events that are—or appear to be, or at least are experienced as being—particular, specific, and unique, the concrete realities that make up individual experience, as against theoretical or abstract experience. After all, clinicians set out to explore individual lives, not theories. It is in this search that the notions of moments- and schemas-of-being-with take their place.

CHAPTER 7

The Therapist

THE PRESENCE of the therapist is the final element of the clinical situation that we must consider. The place and role of the therapist have some unique aspects in parent-infant psychotherapy. Where is the therapist situated in the model we are constructing? For the sake of visual clarity, we will concern ourselves with schematizing a minimal cast of characters: mother, baby, and therapist.

The verbal and nonverbal exchanges between therapist and mother constitute the overt behavior between them. This talking makes up the vast majority of the therapy. The therapist may also have verbal and, even more, overt nonverbal interactions with the baby. These exchanges with mother or with baby are both coded in our model as T_{act}.

And in keeping with the model, the therapist has a representation of the mother, of himself, and of his interaction with her. Similarly, the therapist has a representation of the baby and his interaction with the baby. These are coded as T_{rep}. In addition, the mother has a representation of the therapist and of herself in interaction with the therapist, as does the baby. These can be coded as M_{rep}^2 and B_{rep}^2, respectively (see figure 1.4). Let us look more closely at how these sets of representations function in the clinical situation.

In this chapter I will refer to the therapist as *he*. Thereafter *he* and *she* will be alternated in successive chapters.

The Mother's Representation of Herself When Interacting with the Therapist (M_{rep}^2)

The mother's representation of herself in the clinical situation is a key new element for effectuating therapeutic change and requires further discussion. When the mother is in the presence of the therapist (i.e., interacting with him in reality or in imagination), she will see and feel herself to be a somewhat different person and different mother from the one she feels herself to be when she is alone with the baby. The capacity of the therapy to generate, enable, permit, facilitate in the mother alternative (and more positive) views of herself-as-mother is one of the cardinal products of the therapeutic relationship. What this implies is that M_{rep}^1 (how she sees herself-as-mother when alone with the baby) and M_{rep}^2 (how she sees herself-as-mother when in the therapeutic relationship) are different and can be compared with each other. It is exactly this comparison between M_{rep}^1 and M_{rep}^2 that may direct the mother toward therapeutic change.

Put more simply, the mother's engagement in the therapeutic relationship provides her with several other possible mothers that she could realistically be or become and with several other mothers she could stop being or avoid becoming. No matter what therapeutic approach is adopted, if a therapeutic relationship is established (and there can be no therapy if it is not), an array of multiple possible mothers for the mother to become will open up. Because of the therapeutic importance of M_{rep}^2 (the mother's representation of herself when in the therapeutic relationship), it is important to discuss some of the decisions that the therapist must make that will ultimately influence the M_{rep}^2.

First of all, it is to be determined which interactions with the baby are to be considered as legitimate or fruitful subject matters for the therapeutic work and which would be obstacles to that work. The possibilities include playing with the baby, feeding, setting limits, diaper changing, and so on. Which of these merit consideration for their therapeutic potential? None? All? Some? (Such questions would never arise in traditional family therapy, where all interactions are grist for the mill.)

Is the baby an interlocutor for the therapist? Will the therapist develop a relationship with the baby and use it therapeutically? Therapists differ greatly here. Some direct almost all their attention and action toward the parents, stopping only for a brief moment when the infant makes a clear and inescapable appeal to them directly. Others engage in play and other interactions with the baby as part of a diagnostic exploration as well as a therapeutic maneuver directed either toward the infant—to give him an alternative interactive experience—or toward the parent—to model for them possible behavior with the infant.

The physical positioning of the people present is important and revealing. When the therapist and mother are seated in chairs and the baby is on the floor, the mother-as-a-person is generally the focus of therapy. When all three are on the floor, it is more likely that the focus of therapy is on the mother and baby, or the mother-as-mother. Frequently one sees the therapist seated and the mother and baby on the floor together. This is a largely unstable pattern, most often indicating a difference in agendas between the mother and the therapist.

If the therapist largely ignores the baby, in positional arrangement and focus of action, he is sending a very clear message that the problem—or at least the cure—lies with the parent alone. And, indeed, this is the basic assumption of many approaches. Such a stance renders the therapy closer to a form of focused adult psychotherapy. The baby and his problems become a sign or symptom of conflicts existing within the parent. The fact that the baby is present does not in itself make the therapy a parent-infant psychotherapy.

If, on the other hand, the therapist does make the baby a direct interlocutor, a different set of possibilities is put into play, with various consequences for the M_{rep}^2. Perhaps the most important is the parent's view of the therapist as a real or imagined "baby expert" in comparison with herself. When a mother—in her own eyes—is failing or inadequate in her caregiving functions and the therapist shows her "how to do it" (feed, calm, make smile, whatever), the therapist runs the risk of becoming the "better mother." (The Lieberman-Pawl and McDonough approaches, described in chapters 8 and 9, take great pains to avoid this risk.) Being seen as a better mother may color the central nature of the parent-therapist relationship and alliance and thus the M_{rep}^2 in various ways: the therapist can become an object of jealousy, envy, and competition; the parent may feel devalued as a parent; or the therapist may be seen as a kind of idealized grandparent who will teach the mother and father (as student-children) how to parent. In each case, the nature of the therapeutic relationship and transference hangs in the balance, and with it will be determined the probable maternal perceptions of herself-as-parent when in the therapeutic relationship.

There is a related question. Who is the real patient in the parent's mind? Usually the answer is not clear. (Who the real patient is in the therapist's mind will be taken up in chapter 10.) A mother may fear that she is at fault or deficient—that is, that she is the real patient. She also secretly or openly hopes that this is true, because in that case the essential problem does not reside in her baby, who gets spared, and she is also better able to rectify the problem. The identity of the real patient can thus be obscured by maternal altruism and identification with the baby.

These phenomena also can change aspects of the normally present defenses against and resistances to treatment and to the therapist. Parents may be far less defensive to change what they do or feel or think when it can be shown to impact clearly on the baby than when it impacts only on them. As long as the therapy is acting on the parent-as-parent, and not on the parent-as-person, it will usually meet less resistance. It is for this reason that most therapeutic alliances can be made rapidly and secured solidly if the central focus of the alliance is to make the parent a better parent. To take advantage of this situation, the therapist must be seen as a parenthood-enhancing agent congruent with the major life task of the parents at this point in their lives. (We will take these issues up again when considering the motherhood constellation in chapter 11.)

In summary, there are several aspects of the mother's relationship with the therapist that are either interdependent or overlapping: the conception of the baby or mother as the real patient, the therapeutic use of interactions with the baby by mother and therapist, the presumed and utilized expertness of the therapist, the complexion of the transference, and the range of different possible mothers-to-become or to-avoid that will become apparent to the mother during therapy.

The Baby's Representation of Himself and of the Therapist-as-a-Partner ($B_{rep}{}^2$)

In some therapies, described in chapter 9, the therapist interacts directly and purposely with the infant. The infant then is forced, as the mother was, to form a representation of the type of interaction he has with the therapist ($B_{rep}{}^2$) and to compare it with the representation of the type of interactions he usually has with his mother ($B_{rep}{}^1$). Here, too, the comparison between the two may play a large therapeutic role. Essentially, if the infant can learn to interact differently with someone besides the mother, he may be able to apply that new manner of interacting into the old relationship with mother and thus alter his network of schemas-of-being-with-mother. Behavioral therapies depend on this generalization.

The Therapist's Representations of Himself, of the Mother, and of the Baby (T_{rep})

The introduction of the therapist's representations into the clinical situation makes the processes of countertransference potentially part of the clinical system. Theoretically, an alteration in how the therapist views the mother-as-a-mother could have an impact on how she will ultimately see herself, as we will see in part II.

In sum, the role and position of the therapist in this new clinical situation are basically similar to what one expects in any clinical situation, although there are several relatively special aspects. With this final element of the parent-infant clinical system in place, we can now proceed to an examination of how these elements are used differently in various therapeutic approaches.

THERAPEUTIC APPROACHES IN PARENT-INFANT PSYCHOTHERAPY AND THEIR COMMONALITIES

CHAPTER 8

Approaches That Aim to Change the Parents' Representations

I N PART I, the six basic elements making up the parent-infant clinical system were described. In part II, a variety of therapeutic approaches will be described in terms of two aspects. The first aspect is the theoretical aim or target, the basic element of the system that the therapist wants ultimately to be changed. This element is largely determined by the therapist's theory of how change comes about. She does not necessarily have to focus clinically on it, but it is the key element that her theory tells her must be changed if there is to be clinical improvement.

The second aspect is the port of entry into the system. This is the technical clinical focus, the basic element of the system that is the immediate object of clinical attention. It is where, or the element through which, she enters into the clinical system. It is what the participants most talk about or work on, and it provides the major source of shared clinical information.

The port of entry and the theoretical target may or may not be the same. The port of entry is the way of reaching the theoretical target. For instance, one can try to alter a mother's unrealistic representations of her baby (M_{rep}) by showing her what the baby's capacities really are, what he can do—that is, by holding the clinical focus on the infant's overt behavior (B_{act}). Or one can try to alter a mother's representations of her baby by exploring them directly—that is, making them the port of entry as well as the theoretical target.

An initial attempt to describe different therapeutic approaches in terms of theoretical targets and ports of entry has already been made and proved helpful (Stern-Bruschweiler & Stern, 1989). In that original report, what I am now calling the "theoretical target" was called the "locus of therapeutic action," and what I am now calling the "port of entry" was called the "source of clinical information." What follows is an expanded and elaborated version of that original description.

There are several advantages to classifying therapeutic approaches in this manner. First, it permits the many different approaches to be situated relative to a referent clinical model and allows for easy comparisons at the descriptive level. Moreover, using the same basic elements allows diverse approaches to be seen in terms of which elements are privileged for what therapeutic roles: that is, what therapeutic route is taken to alter what theoretically key element. This view permits us to see differences in technique as secondary to the theoretical choices that underly techniques. It also permits the therapies to be grouped under the main theories that inspire them, since the choice of the theoretical target is a good index of the underlying theory. For example, psychoanalytically oriented approaches will choose the parents' representations as the theoretical target and as the clinical focus.

While I have grouped the approaches in terms of theoretical target, I could also have grouped them in terms of port of entry into the system. This arrangement would have resulted in creating families of similar techniques rather than families of (somewhat) similar theories. My aim is not to create or discuss a classification of approaches, however, but rather to illustrate the range in one (of many possible) coherent fashions.

For the present we will treat each different therapeutic approach as complementary to all the others and focus on how each approach attempts to enter and alter the clinical system. The approaches selected for description represent a wide spectrum of parent-infant psychotherapies. This selection is not intended to be exhaustive but rather to illustrate the main ports of entry and therapeutic targets of the clinical system. I will describe in a summary fashion how each therapy is presumed to work. For a greater knowledge of the conduct of these therapies and a deeper exploration of the theories underlying them, the original sources will be identified.

All five approaches described in this chapter consider the parents' representations as the key element to be changed. In this sense, they are in agreement as to what is the theoretical target of the therapy. They differ, however, in which element of the system will be used as the port of entry to influence the parents' representations.

I will first discuss two therapies that use the parents' representations as both the port of entry and the theoretical target. I will then discuss therapies which, while finally aiming to alter the parents' representations, choose other ports of entry into the system, such as via the infant's overt behavior; via the parent-infant interaction; via the therapist's representations (a sort of countertransferential route in); and finally via the infant's representations.

The Parents' Representations as Both Port of Entry and Theoretical Target

Two different approaches will be described: "infant-parent psychotherapy," as described by Alicia Lieberman and Jeree Pawl (1993), and "brief mother-baby psychotherapy" ("psychothérapie brève mère-bébé"), as described by Bertrand Cramer and Francisco Palacio-Espasa (1993). I will start with infant-parent psychotherapy, because Lieberman and Pawl are figuratively the direct descendants of Selma Fraiberg and are continuing the program begun by Fraiberg in San Francisco. There is a second reason: This approach is an excellent representative of many programs that are psychoanalytically inspired but adjusted to a wide range of patient populations seen in infant mental health programs. The end point of this psychotherapy is to "free infants from the distortions and displaced affects engulfing them in parental conflict" (Fraiberg, 1980, p. 70) or, in Lieberman and Pawl's words, to "change the parent's internal representations of himself or herself and of the child" (1993, p. 430).

To illustrate how Lieberman and Pawl privilege the representation as the key element for change, I will use one of their examples. The mother of a 22-month-old boy was constantly angry at and rejecting of her son. She thought of him as a "monster." This was presumably a key cause of his tantrums and other difficult behavior. The pathogenic representation on the mother's part was the notion that being a mother was demeaning and interfered with "becoming someone important"; her son stood in her way. This representation came from her own mother, who was contemptuous of motherhood, of her daughter (the mother in question), and her son-in-law (the father). Until this mother could see her identification with her own mother and the consequences of these shared representations, she could not change her behavior toward her son. Only when her representations of her child and of herself as a mother were changed could she see her son differently and act differently toward him.

The boy's father was represented by the mother (and by the mother-in-law) as a "weakling." This representation of him—which he partially shared—was potentially pathogenic in the following way. The boy often climbed on his father's back to be carried, a game they both enjoyed. At times, however, the father feared that his back would go out. He could not tell this to the boy for fear of being a weakling. Instead, he would get angry and would put the boy down briskly, causing him to cry. Again, a specific representation was the engine for the troublesome behavior.

It is in this sense that the parents' representations are potentially the pathogenic agent. Lieberman and Pawl would probably want me to nuance this last statement, because they are extremely sensitive to the baby's contribution to the clinical picture, and they conceptualize the parent-infant relationship as the "patient," not the parents alone with their private representational worlds. They even call the therapy "infant-parent psychotherapy" and not "parent-infant psychotherapy." This emphasis is not misplaced, because they treat a severely disadvantaged population. It is therefore imperative to avoid "blaming mother" in any way, which approaches that target the parents' representations may have a tendency to do. These authors consciously and with great effort avoid it, because so many of the mothers they work with have been criticized, invalidated, and penalized by the mental health and legal systems, so that anything that smacks of blaming mother would either prevent or break the therapeutic relationship. Nonetheless, in spite of this clinical necessity, the representations of the mother and father remain the main target of their therapeutic action and the key element in their conceptualization of the clinical situation. They are always aware of the parents' network of schemas-of-being-with-others, though it is often in the background.

The process that is thought to change the parents' representations, in this approach, is the "corrective attachment experience of the therapeutic relationship" (p. 430). The San Francisco group also gives a role to interpretation, to the empathic emotional availability of the therapist, and to increasing the parents' self-esteem, knowledge, and skills, but the corrective emotional experience of the therapeutic relationship is considered the most important mutative process in altering the parents' representations. And as we will see later in this chapter, this leads these therapists to make the therapeutic relationship and the M_{rep}[2] the central port of entry.

This view of the change process puts much importance on forging and maintaining an optimal therapeutic alliance and on creating transference/countertransference conditions that allow for a new and better experience of self in relationship with others, especially with the baby. This emphasis on the parent-therapist relationship gives a special flavor to this therapeutic approach.

Within the large spectrum of psychoanalytic traditions, these therapists could be considered post-Freudian, in the sense that their conceptions and techniques for effecting change rely less on interpretation and making the unconscious conscious, as in earlier Freudian views, and more on the object relations aspects (corrective attachment experiences) and on self-psychology (empathic availability and self-esteem).

Before discussing further the clinical focus the San Francisco group uses, it is more instructive at this point to compare the theoretical target of this approach with that of a second one. Brief mother-baby psychotherapy, the second approach to be considered, is practiced in Geneva by Bertrand Cramer and Francisco Palacio-Espasa (1993). Similar psychoanalytically inspired approaches could have been chosen for discussion, in particular the approaches practiced and inspired by Serge Lebovici (1980, 1983) and Leon Kreisler (1981; Kreisler, Fain, & Soulé, 1974). The approach of the Geneva group is largely inspired by the above French therapists and Selma Fraiberg. It is chosen because it is the approach used in an outcome research project that plays an important role in our story later in the book and because it attempts to adhere as close as clinically feasible to classical psychoanalytic tenets, its practitioners all being psychoanalysts.

In the Geneva approach, the theoretical target is the parent's representations and the identifications and projections that are seen as part of these representations. A vignette of the case described in chapter 3 illustrates this. A mother is experiencing her 13-month-old son as aggressive and as hurting her. She has always seen him that way. She experienced the pregnancy as painful. As a newborn baby, he hurt her when he sucked at her breast. And now, at 13 months, she interprets much of his assertive exploratory behavior as aggressive. In turn, she either rejects him or is aggressive with him. This response presumably results in his tantrums, difficult behavior, and aggressiveness.

The theoretical therapeutic target in this case is the network of representations that account for the way the mother interprets and reacts to her son's behavior. It is further assumed, from the psychoanalytic model, that pathogenic representations exist and that they consist of unresolved conflicts dating from the childhood of the parent. These have remained and been elaborated as core conflictual themes, and they are now being activated and enacted in the current interaction with the infant. The "red thread" that is sought is the thematic connection between the mother's childhood conflicts (memories and representations), her current core-conflictual themes, and the current mother-infant interaction. In the clinical example given, the therapist ties together the mother's representations of her son as aggressive and hurtful and herself as being physically vulnerable, her childhood experiences of repeated hospitalizations and surgical penetrations, her lifelong vulnerability to physical aggressions as a core problem existing in other contexts (e.g., sexual), and the interactive events that the parent and therapist can observe and that enact the thematic material. The main pathogenic influence lies clearly within the mother's psyche, even if its effective manifestation is in the parent-infant interaction. This basic supposition casts a long shadow, as we will see in chapter 11.

It follows clearly that in such an approach interpretation is considered the cardinal force for change. Corrective emotional experiences, empathic availability, and so on may be helpful in an ancillary way, but interpretation linking the past to the present and the mother's representations to the mother's interactions—in other words, making the unconscious conscious—carries the major therapeutic weight. To change the parent's representations, interpretation is necessary and at times could even be sufficient, given a therapeutic context that prepares the way for it.

In a sense, the therapists of the Geneva group use a psychoanalytic model that is, in many of its essentials, close to an early Freudian classical position, with their view of thematic enactment of childhood conflict and their emphasis on interpretation. In fact, many of their clinical cases sound remarkably like Freud's early cases in his *Studies on Hysteria*. It is a model designed for treating neurosis. And, indeed, they have traditionally considered patients with major affective disorders, moderate to severe character disorders, psychoses, and retardation or lack of psychological insight as not appropriate candidates for their treatment, just as traditional psychoanalysis would.

In contrast, the therapists in the San Francisco group rely on post-Freudian psychoanalytic models. They have evolved a model better designed for treating character disorders, affective disorders, and even psychoses. Their clinical cases sound more like cases from the British object relations school, from schools of self-psychology, or from those who treat borderline patients.

Some of these differences between the two groups stem from the differences in the populations they treat. The San Francisco population is relatively disadvantaged with lower socioeconomic status, more single mothers, drug problems, and minority status. Many parents have already had disappointing experiences with the mental health establishment and may even be mandated by the courts to seek infant mental health services. (Other therapies to be discussed later in the next chapter, such as McDonough's "interactional guidance," encounter the same population, which forces some of the same design features.)

The Geneva sample is far more advantaged, consisting mostly of intact nuclear families of middle socioeconomic status, who seek psychotherapy of their own volition, usually on the recommendation of the pediatrician or local nurses. The differences in motivation for treatment and the expectations for the patient-therapist relationship are thus important.

These differences in population have resulted in some curious paradoxes. In order to get and hold patients in treatment, the San Francisco group pays exquisite attention to the formation and nature of the patient-therapist relationship, real and fantasized. They have to. The establishment of a workable therapeutic alliance and acceptable transference/countertransference conditions therefore becomes the primary therapeutic goal. It requires most of the therapist's attention during a long beginning phase, and to accomplish it the therapist is willing to utilize a wide variety of techniques that may fall outside the pale of what the Geneva group would accept: advice, concrete help, home visits, and the like.

The Geneva population and therapists, on the other hand, expect therapeutic engagements similar to those seen with neurotic patients coming voluntarily for a traditional psychoanalysis. Accordingly, the therapists in the Geneva group do not feel the need to spend the same large amount of time and effort on the therapeutic alliance or to regulating the transference and countertransference. An adequate therapeutic alliance is, in a sense, assumed and assured in advance. And it is taken for granted that a generally positive transference will usually emerge on its own if permitted to.

The result is that the San Francisco group is very rigorous about certain psychoanalytic parameters but rather free with others. In a sense, the therapeutic approach of the San Francisco group is built on the presumption that in that population the major obstacle to a successful treatment will be a negative transferential reaction. The therapeutic approach of the Geneva group is rigorous or free with other psychoanalytic parameters. They assume that in their population the major obstacle to treatment (as in the case of classical neuroses) will be the positive transference. These differences in approach are more than practical or technical, based on population differences; they also derive from diverging theoretical positions. The nature of the transference anticipated has far-reaching consequences for the way therapy is conducted. This issue will be discussed in detail in chapter 9.

These population differences also have implications for the port of entry chosen to get to the theoretical therapeutic target and to enter into the clinical system. The therapists using the infant-parent psychotherapy in San Francisco want ultimately to change the parents' representations. They are willing—and find it necessary—to use almost any and all sources of clinical information and routes of entry into the system to achieve their target. The therapeutic relationship, itself, however—that is, the mother's representation of herself when she is with the therapist—is the privileged clinical focus. That is what provides the "corrective attachment experience." And this corrective experience is assumed to become progressively internalized to alter the parents' representation of self, especially self as parent, and of the infant.

This approach attempts to alter the parents' representations in two steps. First, the mother's representation of herself-while-being-with-the-therapist is altered. This is the M_{rep}^2 of chapter 7. It is the corrective emotional (attachment) experience that flows from the experience of the clinical focus on the therapeutic relationship. This altered experience and new representation of self then is transformed into an altered representation of self-while-being-alone-with-baby (M_{rep}^1).

This process is diagrammed in figure 8.1, where the solid arrows show the ports of entry and the dotted arrow shows the theoretical therapeutic target.

FIGURE 8.1

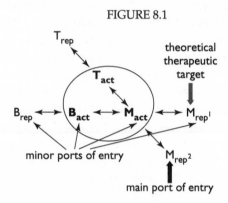

The San Francisco therapist will, if need be, enter the system by using as a source of shared clinical information the infant's assumed representations of what is happening. The therapist may, for example, take the infant's "voice," as if she were speaking from inside the infant's mind, explaining something about how the infant may feel to both the parent and the infant. (This is the privileged port of entry for some treatments, as we will see.)

The therapist is also willing to use the infant's and the parent's overt behaviors as a port of entry. And of course, the therapist wants to discuss the relevant representations of the parent, when that is possible—and it need not be. Even though the parent's representations are the conceptual target of the therapy, they do not have to be the main port of entry. In sum, the San Francisco therapist is willing to use almost every one of the basic elements of the clinical situation as a port of entry into the system, even though the parent's representations remain the privileged port of entry and therapeutic target.

The Geneva group, on the other hand, adheres more closely to classical psychoanalytic parameters in many respects but not in others. The therapists in this group identify more with psychoanalysis, and unless they find convincing clinical reasons to the contrary, they will opt for a classical psychoanalytic solution, with full knowledge and in spite of the fact that the clinical situation they work with is not at all that of a psychoanalysis. The only clinical focus and port of entry into the system they consider legitimate is the mother's representations, M_{rep}^{1}. And indeed, most of the time is either spent directly discussing or preparing for a discussion of how the mother feels about and interprets events, what in her past contributes to these feelings, and so on. The mother's representations are seen as particularly open to change during this phase of life. This approach is diagrammed in figure 8.2.

FIGURE 8.2

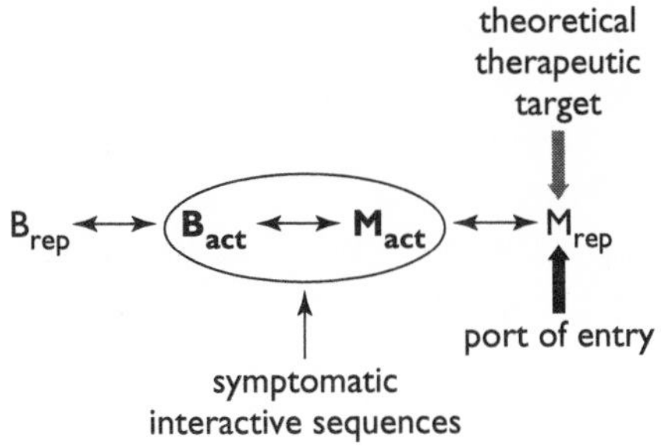

This group does, however, use the overt behavioral interaction as a clinical focus, although in a special way. They seek to identify overt behavioral interactive sequences between mother and infant that can be viewed as manifestations or enactments of the core conflictual theme, putting it into behavioral terms. This interactive sequence is then treated like a symptom within a psychoanalytic model. In fact, these selected behavioral episodes are called *symptomatic interactive sequences*. They are used as a shared clinical focus, but they are valuable, in this approach, only to the extent that they lead the clinical inquiry directly back to the already identified underlying representations, that is, the target. They are used as examples, or instantiations, of what is already known.

The therapeutic alliance or transference, in the form of M_{rep}^{2}, is not used as a clinical focus, as it is in traditional psychoanalysis. Rather, it is left alone, even if it remains operating strongly at the end of treatment. (Other psychoanalytically inspired mother-baby psychotherapeutic approaches, such as that practiced by Serge Lebovici and his colleagues in Paris, freely use the transference as a source of shared clinical focus and as a port of entry into the system.)

In general, then, the Geneva group attempts to maintain a psychoanalytic frame as long as possible under these clinical conditions. Giving advice and concrete physical help, maintaining a positive regard, providing education, and other such techniques are not simply not used; they are considered violations of the psychoanalytic frame. On the other hand, certain essential features of psychoanalysis such as the active clinical use of the transference are not much used, while practically they could be. It is not always clear whether the treatment modalities have been chosen because of the exigencies of the unique clinical situation or for theoretical reasons determined by the psychoanalytic inspiration. There are necessarily inconsistencies in adherence to a traditional psychoanalytic model.

To summarize, Lieberman and Pawl use M_{rep}^2 as the port of entry to ultimately change M_{rep}^1. They give greater weight to the realities of their particular population and of the parent-infant clinical situation than to the established practices and concepts of psychoanalytic theory, which still guides their approach. Cramer and Palacio-Espasa use M_{rep}^1 as both the port of entry and the theoretical target of change. They have chosen to let the established psychoanalytic theory and practice have the upper hand so far as that is possible and acceptable in this clinical situation and with their population. These different choices, plus the differences in populations, result in two quite different therapies, which nonetheless agree that the ultimate goal is to change the parents' representations of self-as-parent and of their child.

The Infant's Behavior as Port of Entry

What is most characteristic about this approach is the clear focus on the behavior as the port of entry. Most frequently the clinical interviews with the parents take place during an examination or evaluation of the infant. The evaluation setting could be in the form of a routine pediatric examination (Keefer, personal communication, 1994), or a Neonatal Behavioral Assessment Scale or a Bailey or other such evaluations that lend themselves to stopping and starting after each item to discuss what was observed. The infant's behavioral responses to the test situation become the subject matter to initiate much of the discussion, which can then lead toward the parents' representations, or parents' behavior or medical problems, depending upon the inclination of the interviewer, the situation, and the material triggered by observing the infant's responses.

For the purpose of this chapter, I will comment on only one version of this approach, one that leads from the infant's behavior toward the parents' representations. The emphasis on the mother's representational world owes much historically to psychoanalysis. A problem with assigning a psychoanalytic inspiration to a particular approach today is that some of the basic ideas of the psychoanalytic "movement" have been so widely accepted that they have been folded into other ways of thinking.

The approach selected here aims ultimately to change a mother's representation of her infant and of herself as a mother (M_{rep}) by focusing clinically on the overt behavior of the infant (B_{act}). This is an approach described by T. Berry Brazelton and his colleagues in Boston (Brazelton, 1984, 1992; Brazelton, Yogman, Als, & Tronick, 1979). This form of behavioral pediatrics is only one among many. It is used here as an example of an approach, not as an exemplar of the entire pediatric approach.

Two examples will illustrate. In the first, a mother gives birth to a small-for-gestational-age baby. Characteristically, these babies become easily overstimulated, hyperexcited, distressed, and disorganized. In this situation, it often happens that the mother finds her newborn extremely difficult to handle, and routine efforts at regulating the baby become a nightmare. The mother begins to represent the baby as difficult, unrewarding, impossible, a bad baby of one sort or another. At the same time, the mother's representation of herself as a normally competent mother can suffer greatly. She may experience growing fears of being insensitive, bad for the baby, or outright destructive. A vicious circle may be established in which progressively more unsuccessful and unsatisfying interactions provoke a deterioration in her representations.

In such a situation, in Brazelton's approach, the clinical focus is placed on the baby's behavior. The therapist might advise or show, for instance, that such babies cannot tolerate stimulation in more than one sensory channel at a time and that they will calm down and tolerate an interaction better if it is conducted in only one channel—touching, or talking, or rocking, but not all three together. The clinical focus is to demonstrate the baby's current interactive capacities and limitations and teach the mother how he can best be helped along at this time.

The unstated aim of these efforts is to alter how the mother sees her baby (M_{rep}) so that she can take advantage of the advice and information given. In other words, the mother's representations of who her baby is and who she is as a mother are the hidden target of the approach. Once she begins to see her infant's behavior and her previously unsuccessful ministrations more objectively, she can start to undo the troublesome representations that were forming or becoming established. (One could always argue that she simply learns how to readjust her behavior without making any appeal to altered representations.)

A second example is perhaps more revealing. An unmarried, disadvantaged, teenage mother has a baby girl. After vacillating back and forth, she decides, without much commitment, to keep the baby. While the choice has been made legally, it has not yet been made psychologically. The mother shows little interest in the baby and makes few initiatives to start the bonding process. The family and staff become worried that this mother may not make a sufficient attachment to her baby or do it in time. At this point, the mother's representation of the baby is of a somewhat unspecified person to whom she can later, in her own time, make a commitment.

The therapeutic approach in this situation is once again to place the clinical focus on the infant's behavior (B_{act}) so as to touch and jog the mother's representations of the baby. In this case, as described by Brazelton, the shared clinical work is to hold the infant, face up, with Dr. Brazelton on one side of the baby and the new mother on the other side. They then both say "Hi, baby" (or her name) repeatedly. The baby will slowly turn in the direction of her mother's voice. (Infants do this because that voice is already familiar to them from the womb and because newborns prefer voices in the alto range in any case.)

The mother is generally surprised by this response on the baby's part. Not only has the baby chosen her to look at, but she has done so in preference to the famous pediatrician (whom the mother may well have seen in magazines or on cable TV that morning). This piece of infant behavior, when well handled, can have a strong effect on mother. She says to herself something like, "My baby prefers me to Dr. Brazelton. She has chosen me already. But I haven't yet chosen her or made my commitment. Now I have to, or else she is all alone." In a very short span of time—minutes—the mother's representation of her baby, and of herself as mother, has been jogged, focalized, and set off on a new course of construction. It is extraordinary to realize that such limited, focused events can have such impact on the representational landscape. Certainly, much of this effect is permitted and prepared for by the conditions of normal crises that new mothers experience and that so many clinicians have been impressed with. (We will discuss in chapter 10 the issue of the duration of changes in the mother's network of schemas-of-being-with.) The important point is that the mother's representations of her infant can be radically altered by placing the clinical focus exclusively on the infant's overt behavior.

The Parent-Infant Interaction as Port of Entry

Any element of the clinical situation can be used as the privileged port of entry. This of course includes the interaction that takes place during the session. As we saw earlier in the chapter, the interaction is used in the San Francisco group's infant-parent psychotherapy along with other clinical foci. It is also used in the Geneva group's brief mother-baby psychotherapy, but as a secondary symptomatic focus. Here I will describe an approach that uses the parent-infant interaction as the privileged and even exclusive clinical focus.

I became aware of the possibility of accessing the mother's representations by focusing in a special way on the interaction during a research pilot that helped lead to the microanalytic interview technique mentioned in chapter 3. One case consisted of a mother and an 18-month-old son in treatment with another therapist utilizing brief mother-baby psychotherapy. One of the mother's main complaints was that her infant was not attached to her and did not love her; he could run to any woman in the park and be made to feel just as secure. I was exploring the memories and representations attached to her interactive behaviors, as part of the research project. At one point in the therapy session (which was videotaped), the infant got bored with being on the sidelines as his mother and the therapist talked together and decided he needed more attention from mother. He dragged a kiddie chair between mother and therapist, blocking their views of each other. He climbed upon the chair and reached his arms out toward his mother, indicating clearly that he wanted to be brought into her lap. She did not pick him up. Instead, she reached her arms out to him, the palms of her hands facing up. The infant, while standing on the chair, posed his hands, palm down, on her hands. She then simply led him by the hands off the chair down onto the floor and to the side. The mother then immediately resumed talking to the therapist as she had been before, as if no interruption had occurred at all. The boy, finding himself back where he started, on the sidelines, let out a long breath and lowered his head. His posture crumpled, as if he were being deflated. He stared at the floor, immobile, for several seconds and then gradually resumed his activity at the periphery of the mother-therapist dyad. He had had a kind of microdepression. (Several seconds in such a position is—subjectively speaking—very long.)

I was intrigued by this interactive sequence, and several days later during my research sessions with the mother I reviewed with her the video of this episode. She saw immediately that her son had been disappointed in being put aside and that he had had a depressive reaction.

I then took this piece of overt behavior and used it to get directly back to her representations and memories, with questions like, "Did seeing that video evoke anything from your own past? Did you ever experience something like that?" She answered with a memory. At the age of 4 or 5, after her father left the family, her mother placed her with an aunt (the mother's sister) to live. The aunt lived at a considerable distance, and the mother came to spend every other weekend with her daughter. The mother was seen by her daughter as hystrionic, unreliable, and overdramatic, a woman who wanted to have a life of her own. She would cry and carry on about how much she missed her daughter, while the girl wondered why she then continued to live so far away.

On Sunday, at the end of the weekend visit, as the mother prepared to leave her daughter again for two weeks, she and the girl would walk to the train station together. Before parting, the mother would hug and kiss her little girl, sobbing endearments. The girl would stay rigid, and let herself be hugged, showing no emotion. She could not—would not—hug back. Then the mother walked away waving and disappeared from sight around a corner of the station. The girl meanwhile walked away in the opposite direction around the corner of another building. As soon as she did that and the good-bye was over, she lowered her head, let out a long breath, and stared at the sidewalk immobile. Her posture and spirit deflated. She had a microdepression.

After the girlhood memory was evoked, the mother realized that in the video episode her son must have experienced something like what she had as a girl. She then said, "He does love me. He is attached to me. He does miss me. It is so clear."

There were three striking aspects to what happened. First, reexperiencing the memory had an immediate impact on the mother's previously hard-to-open-up (let alone alter) representation of her son's state of attachment to her. Second, it opened up an entire period in her life—of clear clinical relevance—that she had not yet had occasion to broach in her regular therapy sessions. And thus third, this use of the interaction as a port of entry was basically different from how interactive sequences are used in the therapy described in the last section. There, the interaction is used to illustrate how an already identified core conflictual theme is manifested and instantiated, that is, enacted. Here, the interactive sequence is used as the starting point, not the end point, of a search into the mother's representational world.

From this example as a seed, I have increasingly used this port of entry and technique, applying it to chosen interactive sequences to gain entry into and explore the mother's representations. Until recently the technique was used as a variation added to more traditional approaches. Currently, however, Steven Bennett, who has been one of the collaborators in the use of the microanalytic interview with mothers, is developing a brief psychotherapeutic intervention that uses, almost exclusively, the microanalytic interview as applied to an episode of overt behavioral interaction to alter the mother's representations (Bennett et al., 1994).

The Therapist's Representations as Port of Entry

In an approach practiced largely—perhaps exclusively—in Europe, the observer-therapist's representations, thoughts, and feelings are themselves the main port of entry. Such an approach could be called a countertransferential approach, such as has been used in various psychodynamic frameworks. The work described here is mainly inspired by the work of Wilfred Bion (1963, 1967) and his notions of the mother or therapist acting as a "container" for the mental activity of the baby or patient. It is also informed by the method of observing mothers and infants of Ester Bick (1964).

In this approach, the therapist may be more or less an observer but always with a therapeutic function. In one variation, hour-long home visits are made weekly for the period of 2 years (Pourrinet, 1993). The therapist is a fairly passive observer of all that occurs concerning the baby. The main work and focus performed by the therapist is upon her own "subjectivity"—that is, her inner experience of the baby—in order to understand the baby fully. The therapist's reactions, as well as a description of what happened, are recorded and are the subject of regular supervisory sessions (in this case with Didier Houzel). This approach takes seriously and concretely the notion that in a psychoanalytic framework the psychic functioning of the analyst is the most essential element.

How could such a focus work? The manner in which the therapist watches, listens to, and reacts emotionally to the baby and mother are behaviorally evident to both baby and mother. So is the fact that the baby is a worthy subject of attention and reflection, as is the mother. It is not lost on the mother—and to a different extent on the baby—that the observer-therapist chooses to maintain this weekly relationship over a 2-year span. The mother and baby are held in a positive benign regard that is concretely manifest. The work that the therapist-observer performs on her own "subjectivity" as it concerns the baby is also certainly translated into her overt observational stance.

The practitioners of this approach are often not concerned with demonstrating how, operationally, such a procedure works, so long as they feel that it does. While this clinical focus appears to be the most distant from the goal of changing the mother's representations, it is easy to speculate that the observational focus of the observer-therapist is translated into her overt behavior with both the baby and the mother. The mother then would come to experience herself in a relationship where a positive regard and a positive therapeutic alliance, as well as many aspects of modeling, are present and functioning.

The Infant's Representations (as Imagined) as Port of Entry

A technique used in several forms of treatment is for the therapist to assume the infant's "voice," as if she were speaking from inside the infant's mind and with the infant's words, if he had them. The therapist directs this borrowed, imaginary voice of the infant, explaining a situation such as the effect of parental fights on him: "I feel so alone and scared and insecure when you two fight like that." The dramatization of the infant's conceivable inner experience is usually intended for the parents' ears and is aimed at their representations of their infant. This technique can be very effective in claiming more representational space in the parents' minds for important concerns of the infant that are being neglected or denied.

The school of Françoise Dolto (1971), which has a considerable following in France, uses this technique but intends it for the infant's ears as well as the parents'. Their approach includes outright verbal interpretations to the infant that they assume can be understood when well placed. It is easy to imagine how the paraverbal and especially the prosodic aspects of the therapist's vocalizations to the infant could alter the baby's behavior. But it is very hard to imagine how the verbal content of these productions could have any impact on the baby, especially when nature has wisely made very certain that the infant does not have to deal with the verbal-symbolic content of communication until after the first 12–18 months or so, when he has fully established the more fundamental aspects of interpersonal communication carried in position, gesture, regard, facial expression, and prosody. The verbal communications to the baby in the mother's hearing can, of course, greatly influence her overt behavior with the baby and thus his behavior.[1]

There is another version of this approach into the clinical system, and that is to view the parent-infant interactions from the baby's perspective, so far as possible. One takes what one knows of the infant's construction of his own representational world, as described in chapter 5, and applies it to an ongoing interaction. This involves searching for the cues—the elements of experience, that is, the invariants—that might differentiate for the infant the different ways-of-being-with his parent that are manifested in the interaction.

The process can be illustrated by the case of a young single woman with a 5-month-old girl. She lives alone, far from family, with few friends, without a telephone. When she got pregnant, her boyfriend gave her a choice: the baby or me. She chose the baby, and the boyfriend left. During the interview with the therapist, the dyad's interactions suggest three distinct ways-of-being-with mother, from the infant's perspective.[2]

First, one can imagine the infant representing certain interactions as the fully connected dyad, or the full mother. In these, the mother and baby are face-to-face in mutual regard and fully oriented to each other. This is the most intense and intimate of dyadic states. With this couple, this full state is of very short duration. The mother takes a position too close to the baby's face and overstimulates her. The infant quickly turns away and down but puts up no further fuss. For the infant then, one of the invariants of this way-of-being-with is a forced partial withdrawal to modulate negative affect. The pattern almost always happens when there is a full engagement, that is, when the mother makes a full engagement.

In other interactions, the way-of-being-with, from the infant's perspective, would appear to be the partially connected dyad, or the half-mother. In these, the baby is generally on the mother's lap, turned and faced partially out toward the external world. The mother is absorbed in her talk with the therapist. She signals her peripheral presence to the baby by occasionally caressing her leg or playing with her foot ("absentmindedly") or readjusting her position. All this is rather normal. What is striking is that this dyadic state of partial connectedness seems to be the most comfortable one for both mother and daughter. In it, they achieve their most positive

---

[1]From early on, certain words may get recognized as sound packages and these sound objects may get associated with certain situations, so that the infant may be able to associate the words to various situations via the sound. It is the music of the word, however, and not the meaning that is the effective agent here.
[2]This vignette comes from a case of Michelle Maury (Stern, 1994c.)

affect states, and it appears to be a stable, acceptable way of being together. But every now and then the mother, as if feeling the need to reestablish the first, more intense way of being with her daughter, abruptly turns her face to the baby and touches her on the nose. The act is not sufficiently prepared, however, so it does not work and is not positive. Both partners then seem relieved to return to a less connected state.

Another striking aspect is that the mother and infant seem to have worked out a large repertoire of states of partial connectedness. One cannot help imagining that much of their time together is spent in this way: sitting together, listening to music, watching television, looking, eating, reading. The mother is moderately depressed. She doesn't know how to be fully with her daughter or cannot tolerate being so. (There is evidence that it would evoke much ambivalence.) Nor can she be away from her daughter, who acts as a partner, a living presence, an anti-depressant of a background kind. From the infant's point of view, she gets the most from the relationship with her mother and the most enduring positive affect when they are partially connected.

The situation is like that of the older infant discussed in chapter 6 who is classified as an avoidant child, who does not react when the mother returns to the room after a separation and makes no effort to reestablish contact in a greeting ceremony. It is currently thought that such avoidant infants know that if they did try to greet the mother or respond positively when she returned, the mother would be likely to move yet farther away or ignore the solicitation. So, in a sense, the child gets the most out of the situation and minimizes negative experiences (such as rejections) by doing nothing at all. In a similar fashion, this infant is content to maintain the dyadic state of partial connectedness to optimize her relationship with her mother. It is acceptable and comfortable, and it avoids the negative alternatives of a fully connected dyad or of that of a fully disconnected dyad, which is the third way-of-being-with her mother.

One cannot help but speculate that years of early experience of optimizing this partial way of being together will become the child's sought-after mode of relating, or at least the one in which she feels most deeply comfortable. It would not be surprising if her later object choices reflected this preference. Some styles of successful marriages rely heavily on partial ways of being together (see, e.g., Parke, Power, & Gottman, 1979). It should be added that the girl's temperament, which was on the passive, more timid side, permitted her to develop this way-of-being-with.

The overall point is that if one listened carefully to the mother and explored her representations, one would get the picture from the mother's point of view of a very symbiotic relationship between mother and infant:

that they "live in one bubble," inseparable and psychically fused. The mother also draws a picture of a half-family, that is, mother and child without husband/father. This carries an important intergenerational theme for this mother, who has experienced many versions of half-families.

From the infant's point of view, given the invariant elements available to her, it is not a half-family; it is a whole family consisting of a half-mother. And furthermore, a half-mother is better than a full mother or none at all. From the child's point of view, this is not a picture of symbiosis at all. It is making the best of things. In any event, the perspective gained from imagining the elements in the parent-infant interaction that would permit the infant to construct representations of the many ways-of-being-with a parent reveals a parallel world that can be of enormous clinical use.

In this example, the child's representations as imagined by the therapist have been the port of entry. Once this information has been gathered, the therapist can use it just as one might in the San Francisco and Geneva approaches. The point is that it has been gathered differently.

We have explored six different approaches, each taking theoretical therapeutic aim at the parents' representations but each entering the system via a different point of access (port of entry). It appears that even when there is agreement about which element of the system is theoretically privileged as the target, there are as many routes to it as there are elements in the system. It is the port of entry that determines to a very great extent the techniques employed and the general guidelines of the therapeutic approach.

It is evident that each port of entry dictates different kinds of technical maneuvers. It is less evident what role the ultimate theoretical therapeutic target, namely changing the maternal representations, plays in determining techniques. We will return to this point in chapter 10. First, let us explore approaches that have different theoretical therapeutic targets.

CHAPTER 9

Approaches That Aim to Change the Interactive Behaviors

THE APPROACHES described in this chapter consider the overt interactive behaviors as the key element to be therapeutically altered. They differ in how they enter into the system to change this target element.

The Mother's Overt Behavior as Port of Entry

Approaches that focus on the mother's overt behavior assume that there is a very high degree of reciprocity between the parents' interactive behavior and that of the infant. Accordingly these therapies conceptualize the real target as the interaction or relationship (Sameroff & Emde, 1989) and not just the mother's behavior. Nonetheless, because it is generally easier and more practical to get the parents to change their overt interactive behavior first, this becomes, effectively, the main therapeutic target as well as port of entry.

A variety of excellent interventions falling into this general group of approaches could have been selected as illustrative (e.g., Clark & Seifer, 1983; Field, 1982). I have chosen the approach called interaction guidance of Susan McDonough, however, because it plays an important role in chapter 10 that follows and has been demonstrated to be effective in parent-infant disorders in diverse populations. As in the previous chapter, I will summarize selected features of this approach. Readers may consult the original descriptions for details and elaboration (McDonough, 1991, 1992, 1993; Zeanah & McDonough, 1989).

It is important to note that this approach grew out of clinical work with mothers and children who were multiply disadvantaged. I believe that these origins have played an important role in the present form of the treatment, even though the approach has proved successful with populations of parents and infants that are at no particular risk. Some of the first populations worked with included unmarried, socioeconomically and educationally disadvantaged young mothers. And with this population—as we see in the experience of Lieberman and Pawl—the first treatment problem is always to get and keep these parents in treatment. And indeed, the establishment and maintenance of a therapeutic alliance is the first priority in interaction guidance. The demands of the therapeutic alliance will even determine who will be invited to participate in therapy sessions. McDonough (personal communication, 1989) described a case in which a slightly retarded single mother moved with her infant daughter into a small apartment house run by a lesbian who to a considerable extent took charge of the young mother's life, at least at the practical level. Although this woman provided an important support system to the mother and baby, most of the therapy staff was concerned about the destructive potential of this relationship for the mother. McDonough, on the other hand, saw the lesbian woman's approval and support of the treatment as crucial, both in terms of the practical aspects such as transportation and in terms of maintaining the mother's motivation without interference. Accordingly, McDonough insisted that this woman participate in the treatment process directed at the mother and child. After several sessions, the woman was convinced that the treatment was good for the mother and child and that she was not being excluded as a supporting friend. She stopped coming to sessions but helped importantly in consolidating and permitting a positive therapeutic alliance to be instituted. She became a very positive influence in the treatment.

Thus, the choice of participants in the therapeutic visits was made on the basis of the needs of the therapeutic alliance. A positive therapeutic alliance is of primary importance, and the therapist will employ any reasonable means that are necessary to that end. These may include home visits, education, advice, practical help, support, and intervening with other agencies.

The next major feature of this treatment is the positive reinforcement of maternal behaviors that are good, appropriate, or even just adequate. This process of positive reinforcement in the large sense includes identifying potential positive parental behaviors—that is, finding them in the mother's repertoire and helping them to emerge.

The parental overt behaviors to be worked on are found in the interaction with the baby, initially with the aid of videotaping and replay. In general, the parent or parents and child are asked to interact (exactly how depends on the age of the infant and the problem). The interactions last 5 to 15 minutes and are videotaped. Immediately afterwards, the therapist and family review the video recording, and the behaviors identified there become the subjects of therapeutic work. All the advantages of video (freeze frame, slow motion, and so on) are used as they are deemed helpful.

During this review particular interactive behaviors are chosen for discussion. For instance, the mother of a 9-month-old (birth age) premature baby with a significant developmental delay is referred for being over-stimulating and intrusive with her baby and becoming anxious and depressed herself. The mother has, in fact, been told by the medical professionals involved to provide constant stimulation for her baby so he will "catch up." This directive suits her personality and is too easy for her to do. When viewing the interaction, the therapist finds that, in general, this mother gives very little space to the infant. For instance, when the infant has stopped being interested in one toy and puts it down, his attention floats for a while, and it takes several seconds or more before he alights on a new object of interest. The mother tolerates this delay poorly and jumps in to direct his attention to a new toy, which she has picked. In such a situation, the task of the therapist is not to identify the behaviors that can be criticized and corrected; they are evident enough to everyone, and plentiful. Rather, the task is to find a behavior that is positive enough that it can be built upon. In this case, for instance, if on one occasion when the infant is floating between foci of attention the mother hesitates or holds herself back, even for only a split second, before jumping in to stimulate him, that will suffice as the port of entry. The therapist might then say something like, "Right there, you seemed to be sensitive to his slow pace of transition between objects of attention and gave him some extra time."

Such a mother is likely to be surprised by this intervention. She had not realized that she was doing something "good" or "right," even if only a little bit so. This usually has the result that the mother herself brings up the whole painful issue of her need and desire to overstimulate her baby and not knowing how to restrain herself—or if she should—and how it wears her down. She can now talk about it, because the therapist has shown her that she does, indeed, have at least the beginning of the ability to remedy the situation. The subject has been raised. The mother's ability and even the means to correct the situation have been identified and reinforced. And the positive supportive nature of the therapeutic alliance has been furthered. The effect on the mother and on the therapeutic alliance of this approach into the system would have been quite different if the therapist had criticized her behavior, or asked her—in one form or another—why she thought she did such a (read in "terrible") thing, or even simply told her, in strict behavioral terms, how to stop doing it.

This kind of work on the overt behaviors that characterizes interaction guidance makes every attempt to keep intact the positive therapeutic alliance, which has been constructed with so much work. In this vein, the therapist does not interact with the baby to model behaviors for the mother; this could sabotage the mother's self-confidence and destroy her view of the therapist as her ally, making him her successful competitor or a better or more expert caregiver.

Working in this fashion, the therapist focuses his therapeutic interventions on the interactive behaviors happening in the therapy session. Progressively, the use of the video is diminished as the interaction can be talked about readily without it, but the focus remains on the interaction. The therapist has no particular interest, technically or theoretically, in the parents' past history or in their representations. If the parent brings these up, they are generally used to enrich the understanding of what is happening here and now, overtly, behaviorally.

The theoretical therapeutic target and the ports of entry for this treatment are diagrammed in figure 9.1.

FIGURE 9.1

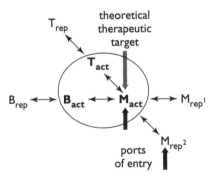

Obviously this approach owes much to a behavioral and educational tradition. However, it adds to a behavioral approach a rich consideration of the role of the therapeutic relationship in the treatment process. For a brief form of treatment, it often pays more attention to the issues of transference and countertransference than comparable short-term therapies that have been psychoanalytically inspired. This appreciation came initially, perhaps, from the nature of the population treated, but in the course of the evolution of this approach it has become a cardinal feature, in itself, regardless of population. The efficacy of this form of treatment has now been demonstrated in several diverse populations and will be further discussed in chapter 10.

The Entire Network of Family Interactions as Port of Entry (A Systems Theory Approach)

It is first important to distinguish a family therapy approach from a systems theory approach. A family therapy approach includes all the relationships of the family members, which can be viewed psychoanalytically, behaviorally, or systemically. A systems theory approach is a way of viewing the organization of separate, interdependent elements that make up a system. The elements could be those that we have described in part I, in which case only two family members are needed, or it could be all family members.

The example that I will use is the approach developed at the Centre d'Etude de la Famille (Center for the Study of the Family), Hôpital de Cery, Lausanne. It is both a systems theory approach and a family therapy, focusing on the organization of the interactive behaviors of the family members, who in this case are the mother, father, and baby, a new nuclear family (see Corboz, 1986; Corboz-Warnery, Forni, & Fivaz, 1989; Fivaz, Fivaz, & Kaufmann, 1982; Fivaz, Martin, & Cornut-Zimmer, 1984; Fivaz-Depeursinge, 1987, 1991; Fivaz-Depeursinge, Corboz-Warnery, & Frenck, 1990).

It is surprising that a family and systems theory approach has been applied relatively little to the family with a very young child—that is, to the nuclear family at its very point of origin, when the emerging organization of nonverbal interactive patterns are what largely characterize the clinical material. Elisabeth Fivaz-Depeursinge et al. (1990) comment on the poverty of the literature in this area, with the important exception of the work of Eleanor Wertheim (1975), whom the Lausanne therapists cite as a precursor to their work. The work of John Byng-Hall and his colleagues at the Tavistock Clinic is another important exception (Byng-Hall, 1986, in press). Byng-Hall works within the family therapy and intergenerational tradition but adds to it an important role for attachment theory in the underpinnings of the early family patterns (Byng-Hall & Stevenson-Hinde, 1991). Other approaches are soon to come.

These exceptions notwithstanding, the established family therapies have traditionally dealt with families with older children and adolescents and have been most inspired by general systems theory. They did not start at the beginning of the family's ontogeny, with the result that family therapy has never evolved a sufficient developmental theory to rest upon. Parent-infant psychotherapies, on the other hand, as other and more recent varieties of family therapy, have been greatly inspired by the observations and theories of developmental psychology. Perhaps in the encounter of this new form of family therapy with the more traditional forms, some new developmental notions will emerge that prove valuable and enriching to both.

The approach of the Lausanne group at the Center for the Study of the Family can be summarized as follows. The first step is to begin establishing a therapeutic alliance that is positive and that permits the family to be confident about the setting and process they are entering. In this regard, these therapists, too, are exquisitely aware of the efforts needed to create a working alliance in this particular clinical situation; they deem such an alliance an absolute necessity that cannot be taken for granted. As the alliance forms, the therapist observes the configuration of interactions between the members of the family and self as the therapist.

The second step is to create a physical frame for the interactions. The physical framework is crucial for observing, in a systematic clinical manner, the interactions that unfold within the confines of a fixed physical-temporal setting. The Lausanne group has created a framework in which the infant is placed in a baby seat on a table and the two parents are seated facing the baby, so that the three of them roughly make an equilateral triangle. The parents are then instructed to interact in a sequence of phases: for example, mother interacts with baby, father observes; father interacts with baby, mother observes; all three interact together; and so on. This kind of framing permits the therapist to observe systematically and comparatively not only the configuration of the three family members during each of the phases but also the patterns that they use to make the transitions from one phase to the next. This latter observation has proved especially fascinating. For instance, when the family goes from mother interacting with baby, with father observing (dyad + 1) to all three interacting together, the manner of the transition tells much about the cooperation or competition between the parents for exclusive interaction with the baby—that is, about the process of triadification (Corboz-Warnery & Fivaz-Depeursinge, in press).

This physical and temporal framework that limits and channels the family's interactions serves the same kind of clinical-research function as does, for instance, the Ainsworth Strange Situation (Ainsworth et al., 1978). Just as the Strange Situation is a paradigm for exploring the nature of attachment, the Lausanne Triadic Play Situation is a paradigm for exploring the early interactive patterns of the nuclear family as a triad, and in particular how the multiple configurations possible in a triad are formed and altered. An important clinical part of the framing function of the Lausanne Triadic Play Situation is its constraints. When a clinician or researcher can watch many families negotiate this same fixed situation, interactive pattern recognition becomes far more acute and clinical acumen sharper.

The place and position of the therapist as the fourth member of the group (nuclear family plus therapist) is also an important clinical aspect of this approach. The therapist remains aware of the family's wishes and fears concerning the role and place of the therapist in this context. The therapist must also explore how he feels about membership and role in this grouping and must find a place in this quartet. Stated differently, the transference of the family—collectively and separately—and the counter-transference of the therapist play very important roles in this approach, since the therapist cannot act without knowing from what position and in what role he is acting.

Once the therapeutic alliance has been addressed and the therapist has been able to observe within the framing context the characteristic interactive configurations that prevail in the family (and that reflect or manifest the psychopathology), he is then in a position to change the interactions of the family members. This represents the third and final step in this treatment approach. The goal is to change the family interactions, not the members of the family. For this reason, this form of therapy is grouped with other approaches that target the overt behaviors.

An example of how the therapist intervenes to change the interaction is illustrated in a single therapeutic maneuver that was part of a whole treatment. A videotaped record of this family was shown to me by Elisabeth Fivaz; the therapist-supervisor was her collaborator, Antoinette Corboz. The case involved a mother who, after the birth of her first baby, had had a depression requiring hospitalization. The result was a father who was sure of himself as a caregiver and a mother with little confidence in herself. At this point in the evolution of the family, the mother deferred to the father at many points in the family interactions seen in the triadic play situation. She let him take the lead and be the more active one. He accepted this role and was gratified by it. In this sense, he maintained the current imbalance in their caregiving roles and even aggravated it. Corboz was at this point fully aware of this pattern. Her intervention occurred at a point when the family triad configured itself as "two (mother plus infant) plus one," with the father pulled back in his chair as observer. At such moments the father had the tendency to lean forward and reenter the action, either making it a triad or effectively forcing the mother to back off—as she willingly did—to be the observer, resulting in a different "two plus one." He would do this with the conscious idea and (often enough) the result of making things go better with the baby, to "help out"—the baby, but effectively not the wife.

At this point in the videotaped session, Corboz quietly slid over behind the father's chair (she was standing) and gently, from behind, rested her hands on his shoulders. The already established therapeutic alliance permitted this action. The effect was to restrain the father from leaning forward and reentering, but not in any forceful, constraining manner. Rather it was more in the spirit of "You don't really have to go in there. Let us both, together, watch your wife and child interact. I have confidence they will do well and it will be fine." And he accepted without words.

The result of his acceptance was that the mother did, indeed, have a successful interaction and had it under the benign regard of her husband and therapist, who had united as confident, appreciative observers. The father had the experience of not jumping in but rather taking pleasure in his wife's success. And the baby had the experience of an active engagement with his mother in the passive presence of his father.

For a moment, a key moment, the therapist had altered the behavior and experience of the family. To the extent that the maneuver worked well, the probability of the reoccurrence of the behavior went up. A behavioral change was initiated in the direction of altering the family interaction.

Such changes are viewed not in terms of reinforcement but in terms of altering the framework or context, thus permitting or favoring new interactive patterns to emerge. It is the interactive pattern that has been changed, not the people. These therapists are well aware that changing interactive patterns may lead to changing representations, but that is beyond their stated field of action.

One of the more fascinating aspects of this work on the formation of a nuclear family is the light it may shed on the triad or triangle. Triangles have occupied a special place in psychoanalytic thinking. The "third" has been viewed as a necessary element for socialization and acculturation in the broad sense of an agent that opens up the exclusive dyad of mother and infant. More specifically, this is the traditional role that psychoanalysis has given to the father, resulting in the Oedipal complex, which has always been assumed to begin around the third year of life. These studies, however, make it clear that the process of becoming a triad must begin very early, roughly in parallel with becoming a dyad, under normal nuclear family conditions. As Robert Emde points out (1994), there are many things one can be excluded from in a triad, such as attentional space or mastery space. And these exclusions subjectively may long precede the exclusion from a love or intimacy space.

The work of the Lausanne group suggests that patterns of interaction involving mother, father, and baby—such as shifting from a dyad plus one to a triad—are fairly ritualized events very early on. There is no reason to believe that the infant's capacities to identify the invariants that describe dyadic patterns (see chapters 5 and 6) would not operate on triadic patterns of interactions as well.

When considering the triad we must make the same distinctions between the behavioral and the intrapsychic that we observed for the dyad. This requires a new terminology. The group mentioned in chapter 3 studying the "interfaces" between different levels of analysis, inspired by the suggestion of Serge Lebovici, has provisionally taken to calling the behavioral process of forming a triad *triadification* and the intrapsychic process of experiencing a triad *triangulation*. The process of triangulation, then, as well as of triadification, must be studied across all the changes most likely to be suffered with the onset of intersubjectivity, of verbal and symbolic ability, and so on. What psychoanalysis has taken to be the Oedipus complex is surely the end result of many developmental transformations that need to be studied, as well as the starting point for other developmental lines.

To return to the central thrust of this chapter, there are many other therapeutic approaches that aim to change the behavior of the parents and infant, both directly or indirectly—for example, through support systems (see Meisels & Shonkoff, 1990, for an overview). For our present purposes, however, these two examples will suffice. And we can now proceed to examine what all the therapies mentioned in this chapter and the last have in common and to explore whether these commonalities account for the far-reaching therapeutic effects of the nonspecific factors.

CHAPTER 10

Commonalities Among the Different Approaches

I N THIS CHAPTER, I will explore those aspects of the therapy that are common to all the approaches mentioned in the last two chapters. The rationale for doing so is the strong impression that all the approaches, when well done, seem to work. This book is in large part inspired by the idea that it is the nonspecific aspects common to all therapies that account for the largest part of their efficacy. To the extent that this is so, it is necessary to identify, where possible, what is specific and what nonspecific to any approach and to try to understand more fully the nonspecific commonalities revealed. It is also my hope that the factors that are shared and nonspecific among the various approaches will tell us more about this new domain of parent-infant psychotherapy than a comparison of the differences in approaches. What, then, are these commonalities?

The Nature of the Clinical System Itself

We have argued that the clinical system is made up of various elements: B_{act}, B_{rep}, M_{act}, M_{rep}, F_{act}, F_{rep}, T_{act}, and T_{rep}. We have further argued that these elements are interdependent and exist in a state of constant, dynamic mutual influence. If therapy alters any one element, it will have an impact on all the elements within the system because of the dynamic interdependence of the elements. It is this property of the system that leads me to suggest that the nature of the system itself is such that it will distribute throughout all its parts any influence that impinges at any one point, regardless of where that point is. Can this be shown to be true?

There is an outcome study that sheds light on this question (Cramer et al., 1990). A brief history of this study is in order. The staff at La Guidance Infantile in Geneva wanted to conduct an outcome study on their psychoanalytically oriented therapy (mentioned in chapter 8). Together, we designed a study to evaluate changes in the mother's representations and overt interactive behavior brought about by therapy. We also measured the baby's interactive behavior, as well as the baby's symptoms that prompted treatment. In other words, many of the different elements of the system were to be evaluated.

The biggest practical problem was in finding a suitable control group. The usual nontreated control groups, such as families on a waiting list, proved to be either not feasible or not ethical. Accordingly, we looked for the most interesting second treatment group, from a comparative point of view. The research design thus became a comparison of therapeutic outcomes between two different therapeutic approaches.

The choice of the second therapeutic approach is key to the central argument. I chose the approach of interactional guidance as practiced at the time in Providence, Rhode Island, and now in Ann Arbor, Michigan, by Susan McDonough (described in chapter 9). This choice was made for several reasons. The two approaches—psychoanalytically inspired brief mother-baby psychotherapy (Geneva) and interactional guidance (Ann Arbor)—differed in the following important respects. The theoretical therapeutic goal for the Geneva group is to change the mother's representations, while for the Ann Arbor group it is to change the mother's overt behavior. The port of entry into the system for the Geneva group is the mother's representations and past memories. For the Ann Arbor group, it is mainly the mother's overt behavior but also that of the infant. The Geneva group does not, or need not, focus on the overt behaviors that make up the interaction unless they corroborate or illustrate themes already developed elsewhere. That is to say, these therapists never suggest or explore or demonstrate ways that the interaction, as behavior, could be altered. The Ann Arbor group, on the other hand, never explores the mother's representations about what is happening in the interaction and how the behavior is related to the mother's past or other representational structures of the mother. For them, the mother's representational world is of small interest, in terms of technique, and nonessential for the therapeutic activity. (See chapters 8 and 9 for more details on each approach.)

In effect, then, the two therapies are diametrically different in focusing their theory and technique on changing either the mother's representations (the Geneva group) or the interactive behaviors (the Ann Arbor group). This divergence is not unexpected, since the Geneva group comes from a psychoanalytic tradition and the Ann Arbor group from an educational and more behaviorist tradition. This basic difference, however, was ideal for pursuing the central question.

It is worth commenting that the reasons why one would enter one's favorite therapy in an outcome competition are complex. Without mentioning all the obvious good and less good reasons for doing so, I will simply note that it is certainly easier to do when one is convinced that their treatment approach is either better in general or at least better for a specific subpopulation. And this was naturally the case for this outcome study.

There were, in fact, three different beliefs in play at the start. Many of the psychoanalysts in the Geneva group could not imagine that a nonpsychodynamic, behavioral approach could achieve a result that was either as general, long-lasting, "profound," or subjectively satisfying to the patient as the results they were used to seeing with their own approach. At a minimum, they were convinced that the psychodynamic approach would prove superior for some important and identifiable subgroup.

Some therapists in the Ann Arbor group, on the other hand, could not imagine that a psychoanalytically inspired approach would work except in a very small, special subgroup of the population. They assumed that their approach was more generally applicable as well as probably superior for certain families.

A third group, including members on both sides, had no prediction as to which treatment would prove generally more effective, but believed that (1) each treatment would prove superior for some identifiable subpopulation and (2) it was likely that the Geneva group would—generally speaking—effect a greater change in the maternal representations, while the Ann Arbor group would—generally speaking—effect a greater change in the overt maternal behavior. After all, those were the specified therapeutic targets of each treatment.

The results: Everyone was wrong. Both treatments did work, but there were no important differences between them. And what was most telling for the main argument being pursued here, the Geneva treatment changed the mothers' overt behavior as much as the Ann Arbor treatment did, and the Ann Arbor treatment changed the mothers' representations as much as the Geneva treatment did. In other words, it did not matter where the treatment entered the system, nor where it applied its clinical activity, nor what element of the system it had theoretically targeted for change. If the treatment achieved its stated, limited goal, it also changed all the elements of the system. The system itself distributed any local effects throughout the entire system, so that the final result of the approaches was the same and any initial differences in approach were effaced.

Before discussing these results further, a description of the study in slightly greater detail is required. (For full details, see Cramer et al., 1990.) The study, directed by Bertrand Cramer, Christiane Robert-Tissot, and myself, was conducted at La Guidance Infantile in Geneva. It consisted of 80 families of mostly moderate socioeconomic status, with children between the ages of 6 months and 2½ years who were referred mostly by local pediatricians and other health agencies for largely psychofunctional problems (sleep, eating, attachment, behavior) that could not be handled by the referring professionals. (We established in a separate study that these families suffered from a level of symptomatology well in excess of that seen normally in the community. We were not treating "normals.")

Once the decision was made that the family met the criteria to be included in treatment, they were assigned at random to one of the two treatment groups. The first group received brief psychoanalytically oriented psychotherapy, which was the traditional approach used at La Guidance Infantile (the Geneva approach). The therapists were four psychoanalysts and child psychiatrists fully experienced in the technique. The second treatment was interactional guidance, conducted by two members of the staff (a psychologist and a psychologist–speech therapist) who had had an intensive 6-week course in interactional guidance by Susan McDonough (the Ann Arbor approach). They were supervised during their treatments by two of the senior authors who also are trained in the technique of interactional guidance.

All treatments were brief, lasting no more than 10 sessions, usually once a week. The families were evaluated before the onset of treatment, 1 week after the end of therapy, and 6 months later.

The nature of the evaluation is most important here, since we wished it to cover as many of the separate elements of the clinical system as possible. We evaluated the mother's representations (M_{rep}) with two types of measure. The first was a perceptual-descriptive task. The mother was asked to describe her infant in terms of 20 pairs of contrasting adjectives (e.g., active-passive, easy-difficult, and so on). This is a perceptual task in part, because the two adjectives are placed 10 cm apart on a line and the mother was asked to choose a point somewhere between the two that best rated her infant on that continuum (Stern et al., 1989a).

The mother was asked to fill out five such descriptive lists, each with 20 adjectives. On four of these lists—for her infant as a person, for herself as a person, for her husband as a person, for her own mother as a person—the adjectives are the same. The fifth list contains 20 adjectives for parenting (e.g., controlling-permissive, affectionate-distant). The mother was asked to fill out this list for herself as a mother, for her husband as a father, and for her own mother as a mother to her as a child. This perceptual-descriptive task is not intended to tap any absolute realities but rather to measure any relative changes over time in the way in which separate persons are viewed (represented) in different roles, and to determine if the view of different persons changes together, converges, or diverges over time (e.g., does the baby become perceived as more difficult or easier).

A second method used to evaluate the mother's representations was to elicit her own adjectives and descriptions of her infant, herself, her husband, and her mother.

The mother's and the infant's overt interactive behavior, as recorded on videotape, was evaluated with three separate measures, which were applied to a semistructured interactive sequence between infant and mother at each evaluation. These were the Crittenden (1981), the Ainsworth (1974), and the KIDIES (Kiddie–Infant-Descriptive Instrument for Emotional States), which measures the affective states observed for the infant and mother during the interaction (Stern, Robert-Tissot, de Muralt, & Cramer, 1989b).

The infant's symptoms were also evaluated by questionnaire in terms of intensity and frequency (Robert-Tissot et al., 1989), but that is not crucial to our point here. In brief, the mother's representations (M_{rep}), the mother's overt behavior (M_{act}), and the infant's overt behavior (B_{act}) were all evaluated using several convergent measures.

The results showed that there were no striking differences between the two treatment groups. All measures showed an improvement with treatment. And the overall change in representations or in overt behavior or in symptoms was not more marked in one treatment than in the other.

But these general results leave open the question whether there are identifiable subgroups of families for which one treatment is found to be more effective, either in general or in changing the representations relative to the overt behavior or vice versa. In fact, this was one of the original hypotheses that almost all of us readily agreed upon. To show it, we had sought to find all the indices that might possibly distinguish which mother-infant dyads might do better with one of the two treatments. The usual list of identifying demographics was considered, such as age and socioeconomic status. In addition, we asked if subgroups might be revealed by such indices as the level of maternal depression (Hamilton), psychological insight, estimated ability to form a therapeutic alliance or positive transference, or severity and type of psychopathology. Some of these indices were assumed to be able to predict a subgroup that would do well with the Geneva treatment—for example, good psychological insight, ability to form a therapeutic relationship, not depressed, higher education, and so on—that is, all the criteria that are generally used for analyzability in a traditional psychoanalytic framework. Other indices were thought to be more likely to predict a subgroup that would do relatively better with interactional guidance (see Bachmann & Robert-Tissot, 1992).

In spite of our well-thought-out expectations to discover subpopulations that reacted better to one treatment, however, we did not find any. Broadly speaking, we could not predict who would profit best from which treatment. This finding was quite unexpected, given the different populations for which these two types of therapy were designed.

To summarize, while both treatments worked, they were not markedly different in selectively altering the representations versus the overt behaviors. And they were not markedly different in working better for any identifiable subpopulation.

Almost everyone involved in the study was unhappy or somewhat dissatisfied with these results. After all, it is hard to believe that two such different therapies are so similar in effect, especially when you are heavily committed to one. The most common reaction is to say that negative findings (lack of differences) are hard to prove and perhaps not worth interpreting. One assumes that if only there had been more subjects, or better evaluation measures, or more evaluation variables, or a replication, or a matching of treatment desired with treatment given, or some other refinement, a greater difference would have been found. And, indeed, that is highly probable; in fact, there were some minor differences. The point is that any differences found with further effort would most likely account for only a very small part of the whole effect and would, for all practical and theoretical purposes, be trivial.

In fact, it is the rule among comparative outcome studies to find that the therapeutic effects specific to any one treatment are minor compared to the nonspecific therapeutic effects common to all treatments (see, e.g., Frank & Frank, 1991; Parloff, 1988). (A comparative study of different treatment approaches to maternal postpartum depression has shown some specific treatment effects [Murray, personal communication, 1993], but that is basically an individual treatment, not a parent-infant treatment.) Results such as ours are thus often met with a yawn and a wave of dismissal. They are too basically upsetting without offering a clue as to what to do next or how to dismiss them.

An alternative way of dealing with such results is to assume that the system that was acted upon tends to minimize process differences and wash them out in a final common outcome. If we had only evaluated the diminutions in symptoms (such as sleeping problems), that would have been a reasonable conclusion. But we also measured the separate elements of the system that could have indicated different routes of influence in operation before affecting the symptom. But here, too, we found no important differences. It appears as if the system minimizes the specificity of initial influences. It is not that all paths lead separately to Rome (the symptom); rather, all paths quickly join together to forge one inevitable highway, the altered system.

This situation is the result of the constant dynamic interdependence of the many elements of the system, and it constitutes our first and perhaps the most important single commonality among approaches. The notion of a system here is somewhat different from what is usually meant in systems theory approaches, in that it consists of some parts that are intrapsychic and others that are interpersonal. In dealing therapeutically with the parent-infant dyad, it is necessary to conceive of such systems that cross many of the traditional lines.

While these results and perhaps arguments may be counterintuitive, it is worth asking further why we hold so firmly to the belief that certain therapies work better for certain patients. I think that much of the reason lies in the sense that if the patient believes in and expects a certain form of therapy—if he is acculturated to one approach and/or against others—his preferred approach will probably work best, and vice versa. While this idea is probably true, it reduces the question of therapeutic specificity to cultural, aesthetic, and political considerations. These, however, very much affect the nature of the therapist-patient relationship and play a determining role in the kinds of therapeutic alliance that are possible. This issue is taken up again in chapter 12.

Serial Brief Treatment

In general, parent-infant psychotherapies do not last very long, usually between 3 and 12 sessions when there are no programmatic constraints. These sessions are most often weekly, so the duration of treatment is somewhere between a few weeks and several months. (The special situation of infants with chronic conditions or recalcitrant cases or preventive intervention with at-risk groups or parents with psychiatric diagnoses will be discussed later in this section.)

The most common reason for this brevity is that when things go well, enough therapeutic work is accomplished in a short period of time that

either there is not much left to do or, even if there is, the parents or therapist are insufficiently motivated to continue. Most therapists who work in
settings where they have great liberty to decide the duration of treatment
find that if the initial problem is not significantly ameliorated in several
sessions (up to 10), then the therapy will be of far longer duration, usually
several years. In such cases the therapy tends to slide in the direction of
either a psychotherapy with the mother or a couples therapy, more than a
parent-infant psychotherapy (C. Aubert, personal communication, 1993).
One might then ask, "Well, what are we talking about here? If things get
fixed so quickly and easily, is it worth even considering these therapies?"
As we will see, however, the initial success is most often only the beginning of the therapeutic story.

I asked several colleagues who work in private practice and who treat
many relational and psychofunctional problems of infants and parents
about the time structure or format of treatment they used. In one typical
response, the therapist threw his hands up and said, "There is no real
structure. I see them for 2 or 5 or 10 times or more. It usually gets better
pretty quickly. Some of them come back a few months or a year later, and I
see them again for a short while. Some don't come back. And then I may
hear from them several times more, or I may not. It is not exactly what I
would call a structured format for treatment. Sometimes I don't even distinguish between what is a treatment or an extended consultation." I will
argue that hidden in this response there is, in fact, a very cogent structure
and rationale for this kind of treatment.

Because of the limited duration of treatment (and most often the focus
on one symptom), many have described infant-parent psychotherapy as a
related form of brief-focused adult psychotherapy (see, e.g., Cramer &
Palacio-Espasa, 1993). This association may be misleading, for the two
therapies are very different. In brief-focused adult psychotherapy, the limitation of sessions, usually to about 10, is used to maximize motivation and
thereby accelerate an otherwise lengthy process. The problem in infant-
parent psychotherapy is almost the opposite: how to prolong a treatment
process so that early success does not lead to a curtailing of treatment
before it can be "deepened" or "widened" (i.e., generalized). In other
words, for adults in brief-focused psychotherapy, short duration is a strategy imposed on the therapeutic process; for infants and parents, the
brevity is the natural result of not imposing a strategy.

The major point I wish to make is not that these treatments have to be
brief—brevity in itself adds little here—but rather that the course of these
psychotherapies tends to be serial bouts of brief therapy that stretch
unevenly over months or years. It is most common that after the first bout

of treatment, which we may call the opening phase, some form of therapy is reapplied after 3–6 months or so, a second phase. What usually happens is that several months after the termination of the opening phase, a seemingly new or related psychological problem arises or the original one reintensifies, even though the opening phase was considered successful. (We are not talking about symptom substitution.) Does this mean that the therapeutic effect of the opening phase treatment was only short-lived? Yes and no. Before discussing this double answer, I want to explain why we usually do not describe the situation as I have just done.

Many therapists know and accept that serial brief treatments are needed. At the end of the opening phase, they leave the door open for a later revisit or even plan for a contact 3–6 months later to "see how things are going." The majority of families accept this invitation for a second phase very willingly. Sometimes the second phase consists of only a single visit to summarize what has happened during the treatment pause and evaluate the present situation. The second phase may consist of just a telephone call as a form of follow-up and catch-up, or it may be a reinstituted treatment of 2–10 sessions. Sometimes the second (or third) phase follows the preceding phase almost immediately with either a short pause or only a diminution in the frequency of visits as the sole index of a discontinuous process. What distinguishes one bout of treatment from the next is mainly the topic of treatment. One could say that this is true of any long-term treatment, but here the change in topic is driven by the internal growth and development of the baby and not necessarily by the exhausting of any particular subject matter.

After the second phase, the door is again left open for a possible, or planned, third phase, and so on. In my experience and that of many others, when the door is left open families tend to establish a pattern of serial brief treatments, separated by several weeks, months, or a year. T. Berry Brazelton has spoken of this situation and also described how best to use it as preventive intervention in his notion of "touchpoints" (Brazelton, 1984, 1992). (What I am calling a clinical window corresponds to Brazelton's touchpoint—of reorganization—plus the subsequent phase of consolidation.)

Is this clinical experience of serial brief treatments common? I believe that it is but that many factors have militated against doing it or recognizing it. First, there is the therapeutic prejudice that an episode of treatment is supposed to have an enduring therapeutic effect—if not forever, at least more than several months. Indeed, psychoanalytic and psychoanalytically inspired psychotherapies aim not only to correct a problem but to give the patient the self-righting introspective tools for avoiding similar problems later, even in novel life circumstances as they might arise in the future.

From this point of view serial brief treatment looks like an utter failure of the therapeutic process, resulting in only superficial and temporary changes. For many practitioners who share—or at least were trained with—this prejudice, the serial nature of many of their treatments (if they permit it) is simply not addressed.

The other familiar scenario is that the therapist does not feel that serial—or repeated—bouts of therapy are necessary. She believes that her treatment has more lasting effects—or ought to if it was successful. In such situations, the family is not invited to come back, nor is the door left open; in fact, the message is often that the cure ought now to be permanently in place. What frequently happens is that several months later the family again feels the need to consult a therapist but naturally goes elsewhere. They are then lost to follow-up, and the serial nature of their treatment is hidden from view, because each bout of therapy occurs at a different treatment site. This is far more frequent than is reported, I believe, because the initial therapist doesn't learn about it and the case falls wrongly into the category of her permanent (i.e., long-lasting) cures. It becomes a false long-term success. The second treating therapist either considers it a new case (as is the tendency) or a treatment failure of the first therapist, which it need not be.

I believe that serial brief treatments are not failures of the therapeutic process but rather the very best way in which parent-infant psychotherapy can be delivered. They represent the family's success (and sometimes that of the therapist) in finding a temporal format of treatment best adjusted to a psychotherapy that involves a rapidly developing organism (the baby) and system (the family). I am suggesting that serial brief treatment is the desirable way to treat most parent-infant problems, a necessary adaptation to the nature of early development.

In psychoanalysis the notion of *working through* is an essential feature of the therapeutic process. In nonpsychodynamic therapies one also recognizes the need for such a process under different names, most usually *generalization*, using the learning model.

By working through is meant dealing with and resolving a key issue in all the spheres and arenas of living in which it is manifested: in the workplace, in the home with the spouse and nuclear family, with the family of origin, in the reconstruction of the past, and most important for the psychoanalytic perspective, in the transference. In most treatments the same issue is worked on almost simultaneously in these different arenas. There are no fixed sequential rules or limitations. The issues are dealt with transversally in time, so to speak.

With an infant or a parent-infant relationship, one cannot work through transversally in time because of the nature of development. At any given time the infant and parent have many new arenas of living together yet to be experienced. Until the infant's capacity to operate in a new arena unfolds in time, it cannot be worked on or worked through.

For instance, it is a common experience for a family to come to a therapist with an eating problem when the infant is 2 months old. Let us assume that the problem is quickly resolved. The family returns 4 months later with a social problem; the infant is "rejecting," frequently refuses mutual gaze, and so on (though the eating problem stays solved). This social problem may result from the almost identical interactional-relational forces that produced the eating problem, but now they are being played out in the arena of social interaction. This problem too is solved in weeks of treatment. Then at 14 months, they return with a separation problem.

The point is that the parent and infant could encounter these three arenas for the enactment of the same basic interactional-relational problem only in a serial fashion. They have to await the arrival at subsequent milestones or phases of development before these different arenas become available for the working-through process. It is in this sense that the working through must be *longitudinal in time* in a rapidly developing system. Berry Brazelton has a complementary view to the one just stated, namely, that at the transition to each new developmental phase the parents and system are especially open to change; ideally one intervenes at such points, "touchpoints" (Brazelton, 1984, 1992; Brazelton, Yogman, Als, & Tronick, 1979). Practically speaking, these two views are convergent.

The discussion of successive clinical windows in chapter 4 is another description of this same reality. The discontinuous nature of infant (and family) development is such that with the advent of new abilities the infant enters or creates new worlds of relatedness that the parents—especially first-time parents—and infant could not have fully predicted or prepared for. And each new world offers different opportunities for the expression of relationship problems. This is what was meant in chapter 4 by the metaphor of the same war as a succession of battles, each fought on a different and novel terrain.

It is for this reason that these therapies are best conceived as serial short-term interventions, each one with short-term effects lasting the duration of that developmental phase. As the next phase emerges with its new version of the problem, a new short-term intervention is needed. Reinstituted in this way, the serial interventions will achieve a maximal generalization (or working through) that the dyad can then itself carry forward in time. One does not know in advance how many versions of the same basic themes will be needed before sufficient generalization or working through is accomplished. One may be enough, but more often several are needed.

Thus, what looks like a therapeutic failure is, in fact, the optimal procedure in a context of rapid development. We are confronted here with a new temporal format of treatment. It must be seen for what it is and why it exists in this clinical context. And we must no longer evaluate it with only the standards and exigencies appropriate to other therapeutic contexts and populations.

The question arises whether in special situations such as those involving chronic conditions—mental retardation, blindness, developmental lag, deafness, and cerebral palsy, for example—the format of serial brief treatment is also used and appropriate. In actual practice, two different temporal formats of treatment seem to be used simultaneously in these situations. There are the evenly spaced visits (e.g., once every 2 months) that continue regularly. And superimposed on that structure is a form of serial brief treatment dealing with the challenges and crises caused by the inevitable discontinuous developmental leaps of the infant and the discontinuous arrivals of external events based on those leaps (e.g., starting school). Accordingly, under optimal conditions, a blind or developmentally lagged baby and his family may have an intensified burst of treatment when the infant starts (or should have started) to walk, when he begins a play group, and so on. After the change-point is adequately dealt with, the frequency of visits falls back to its regular level. In this sense a superimposed serial brief treatment format is used and is appropriate.

In the application of prevention programs for at-risk populations such as premature infants, or at-risk families, this serial brief-intervention format is hard to use for several reasons. The timing of the subsequent phase of intervention (or prevention) is an individual matter in large part and is not easily programmed for a large group prospectively. While most designers of prevention programs are fully aware of the discontinuous nature of things in infancy, they can best cover their bets with regularly spaced interventions over the longest period feasible. Still, it is relevant to note that in an exemplary prevention-intervention program addressed to premature infants, Barnard and colleagues (Barnard et al., 1987) found that an intervention concerning infant state modulation given at the time of hospital discharge was often insufficient unless reapplied six months later. I assume that the problem was not one of maternal memory but of inability to generalize what was learned at discharge for an infant of 1–2 months of age to an infant of 6 months of age.

In a similar fashion, many prevention and intervention programs that are applied for several months after birth (e.g., 0–3 months) prove much less effective than when the intervention is stretched out over a year. The

Clinical Nursery Models Project addressed to at-risk families provides such an example (Barnard, Booth, Mitchell, & Telzrow, 1988; Barnard, Morisset, & Spieker, 1993). Once again, it is necessary to evaluate how much of the inadequacy of the 3-month intervention was due to the parent's difficulty in generalizing to ages beyond 3 months and how much to the loss of other direct effects of the program. Both were probably factors. In any event, prevention programs would do well to take the issue of generalization or working through into account, wherever possible, and consider it apart from simple duration of intervention.

While the format of serial treatments is ideally suited to the developmental realities of infancy, it may also be a legitimate temporal format of treatment in any situation where life discontinuities, of whatever kind, impede continued functioning. (I will take this up in the final chapter on wider implications.) In this regard it is important to note that serial brief treatment conforms to the same longitudinal format used in pediatric well-baby care. It is thus well suited on both practical and theoretical grounds to being coordinated with the medical care and follow-up of infants. In summary, this temporal form of treatment should be considered as more an ideal, in the parent-infant situation, than a failure or deviation from standards applicable to other clinical situations.

The Use of a Positive Therapeutic Alliance, Positive Transference, and Positive Therapeutic Regard

A third commonality of most parent-infant psychotherapies is the way they use a positive therapeutic alliance and a positive transference. These positive processes are encouraged, used therapeutically, and left in place at the end of treatment; that is, they are not undone, or analyzed away. This feature has led to the criticism (mostly from the psychoanalytic perspective) that these therapies work as "transference cures."

In a related vein, the therapist adopts a positive regard toward the family and spends relatively more time on its assets and strengths, searching for, identifying, and focusing on the positive aspects of parenting she observes, than on its pathology and deficits. For this reason, these therapies have sometimes been called superficial, not therapies at all but simply efforts at support.

A third criticism of the use of these positive processes is that while they may be appropriate for disadvantaged and initially unmotivated mothers, they are not necessarily applicable to the rest of the population who need and seek parent-infant psychotherapy. Indeed, some argue that for those parents who do not have a "sturdy sense of self with a more painfully acute awareness of inner conflict about their babies" (Lieberman and Pawl, 1993, p. 433), creating a positive transference and alliance is simply a necessary technique to get and keep these parents in treatment.

I believe that all three of these criticisms are largely beside the point. They arise from a lack of appreciation of this particular clinical situation and from an adherence to criteria that were developed for other clinical contexts. In my view, these positive processes are an integral and indispensible part of parent-infant psychotherapy, for three main reasons.

First, the predominant content of new mothers' transference is different from that of other therapy patients. A brief historical review may be helpful in explaining why the issue of the nature of the transference arises here in the form it does. The notion of positive (especially romantic or erotic) transference first arose in Freud's early experience with hysterics in the 1890s. Initially it was seen as an impediment to psychoanalytic work. With growing experience in the psychoanalytic method and with the realization that several of his most promising disciples were involved in romantic and sexual relationships with their patients, however, Freud was forced to address the issue of transference and countertransference. His papers of 1914 and 1915 on technique contained at least three new emphases: that transference and countertransference were powerful and unavoidable forces; that while they can represent a resistance to treatment, they offer an opportunity for treatment in the form of the "transference neurosis"; and that particular technical measures (abstaining from sexual behavior with the patient, being a reflector for the patient's productions, and adopting a stance of emotional neutrality) were necessary, not only to further the elaboration of the "transference neurosis" but also to keep it safely within the bounds of the therapy proper (see Haynal, 1989; Person, Hagelin, & Fonagy, 1993).

The point is that in the treatment of neurosis, especially of "hysterics," the danger to a psychoanalytic treatment—and to the psychoanalytic movement in general—was an uncontrolled positive transference and countertransference. (An uncontrolled negative transference or countertransference resulted only in termination of that individual treatment. Generations of therapists—and not only psychoanalysts—have been trained with this caveat in mind, with or without the historical perspective.)

With the growing prevalence and theoretical importance of borderline and narcissistic personality disorders in comparison with classical neuroses, new kinds of predominant transference phenomena were discovered, such as the "idealizing transference" or "mirror transference" of Heinz Kohut (1977). The cardinal danger of an inadequately dealt with positive romantic or erotic transference was replaced with the dangers of a lack of an empathic stance. Appropriate shifts in technique were called for (e.g., Kernberg, 1984). A new population had partially reordered the landscape.

We now meet yet another new population: new parents and a baby. For the great majority, the mothers in this life situation, whether disadvantaged or advantaged, have a different predominant reaction to the therapist, namely, a fear of being found inadequate as a mother, of being judged unable to keep the baby alive and healthy and sane. They want and need to be supported and accompanied in this new life phase. (This wish will be discussed in greater detail in chapter 11.) Most mothers with relational problems with their infants know all too well, and painfully, what they are doing wrong, or find themselves unable to do, or can't do naturally. What these mothers don't know is what they are doing right, what assets they have to build upon, and how to reclaim unused parts of their more positive parenting repertoire. The result is that the greatest danger to effective treatment is a negative transference or countertransference. I believe that this is as true with advantaged as with disadvantaged mothers. It is not simply a technique to motivate or hook people to the treatment.

It is in this light that the creation and maintenance of a positive therapeutic alliance and transference must be evaluated. The basic therapeutic posture that was needed to work with the ready positive transference in hysterical neurotics was neutrality and relative emotional deprivation. The basic therapeutic posture required to work with the potentially devastating negative transference of a new mother is support and positive regard.

The basic therapeutic stance against which the transference will occur will necessarily distort the treatment process one way or the other. There is no such thing as a universal (neutral) ideal. The idea is to adjust this therapeutic stance most constructively fit the patient.

This is the major reason behind the very marked emphasis on the positive seen in the approaches of Lieberman and Pawl, of McDonough, of Fivaz, and of Barnard and Booth. While they often speak of the necessity of accentuating the positive to get disadvantaged mothers into treatment and hold them there, they have all understood and relied on the more basic reason that a different therapeutic stance is needed for the transference material appropriate to this life phase for all mothers.

The approach of the Genera group is a partial exception. Because of their commitment to their psychoanalytic roots, Cramer and Palacio-

Espasa often conceptualize this issue as if the traditional psychoanalytic therapeutic stance is to be maintained in spirit (as if the patient were a neurotic), while in actual practice they introduce a somewhat more positive and friendly therapeutic atmosphere than they would with other psychoanalytic cases. This has led to one of the most severe criticisms of their form of treatment, namely, that the Geneva group is basically looking for the memories and fantasies in the mother that "contaminate" her current interaction with the baby so that they can be decontaminated. Accordingly, regardless of the extent to which this may be true, the mothers who grasp this basic working assumption find in it the confirmation of their worst fears, those that animate their potential negative transference. In short, they experience it as just another, more sophisticated way of blaming mother.

My second reason for considering the positive therapeutic alliance and transference essential in parent-infant psychotherapies is that they permit the serial brief treatments described earlier in this chapter.

These relatively short bouts of treatment are interposed between periods of no treatment, during which the conditions for the next bout of treatment mature. As a rule, these periods of nontreatment last several months. How does the family remain "in treatment" during these nontreatment periods? How is the therapeutic relationship maintained so that the family wants to come back at the next appropriate phase and does so, spontaneously or by plan?

It is right here that the positive nature of the therapeutic alliance and transference plays another crucial role. It provides the momentum that carries the treatment process across these nontreatment stretches. That is why the positive nature of this process is left in place at the end of each treatment phase and not analyzed away; it is needed to hold the family in potential treatment. In a sense, the family—or most often the mother—walks away at the end of the last phase of therapy keeping the therapist and therapeutic relationship much in mind. The therapist is, so to speak, carried along with the parent during the nontreatment phase as a positive, benign, potentially available source of help, strength, and support. In this form the mental presence of the therapist not only keeps the door open for a possible next treatment phase but may act constructively in the interim.

The lingering positive alliance and transference clearly constitute unfinished business. It is in this light that they have been criticized as contributing to a transference cure. In the point of view adopted here, this unfinished business does not in itself create the cure but rather permits the treatment conditions—that is, serial treatment for longitudinal working through—that will effect the cure.

Even if the continuing positive transference does play an important direct role in the cure, that need not be a source of chagrin in this clinical context. The parent will soon pass out of this acute life phase, and the mental presence of the therapist as an active force in current life will disappear (more on this in the next chapter). In short, a transient "transference cure with treatment maintenance" is not an undesirable state of events; it is an ideal situation, to be sought in this clinical context.

In most clinicians' minds, this particular use of the positive transference and alliance is rarely stated. But for those who invite or plan a serial treatment format, there is some awareness of the need to create relationship conditions that permit the necessary treatment interruptions.

A final reason why the utilization of a positive therapeutic stance occupies a different position in parent-infant therapies concerns the nature of motivation for therapy. Parents having problems with their infants have a different kind of motivation. They are motivated to help the baby as well as to help themselves. It is difficult to state or predict which motivation will be greater, but they are different, with different defensive structures. The motivation to help the baby can more readily tolerate and profit from a positive therapeutic stance than a neutral one. This is also true for mothers' motivations to help themselves as mothers, but it is even more so for their motivation to help their infants.

The engine for change is also different in this clinical situation. In a traditional therapeutic setting with a single adult patient, the creation and maintenance of the motivation to change is necessarily a primary therapeutic focus. In parent-infant therapy, continuing change is imposed upon the participants by the force of development—in fact, rapid development. Much of the time is spent trying to catch up to intrinsic changes, rather than trying to initiate them.

This situation alters the possible impact of a positive alliance or transference. In the traditional situation, one does not want the patient to change for the sake of, or be gratified by, the positive traffic with the therapist. This is one of the potential dangers of a positive alliance and transference. In the parent-infant situation, rapid continuing change is taken for granted. The question is not how or why to put the relationship in motion but where to direct it. Under these circumstances, the parents work best in an atmosphere of benign regard.

In summary, a positive therapeutic alliance, transference, and regard play different roles in the clinical situation of parent-infant therapy. They offer different opportunities with different dangers courted or avoided. Working with these positive processes with this population is not a mistake nor a compromise treatment; it is what this clinical situation calls for.

This issue raises a larger question. Why is working with the positive more superficial than working with the negative? Why is the negative more profoundly situated? Why are ego strengths so often considered less interesting or important than ego defenses, or symptoms, or deficits? Why are therapists trained so that they become experts at identifying, naming, and understanding all manner of psychopathology but do not even have a meaningful nomenclature for positive aspects of mental life and must fall back on the classical virtues of our culture that have always existed outside of psychology in general: courage, honesty, curiosity, persistence, sense of humor, and so on? Therapists ask themselves these questions periodically, but this new clinical population demands a greater effort in pursuing these basic issues.

Functionally Reconnecting the Representations

It is common clinical experience that long and hard work is required to change a patient's representations. For this reason, many clinicians say that the parent-infant psychotherapies I have described could not possibly change any representations in 3–10 sessions, even if all the therapeutic work is directed to the mother's representations. In this light, these therapies are often judged to be superficial and their effects to be temporary because they do not bring about pervasive, enduring, "profound" structural changes. These criticisms—or better, observations—are mostly true, although misplaced. How then do we explain change?

I assume that there are two different main processes of change: functionally reconnecting the representations that are enacted in the interaction, which can be done relatively rapidly, and altering representations, which takes more time. Let us look first at what I mean by functionally reconnecting the representations.

Most parent-infant psychotherapies are concerned almost exclusively with those representations that are activated and then enacted in the parent-infant interaction. Therapeutically, what one is really interested in is the enactment (i.e., the actions, feelings, vocalizations, and so on) directed toward the infant and those that the infant enacts. This enactment is assumed to be the momentary result of many dynamically interacting activated representations, each a candidate for enactment. Two or more activated representations could act together to strengthen one form of enactment, or they could act to counter or mitigate one another.

In a sense, the activated representations are in competition to be transformed into action. This competition is highly fluid and dynamic and is influenced by the present conditions, which change from moment to moment. (See the summary discussion that concludes chapter 3.) Given this state of affairs, the actual enactment in any given moment can be therapeutically altered in several ways:

1. By inhibiting one or more of the activated representations from being enacted, or by substituting one representation for another to be enacted under specific conditions. For instance, in the case mentioned in chapter 3 of the mother who overinterpreted her son's aggressiveness, one of the treatment goals was to get the mother to see her child's behavior toward her as exploratory and curious rather than aggressive. She already had a representation of the boy as exploratory and curious, and another of him as aggressive. We wished to alter the relative threshold for enactment of these two representations under the same conditions of interaction. Neither representation had to be altered in itself.

2. By strengthening representations that are already activated but enacted weakly or not at all. For instance, the technique of identifying and reinforcing those interactive behaviors that parents can do well (as in interaction guidance, described in chapter 9) is predicated on the notion that the parents already have these behaviors potentially available to them.

3. By discovering representations. By "discovering," I mean the activation of representations that have not in the past been activated in a particular interactive context. For instance, consider the case of a mother who, as a child, had a negative experience with her own mother and now finds herself repeating the old patterns with her child. In this situation, the therapist may try to find some person in the mother's past with whom she had a positive parenting experience and who could serve as an alternative and contrasting model to her own mother—for example, her aunt, grandfather, or older sister. Once discovered, these representations can be explored for their potential to be activated and enacted.

   Another kind of discovery process is initiated when a mother enters into a productive therapeutic alliance with a therapist. She usually finds that certain perceptions, feelings, and evaluations about herself-as-a-mother come to the fore in the therapeutic relationship (the $M_{rep}{}^2$ of chapter 8). These newly "found" representations can then be used therapeutically.

   A third sort of discovery process occurs within the family therapy approach (see chapter 9), when changes brought about in the interactive context activate previously unavailable representations. Many supportive therapies also make certain representations enactable where they were not before.

The important point about all these therapeutic operations is that no representations are altered. One could argue that the representations that emerge in the mother while she is in the therapeutic relationship are the result of a "corrective emotional experience," as Lieberman and Pawl suggest (1993). In that case, these representations can be viewed as new creations and not simply the activation of latent representations. The distinction between these two, however, is not always clear.

In any event, to the extent that the mother's or the baby's representations are strengthened, weakened, inhibited, substituted, disinhibited, or have their threshold for enactment altered, one can speak of *functionally reconnecting* the representational world. This process requires no alteration in the form or content of existing representations and can readily be done in a brief psychotherapy. (Many cognitive psychotherapies are openly based on functional reconnecting.)

Before proceeding, it is worth saying something further about how the enactment of a representation is being viewed here. I assume that enacting a representation is similar to reconstructing and recalling a memory. In the process of remembering, many memory fragments are selected and activated. These fragments are presumably reassembled into several possible reconstructed memories, one of which is brought up into consciousness as the recollected memory. The final form of the recalled memory is greatly influenced by the present context that triggered the reconstruction and recall process to begin with. (The present context may also include what it is like to be with the therapist. This is another aspect of the corrective emotional experience.)

In the process of enactment, several representations are selected and activated. The enactment is analogous to the recall, in that it results from the interaction between several activated representations under the guiding influence of the present context. This context shifts moment by moment, so that different representations may be brought into or dropped out of this dynamic process at a rapid rate. After all, representations are generalized memories. They can result in mental acts (remembering) or physical acts (enacting).

To summarize the fourth commonality, then, all the therapeutic approaches mentioned act directly or indirectly to reconnect functionally the mother's and infant's representational world. The result is that the maternal enactments in the interaction are changed, while the actual representations have not been altered but only rearranged and reordered, to change the determination of which will result in action in specific contexts.

The different approaches explain how they bring about the functional reconnection in terms of different processes: reinforcement, interpretation, corrective emotional experience, altered context, or various combinations of these. This is as true for the infant's representations as for the mother's.

Once the representations have been reconnected so that the enactment in specific situations is different, the conditions are present to alter existing representations or create new ones. As we saw previously, any change in the interaction (due to a new enactment) will feed back to the representations and force an alteration to take into account the changed interaction. New enactments thus lead to changes in or additions to both the parents' and the infant's representations. This process can be more gradual and can proceed after therapy is concluded or between bouts of serial therapy.

Another crucial aspect of changing representations is their progressive generalization. This has been discussed earlier in this chapter as the necessary working through that generalizes the applicability of a representation and thus strengthens its functional power.

We have now viewed many different therapeutic approaches. And we have identified some of the features common to all of them. In part III, that follows, I will attempt the beginning of a synthesis and will start with a reconsideration of the mother as a different kind of "patient." I will suggest that motherhood creates a special psychic constellation, the "motherhood constellation," and that the common therapeutic features that have been identified among the different approaches are those best suited to help someone in the motherhood constellation. It is perhaps along these lines that the field of parent-infant psychotherapy is conveying.

PART III

SYNTHESIS

CHAPTER 11

The Motherhood Constellation

I AM SUGGESTING that with the birth of a baby, especially the first, the mother passes into a new and unique psychic organization that I call the *motherhood constellation*. As a psychic organizer, this "constellation" will determine a new set of action tendencies, sensibilities, fantasies, fears, and wishes. It also forces clinicians to adopt a different treatment framework, with a different kind of therapeutic alliance for the treatment. This new organization is temporary. Its duration is very variable, lasting months or years. But during that time, it becomes the dominant organizing axis for the mother's psychic life and pushes to the side the previous nuclear organizations or complexes that have played that central role. In a sense, a mother passes out of the Oedipus complex (or whatever else is conceived as the nuclear organizing axis) and enters into the motherhood constellation for an important but transient period. The motherhood constellation is not seen as simply another variant or derivative of already existing psychic constructs. Rather, it is seen as a unique, independent construct in its own right, of great magnitude in the life of most mothers, and entirely normal. (The situation for fathers is somewhat different and will be described later in this chapter.)

I further suggest that without an appreciation of the nature and predominance of the motherhood constellation, it is difficult to grasp the main subjective themes that mothers experience, the shape of the problems for which they seek help, and the form of the therapeutic alliance they most need. This last point is crucial, for I shall argue that the existence of the motherhood constellation requires the therapist to establish and work within a therapeutic alliance different from that traditionally sought.

The motherhood constellation concerns three different but related pre-occupations and discourses, which are carried out internally and externally: the mother's discourse with her own mother,[1] especially with her own mother-as-mother-to-her-as-a-child; her discourse with herself, especially with herself-as-mother; and her discourse with her baby. This motherhood trilogy becomes her major concern in the sense that it requires the greatest amount of mental work and mental reworking.

With the birth of her child, the mother experiences a profound realignment. Her interests and concerns now are more with her mother and less with her father; more with her mother-as-mother and less with her mother-as-woman or -wife; more with women in general and less with men; more with growth and development and less with career; more with her husband-as-father-and-context-for-her-and-the-baby and less with her husband-as-man-and-sexual-partner; more with her baby and less with almost everything else.

A new psychic triad, mother's mother–mother–baby, has come into existence and become the dominant organizing axis. The Oedipal triads of mother–mother's mother–mother's father and its new edition of mother-father-baby move from center stage and continue as still important but background issues during this period when the motherhood constellation becomes predominant. (One could argue that the "positive Oedipal complex" issues of the mother's identifying with her own mother and her mother's giving her permission to become a mother herself remain cardinal. And indeed these are important, but they come under the influence of the motherhood constellation, not the Oedipal complex. Most attempts to Oedipalize this phase of a woman's life have been very misguided, both clinically and politically.)

While exploring this phenomenon, it has been eye-opening to me to realize that most mothers in therapy have known this all along. They sense that they have temporarily passed outside of the main and exclusive influence of the Oedipus complex and other such psychic organizations that are used to explain pathology. They know full well that they have entered into a different psychic zone that has largely escaped psychiatry's official systematic theorizing but is perfectly evident to them. And they have most often, when in psychodynamic-type therapies, tolerated the traditional psychodynamic interpretations (e.g., the baby is symbolically the equiva-

---

[1]By "mother" in this context, I mean the main maternal figures in the woman's experience.

lent of a missing penis or a fantasized gift from their own father or from the male therapist) without giving them too much weight, in order to benefit from other aspects of the therapeutic relationship.

With this much said, let us begin to describe the motherhood constellation. When a woman becomes a mother, in our culture, anyway, several related themes emerge:

1. Can she maintain the life and growth of the baby? Let us call this a *life-growth theme.*
2. Can she emotionally engage with the baby in her own authentic manner, and will that engagement assure the baby's psychic development toward the baby she wants? This is a *primary relatedness theme.*
3. Will she know how to create and permit the necessary support systems to fulfill these functions? This is a *supporting matrix theme.*
4. Will she be able to transform her self-identity to permit and facilitate these functions? This is an *identity reorganization theme.*

Each theme involves an organized group of ideas, wishes, fears, memories, and motives that will determine or influence the mother's feelings, actions, interpretations, interpersonal relations, and other adaptive behavior. This organization may also structure aspects of her psychic life far beyond the phase in which it prevails.

Taken together, I will call these four themes and their related tasks the *motherhood constellation* and the three discourses she must bring together the *motherhood trilogy* so that they have names, which we will need clinically.

What sort of a thing is a motherhood constellation or, for that matter, its component themes and tasks? Is it like a complex? a psychic organization? a specific life-phase? We will take up these questions later in the chapter after the constellation has been described, but first some general comments.

The motherhood constellation is not universal, and it is not innate. We know that in other historical epochs and cultures any such collection of themes and tasks would be or is very different or almost nonexistent. Similarly, men could (but rarely do, as will be seen later) elaborate a motherhood constellation when conditions are propitious. I am describing a phenomenon seen in developed, Western, postindustrial societies, and almost exclusively in the mothers of these societies. I am making no claims beyond that, nor beyond the current cultural-political time frame. There are, unquestionably, psychobiological, especially hormonal influences that prime the sensibilities and tendencies of the new parent to develop some form of the motherhood constellation. The social-cultural conditions, however, seem to play the dominant role in how and whether these psychobiological influences will act.

In our society, the cultural conditions that seem to play a major role in shaping the final form of the motherhood constellation as we know it include the following factors:

1. The society places a great value on babies—on their survival, well-being, and optimal development.
2. The baby is supposed to be desired.
3. The culture places a high value on the maternal role, and a mother is, in part, evaluated as a person by her participation and success in the maternal role.
4. The ultimate responsibility for care of the baby is placed with the mother, even if she delegates much of the task to others.
5. It is expected that the mother will love the baby.
6. It is expected that the father and others will provide a supporting context in which the mother can fulfill her maternal role, for an initial period.
7. The family, society, and culture do not provide the new mother with the experience, training, or adequate support for her to execute her maternal role alone easily or well.

It is clear how these sociocultural factors are reflected in the four themes and tasks that make up the prevalent motherhood constellation in our society.

Even under the same sociocultural conditions the emergence of the motherhood constellation is not obligatory. Only most women, not all, will develop a full-blown or even recognizable motherhood constellation, depending on how many children they have already had and other individual differences. The society has a range of tolerance here for the strength and quality of the motherhood constellation that any one mother elaborates, but this tolerance is not very large before behavior passes over into zones of the questionable, bizarre, pathological, or outright criminal (e.g., child neglect or abuse).

The phase of the motherhood constellation is not a critical or sensitive period, either, so far as we know. The psychic organization that emerges during this phase may be permanent, transient, or, most frequently, permanently evokable.

The Component Themes of the Motherhood Constellation

Let us turn, then, to a description of the motherhood constellation as it is most commonly seen in those cultures and groups where parent-infant psychotherapy is practiced as we know it. And let us begin after the birth of the baby, even though the earlier forms of the constellation begin during pregnancy and sometimes even before.

THE LIFE-GROWTH THEME

Concerning the first theme, the life-growth theme, the central issue is, Can the mother keep the baby alive? Can she make him grow and thrive physically? It is this theme that, on the first nights home and for some time after, sends the mother repeatedly to the side of the sleeping baby to see if he is still breathing (even though she may joke about it the next morning); that makes decisions about breast- or bottle-feeding so momentous and success at feeding so vital; that turns superficially annoying remarks from the new grandmother that "his cheeks aren't very chubby" into profound recriminations; and so on.

What is at stake here is whether the mother will succeed as a human animal. Is she an adequate, naturally endowed animal? If she is, as measured in terms of the baby's life and growth, she can take her natural place in the evolution of the species, the culture, and her family. If not, she will fall irreversibly out of these natural currents of human evolution, perhaps forever. I am overdramatizing the situation for emphasis, but the power of this theme is enormous and long-lasting.

It is this life-growth theme that generates a family of fears that are normally a part of the motherhood constellation: that the baby will die or, more specifically, that he will stop breathing; that she will unintentionally suffocate him; that he won't eat and will waste away, or won't drink and will become dehydrated; that he will fall because she isn't sufficiently protective, and so on—in short, murder by profound inadequacy. Or, she fears, the baby will stay alive but not thrive, so that he has to go back to the hospital or she will have to be replaced at home by a "better" mother. The fear is of the failure of animal vitality and creativity. These are the postbirth variations of the related family of well-known normal fears during pregnancy of stillbirth, malformations, and monsters.

It is worth noting here that this life theme is unique in the life cycle; that mother has never before confronted it in its raw form, and may never again. It is not a derivative theme. It is not yet another version of castration, isolation, fragmentation, or one's own death. These other themes do not involve another's life in the same way. It is a cardinal, unique, independent life theme. The traditional themes address individual survival and sexual reproduction. The themes of the motherhood constellation pick up the story from that point forward and are directed toward species survival, once individual survival and reproduction have produced the next generation. (Attachment theory is also addressed to that phase of transmission of the gene pool.)

This point is crucial, for in proposing a new psychic organization, it is important in considering its magnitude that one can see it as directly necessary for the survival of the species.

THE PRIMARY RELATEDNESS THEME

The second theme concerns the mother's social-emotional engagement with the baby, the primary relatedness theme. The central issues are, Can the mother love the baby? Can she feel the baby love her? Can she recognize and believe that it is truly her baby? Can she enter into that state of "primary maternal pre-occupation" described by Donald Winnicott (1957), in which she develops a heightened sensitivity and engages in an intense identification with her baby, so as best to respond to his needs? Can she "read" her baby? Can she relate to her baby in a nonverbal, presymbolic, spontaneous manner? Can she fall or jump into free play? Is she a "natural" as a mother?

By primary relatedness, I mean the forms of relationship that occupy the first year or so of the infant's life before speech. These include the establishment of the human ties of attachment, security, and affection, the regulation of the baby's rhythms, the "holding" of the baby, and the induction of and instruction in the basic rules of human relatedness that are carried out preverbally, such as the production and reception of affect signals and social signals and the negotiation of intentions and intersubjectivity. These are some of the main elements of primary relatedness that must be laid down well before the word and the symbol arrive on the scene, before the infant must get socialized beyond the mother-infant dyad. It is the work of this (preverbal, pre-Oedipal) phase that is accomplished under the influence of the motherhood constellation.

Mothers are generally exquisitely aware of but also fearful of failures in this primary relatedness task, which tends to be highly defined by the culture and may be defined in ways that are not congruent with the mother's private leanings. The fears concern issues such as the mother's feeling unnatural, inadequate, handicapped, deficient, empty, ungenerous, or wanting in some of the basic human repertoire of feelings and behaviors, such as being unable to love, unspontaneous, or ungiving. Concerns for the psychic development of the baby inevitably result from any sense of failure in this task. (Note that what I am calling primary relatedness lasts over a year and includes Winnicott's "primary maternal preoccupation," which lasts only weeks and months after the birth, as initially formulated.)

THE SUPPORTING MATRIX THEME

The third theme concerns the mother's need to create, permit, accept, and regulate a protecting, benign support network, so that she can fully accomplish the first two tasks of keeping the baby alive and promoting his psychic-affective development. This theme, the supporting matrix theme, is unavoidable, given the great demands that both the baby and the society place on the mother, without providing her with the necessary preparation and means to accomplish them. The relative disappearance of the functional extended family for aiding the mother has not been adequately replaced by any other societal unit and certainly not by any medical or health structures. There is thus increased pressure on the husband and couple alone to provide the needed supporting matrix, an almost impossible task.

Traditionally, the supporting matrix, as the root of the name I have chosen implies, has been a female and maternal network. Some of the figures who have played or still play central or supporting roles in this matrix are goddesses of fecundity or childbirth or children, midwives (in French, *sage-femme*, i.e., wise woman), guardian angels, nurses, benevolent grandmothers, experienced aunts and sisters, doulas, and importantly, the mother's own mother (and only more recently the husband). Birth has traditionally been "woman's business"; so has early child care, both among humans and among most primates, the males being kept at a safe (for the baby) distance and only gradually permitted access to the infant, with most species.

In spite of the enormous importance of the husband in this matrix today, it is clarifying to evaluate his role compared to that of the women traditionally included in the functions of the supporting matrix. The first main function of the supporting matrix is to protect the mother physically, to provide for her vital needs, and for a time to buffer her from the exigencies of external reality so that she can devote (to use a word so appreciated by Winnicott) herself to the first two tasks. The husband has always played a large role in this function and simply plays a greater one now that the small nuclear family carries most of the weight.

The second main function of the supporting matrix is more psychological and educative. The mother needs to feel surrounded and supported, accompanied, valued, appreciated, instructed, and aided—each to a different degree for different mothers. The instruction aspect is very large. After all, learning to parent is at best an apprenticeship. These needs arise in large part from the cultural conditions prevailing at this life phase in our society. Without this form of support, maternal function is likely to be compromised. It is this function that a society of women traditionally fulfilled in the name of "woman's business." The modern husband tries to pick up the slack created by the shift in our social history, but there is a question as to what extent he can. We will return to this point later in this chapter.

After the birth of the baby, the mother's main active psychological involvement (besides with the baby) is most often with the maternal figures in her life—those figures who will in reality or in fantasy (for good or bad) provide the psychological and educative aspects of the supporting matrix. Concomitantly, there is less involvement with the traditional male figures in the mother's life and with the traditional themes associated with them (e.g., sexual themes and Oedipal themes). The husband, while more needed for certain things such as protection and support, is pushed into the background for others, such as maternal experience. For some of her new functions she needs a benevolent mother or grandmother more than she needs a husband. If the husband is needed to fill this role too (which he can do only very inadequately), he may be "maternalized" during this phase. The consequences of this development for the later adjustment of the couple are unclear. Many "new" (in the sense of sharing roles) couples feel closer and more equal when the husband has played a large practical and psychological role and been maternalized. It can be a positive experience.

Clinically, it has long been realized that the new mother's relationship with her own mother undergoes a reactivation and reorganization during this time, with the necessary formation of positive and negative models of parenting. Many authors have commented upon and deepened our understanding of this reinvolvement with the mother. Despite their diverse perspectives and different explanations and evaluations, they have agreed that there is a reengagement with maternal figures during the phase of the motherhood constellation (e.g., Benedek, 1959; Block, 1991; Chodorow, 1978; de Beauvoir, 1953; Deutsch, 1945; Gilligan, 1982; Winnicott, 1971). There is still much woman's business to be accomplished, even if intrapsychically.

In this light, the recent work on the patterns of attachment of new mothers to their own mothers is corroborative and not surprising (Fonagy et al., 1991; Grossmann & Grossmann, 1991; Main & Goldwyn, 1985; Zeanah, Mammen, & Lieberman, 1993). As we saw in chapter 2, one of the best predictors of the pattern of attachment that will emerge between a mother and her 12-month-old infant is the way the mother currently talks about her own mother and her own experiences of being mothered as a girl (the Adult Attachment Interview, Main & Goldwyn, 1985). The current emotional distance and atmosphere established by a mother toward her own mother, plus her ability to reflect on that relationship and its memories, become important factors. Is she enmeshed in, autonomous from, or rejecting of her relationship with her own mother? In effect, the new mother's current relationship with the totality of her experience of being mothered becomes a major influence on her maternal behavior toward her own child. In a similar vein, researchers such as Massimo Ammaniti (1991, 1994), Charles Zeanah et al. (1986, 1993), Graziella Fava-Vizziello et al. (1992, 1993), and Deiter Bürgin (personal communication, 1994), in tracing the mother's representations of her own mother during pregnancy and after the child's birth, note that the new mother's perceptions of her own mother undergo major shifts, suggesting that these relationships are the object of active and intense reworking during this life period.

It is in this context that a set of particular fears, wishes, motives, feelings, and ideas arise. The main source of fears is failure to create or keep a supporting matrix. The mother can be criticized and be found wanting as a mother, or she can be judged destructive as well as inadequate, by the supporting matrix. The matrix can criticize, devalue, or even abandon her. One or more members of the supporting matrix can undermine, sabotage, or outcompete the mother in the mothering role, with the result that the mother fears the loss of the baby or the baby's love. The mother may have to pay too high an emotional price to maintain the support of the matrix. For example, she may have to become dependent, or subservient, or fused with her own mother to enlist and maintain her support. The price is usually in terms of self-esteem, autonomy, independence, or dignity.

With her own husband as part of the matrix, there are related but special fears. She may fear that her husband will compete with her as parent or compete with the baby for the mother's attention ("the husband-as-the-second-baby syndrome"); she may fear overparentalizing (overmaternalizing) him; or she may fear that he will flee, opt out, or seek his need satisfaction elsewhere. The couple has a difficult equation to balance. The husband is needed as a physical, practical protection and buffer, as a psychological support, and as a husband-man. The wife occupies the complementary roles. These different roles are not necessarily compatible and are often out of sync for the two partners. The couple's ability to negotiate the frequent shifts in appropriate roles will be instrumental in establishing their adaptability and coping styles for the future as a couple.

One might ask, Why can't the husband simply fulfill the psychological supporting role as a husband and as a man? Why is that role necessarily parental and, even more, maternal? Theoretically he could. But to the extent that the new mother was primarily parented by a woman (her mother), she will need and seek a maternal figure as a crucial part of the supporting matrix when she has her own baby. Some of the reasons for this need are explained later in the chapter, in the discussion of the present remembering context of the motherhood constellation.

THE IDENTITY REORGANIZATION THEME

The fourth theme concerns the mother's need to transform and reorganize her self-identity. Some of the basic issues of this theme have already been discussed in chapter 2 on the parents' representations. In essence, the new mother must shift her center of identity from daughter to mother, from wife to parent, from careerist to matron, from one generation to the preceding one. Unless she can accomplish these transformations, the other three tasks in the motherhood constellation will be compromised. This theme of identity reorganization is both a cause and a product of the reinvolvement with maternal figures of the supporting matrix just discussed.

This reorganization is an obvious necessity if the mother is, indeed, going to alter her emotional investments, her allocation of time and energy, and her activities. The new identity as mother, parent, matron, and so on, requires new mental work. The need for models is evident, and she will revive the long history of her identifications with her own mother and other parental/maternal figures to provide the needed models. Some may become negative models, but models nonetheless. And again, the focus and preoccupation with other maternal figures in her life is likely to be intense. The process of intergenerational transmission takes over and is not so mysterious when one thinks of the baby and the interactions of mothering as a remembering context.

The Present Remembering Context and Its Role in the Identity Transformation

The reflections that follow are prompted by the question, Why is the mother's mother the central parenting model to be followed or rejected? Much of the recent work on memory in the cognitive neurosciences stresses the importance of the *present remembering context*. Researchers such as G. Edelman (1989) and F. C. Bartlett (1964) point out that the experience of remembering happens in the present, not in the past. The present context is viewed as the key to what is evoked from memory and how it is assembled.

From this perspective, the present moment with all its feelings, sensations, perceptions, thoughts, and contextual cues acts as the trigger—or rather many triggers—to activate many different memory networks and to determine which fragments will cohere and emerge as a memory. It is assumed that no memories or memory fragments are lost from storage; rather the crucial step is retrieval, that is, finding or creating a remembering context that facilitates retrieval.

For a mother, the moment-by-moment everyday interactions with the baby constitute the present remembering context. Concretely, they include experiences that belong to the mother as she directly lives them, such as holding the baby in her arms, feeling the baby's head in the crook of her neck, feeling the tug of feeding, being unable to console the crying baby, reacting to his rejections of her, and at times expressing disgust. They also include experiences that belong to the baby but that the mother lives empathically, such as the baby's avid drinking, his slipping into sleep, rageful crying, anxiety and fear at sudden violations of expectancy, and the face he sees of the furious or disgusted mother (herself). Selma Fraiberg (1980) noted some time ago that the baby's presence "in the room" elicits feelings and memories in the mother that would not have been evoked otherwise.

The remembering context is made up of one person's experience of both sides of the interaction or relationship as these occur almost simultaneously: that which is directly felt by one partner and that which is empathically apprehended of the other partner's experience. Similarly, the mother's stored memories or memorial fragments also include both sides of her interaction or relationship with her own mother when she was young: the parts that she experienced directly as a baby, while interacting with her mother, and the parts of her mother's experience of interacting with her that she experienced empathically (via imitation and primary identification).

It is likely that in this manner the daily acts of mothering constantly evoke memories of the mother's infancy and, at the same time, of the mothering she received from her own mother. The interaction with a baby is a very specific remembering context that the new mother may never have had before. Even though she may have baby-sat or been with younger siblings or nieces and nephews, she has not until now been in a situation where empathic immersion and primary identification were fully needed and used.[2] After all, what makes the remembering context the trigger for those early memories is that both of them consist of the experiences on both sides of the interaction—the mother's and the baby's—across a generation. (The concepts of imitation, contagion, empathy, and primary and secondary identification play a major role in this conceptualization [see Sandler, 1987].)

These constantly evoked memories seem to act mostly at a preconscious level and are generally accessible when approached with techniques like the microanalytic interview, mentioned in chapter 3. Sometimes they pop into the mother's consciousness during the routine caregiving activities. For example, a mother is playing face-to-face with her 26-week-old daughter in the company of observers. She runs out of things to do, then suddenly starts a "face game." It consists of singing a song while pointing to each of the facial features that are named in the song. This is a game she has not heard for over 20 years (it is in her mother language, which is different from what she speaks on a day-to-day basis). And she has never played it herself—that is, acted it on someone—before; she has only received it, so to speak. She does not know why the idea or memory arose then. This memory was retrieved spontaneously in that context.

Recently I saw the videotapes of George Engel's famous case of Monica, a girl born with an esophageal atresia who was fed by tube directly into her stomach until her twenty-first month of life, when surgical repair was accomplished. (This viewing was in the context of a reconsideration of this case; see Hofer and Hofer, 1994.) Monica is now in her early forties and a grandmother. As a baby, she was fed lying flat on her back, across her mother's knees, with no attempt to contour her body by her mother's arm or body. This position was largely necessary because it took two hands to feed her well by tube. The procedure stopped when she was 21 months old and able to eat normally. As a girl of 3 and 4 years old, she pretend-fed her doll placing it in that same position across her knees. As a young mother, she fed her baby girls in that position. Her daughter started to feed her own baby (Monica's grandchild) in that position, but then seemed to shift to a more usual holding position. During all this time, Monica did not see these visual records of her feeding, and there is no reason (that I know of) to believe that the subject of the feeding position should have prompted any discussion. Feeding a baby with a bottle appears to have

[2]Sometimes memories of the role of the older sib taking care of younger ones, or the younger sib being taken care of by the older one, are evoked and stand as the important "maternal" events.

acted as a strong remembering context. While this vignette is only an anecdote, it makes the point without proving it.

In any event, such evocations contribute greatly to the mother's working on the relationship with her own mother, past and present. The flow of evoked memories, triggered by this new remembering context, is the raw material for an important part of the mother's reorganization of her identity as daughter and as mother.

There are two other features of the motherhood constellation that provide an effective remembering context. In seeking the support of the matrix, the mother needs and wants to be "held," valued, appreciated, aided, and given structure by a benign, more experienced woman who is unequivocally on her side. To the extent that she receives this support she has approximated some of the conditions that prevailed for her when she was an infant. Similarly, to the extent that the new mother must make order out of chaos with her baby in terms of rhythms, signals, and meanings, and must do so largely by trial and error, she is once again forced to create an emergent order concerning the most basic and rudimentary aspects of living. In this, too, a situation that prevailed during her infancy has been approximated and will aid in defining the present remembering context.

Seen this way, the mother's recalling (and reimmersing herself in) the earlier experiences of her own mothering is not an act of regression. It is more simply the result of finding oneself in a powerful and pervasive present remembering context that has not been experienced since the early years of life. And in this remembering context, the old schemas-of-being-with-mother will tumble out and pervade the new mother's experiences. (Of course, regression in the pathological sense may occur, but that is not what I am talking about here.)

The Nature of the Motherhood Constellation

With this general description of the motherhood constellation and its major themes in place, we can return to the question put off at the beginning of the chapter and ask, What is the nature of this constellation? First, the motherhood constellation is a construct occupying the minds of clinicians, who find it hard to work without some such construct that helps make sense out of a wide variety of clinical phenomena. But does it actually exist in the mother's mind, and if so, in what form? Such concepts are often very convincing and useful clinically, but very problematic scientifically.

There is now a long history of clinical constructs postulating an organized grouping of ideas, interests, desires, feelings, motives, action tendencies, and sensory and perceptual susceptibilities. A brief overview may help in placing the motherhood constellation.

The *complex*, as it arose in psychoanalysis, is an organized grouping of mental phenomena, par excellence. It has, however, not been very helpful theoretically. Its extended use, beyond the Oedipus complex, has been largely discouraged, even by Freud, despite—and in part because of—its wide popularity for connoting pathology (see Laplanche & Pontalis, 1967/1988). It is only for the Oedipus complex that psychoanalysis preserves the unmodified term *complex*, in large part because the organization of psychic life implied by the Oedipus complex is thought to play a uniquely central and universal role in structuring personality and sexuality and in providing the axis of reference for most psychopathology, certainly all psychoneuroses. From a traditional psychoanalytic perspective, then, there cannot be any other main complexes. The Oedipus complex is *the* constellation for viewing and understanding psychoneuroses. Thus, we cannot properly speak of a "motherhood complex," nor would we want to, because of its connotations of pathology.

Psychoanalysis since Freud has focused more on pre-Oedipal constellations and their value in viewing personality disorders and psychoses; one generally speaks of *pre-Oedipal organization*. In a similar vein, the organization given to psychic life by early developmental phases (e.g., psychosexual stages or separation-individuation) can also be seen as different forms of constellations. These, however, are organizations for the infant. The motherhood constellation is an organization for the mother. In this regard, it is more like a life-span stage, phase, task, or issue. Why not, then, leave it at that—as a life-span phase?

Life-span phases or issues tend to be quite general and obligatory within a culture. Erikson's examples are the classical referent (1950). The motherhood constellation is narrower and more specific, and it is not obligatory; women do not have to become mothers. Moreover, the motherhood constellation is not brought about by general internal developmental changes unfolding in a given culture. It is a response to getting pregnant and having a baby in a certain cultural setting. The core triggers are very concrete and specific.

The most telling reason, however, why the motherhood constellation should be considered a type of basic psychic organization rather than simply a life phase is this. Life phases, in the psychoanalytic literature, generally describe developmentally new sets of tasks and concerns, and new sets of capacities for dealing with these tasks. These then act to alter the already exciting, central psychic organization that is Oedipal. They do not replace it with a new organization; they reorient, elaborate, and extend the existing one. The motherhood constellation, on the other hand, involves the creation of a new central psychic organization that, for a time, replaces or pushes to the background the preceding one.

Moving away from the more clinical concepts, one also cannot speak of this constellation as the result of an activated motivational system that organizes mental life. This is hard enough to do with a more delimited motivational system such as attachment, and it would be unwieldy to do with something so diverse as mothering in the broad sense.

The motherhood constellation has some features of a complex, of a psychic organization, of a specific life-span phase or issue, and of the mental organization created by an activated motivational system. We do not know the exact nature of this kind of mental organization, or how it influences ongoing mental life and behavior. (Further clarification at a fundamental level probably awaits advances in the cognitive neurosciences in collaboration with the clinical sciences.) Nonetheless, some such concept is needed clinically and theoretically, especially because the motherhood constellation with its component themes provides the most convincing axis of reference for the mother's side of most parent-infant problems. It occupies the same position for these disturbances as the Oedipus complex has for the classical psychoneuroses.

Clinical Implications of the Motherhood Constellation

THE THERAPEUTIC ALLIANCE AND THE TRANSFERENCE/COUNTERTRANSFERENCE

Perhaps the most important clinical implication concerns the best form of therapeutic alliance and the transference/countertransference considerations that should be applied to someone who is in the motherhood constellation. Generally speaking, in psychodynamic therapies, these issues are dependent on the type of psychopathology present and on the conception of the psychic organization that best explains that psychopathology.

Accordingly, for classical psychoneuroses, as viewed psychoanalytically, the Oedipal complex is seen as the key psychic organizer. Classically, hysteria was the prototype, involving a female patient and a male therapist. In this context, as we have seen, the "transference neurosis" involved the elaboration of a "love" for the therapist (as father) and the transference/countertransference danger to the treatment frame was the acting out of this "love." Many of the classical psychoanalytic techniques on the therapist's part were adjusted to dealing with this situation—for example, the strictures against sexual activity between therapist and patient.

By contrast, for borderline patients and those with a narcissistic personality disorder, the determining psychic organization is assumed to be pre-Oedipal. The transference/countertransference situation is therefore viewed differently, in terms of "idealizing and mirroring transferences" by the patient and an empathic stance on the part of the therapist.

For a mother having a relationship disturbance with her infant, the determining psychic organization is the motherhood constellation. The transference that evolves in this situation involves the elaboration of a desire to be valued, supported, aided, taught, and appreciated by a maternal figure. This desire for such a maternal figure is evidenced in many situations outside of the therapeutic one. Beginning in the hospital with the birth of the baby, mothers very frequently find someone to fill this role or part of it. It is often a nurse, a nurse's aide, the cleaning lady, or someone else who takes a moment to share personal experience and give heartfelt encouragement. It is amazing how important these short encounters can be. They are overwhelmingly with other women more experienced in motherhood. Emotionally they often overshadow the more medical encounters (provided that all is going well). Later, other mothers met in the park may partially fill this role, to say nothing of the mother's actual mother, grandmother, older sisters, and experienced friends.

In the transference situation this seeking and finding is intensified and focalized on the therapist. It has been suggested that I call this form of transference "the good grandmother transference." The danger to the treatment frame and to the therapeutic alliance in this situation is that the therapist will be unable to respond to these wishes and needs, either on personal grounds or because the therapist is adhering to a therapeutic framework appropriate to psychoneurosis but not to the motherhood constellation. Most mothers experience such a lack of response to their needs as a refusal to be supportive, as criticism, or as withdrawal of encouragement, belief in, or appreciation of their maternal functioning. It exacts a heavy price on the therapeutic alliance.

Once this form of good grandmother transference has been accepted by the therapist as appropriate to the motherhood constellation, it does not have to be fought against. The therapist can be more active, less abstinent emotionally, freer to "act out" in the sense of making home visits, giving advice, touching the patient, and so on, and more focused on assets, capacities, and strengths than on pathology and conflicts. This form of transference is ideally suited to utilizing the positive aspects of the transference alluded to in chapter 10. The result is a better therapeutic alliance and with it greater facility in acting therapeutically, including furthering certain psychodynamically guided explorations.

This shift in perspective about the actual psychic situation pertaining in mothers has, in fact, already begun, even if it is not officially recognized. The therapy conducted in San Francisco by Lieberman and Pawl (see chapter 8) has, in effect, shifted from a transference frame appropriate for psychoneuroses to one appropriate for the motherhood constellation, although these therapists explain this shift as largely required by the needs of the particular disadvantaged population they serve. I believe they underestimate the full scope of their framework. In a similar fashion, McDonough has attributed much of her handling of the therapeutic alliance in interaction guidance to its early history with disadvantaged mothers. Nonetheless, she is fully aware that it works with advantaged mothers quite as well. Most of the other treatment approaches mentioned in part II have some modifications in the direction of adjusting to the reality of the motherhood constellation. In a sense, our theories have not yet caught up to our practices.

On the contrary, many of the psychoanalytically oriented therapies have maintained the psychoanalytic framework appropriate for psychoneuroses even when dealing with the motherhood constellation. Too often, this approach results in positive behavioral therapeutic changes but a profound wound to the mother, who feels that the interaction with her baby has been "decontaminated" of her individual conflicts. The mother necessarily senses that this assumption underlies the therapist's basic view, and it aggravates her worst fears of being destructive, inadequate, lacking, criticized, blamed, and unappreciated. To avoid these negative consequences, the mother acts better, and the symptoms disappear. What one gets is in effect a behavioral cure based on the mother's avoidance of negative reinforcement in the therapy, all of which takes place paradoxically in a setting that purports to be psychoanalytic. This problem is at the base of one of the most persistent criticisms of these approaches.

To summarize this clinical implication, I believe that there is now sufficient reason to adopt the assumption that the mother's psychic organization is mainly determined by the motherhood constellation and to let this view provide the paradigmatic transference framework for disturbed mother-infant relationships.[3] Once this conceptual shift has been made, we can go about the business of freely and systematically evaluating its advantages without having to defend it. This shift offers a new approach to a unique set of problems. It marks the point where the growing experience with parent-infant therapies stops being an application of an old framework adjusted to a new problem and becomes, in its own right, a new approach.

Assuming, then, that the motherhood constellation provides the appropriate framework for most parent-infant therapies, what are the full implications? Providing a therapeutic alliance–transference framework to the context of a motherhood constellation will promote most of the commonalities that we discovered in chapter 10. It will permit the therapist to become a special form of supporting matrix that can validate, support, and appreciate the mother and thus "hold" her so that her maternal functions are liberated or discovered and facilitated. Furthermore it can do this without exacting a price from her functioning, self-esteem, or independence. It can help her change or reconnect her representation primarily through corrective emotional experiences as well as interpretations and modeling. It is ideally suited to the exploration and discovery of the previously unknown or unused assets for mothering and to the search for any alternative maternal figures who have played a positive maternal role in her past and can now be used. It can provide her with realistically needed advice and practical help. It supports her capacity to create the necessary "positive distortions" about her baby—those that will become self-fulfilling prophecies.

Finally, the maintenance of a positive transference during the hiatuses in the serial brief therapies poses no practical or theoretical problems for a therapeutic alliance–transference structure appropriate to the motherhood constellation. On the contrary, the maintenance of such a positive transference is desirable during the reign of the motherhood constellation, and its termination poses no problems, because the transference fades away naturally when the mother passes out of the motherhood constellation.

In summary, the argument is that parent-infant therapies may do well to reevaluate what they imagine to be the basic psychic organization of the

---

[3]There will of course be a minority of cases where more traditional psychoneurotic problems remain in the forefront. In such cases the old framework is applicable. Also there will be cases where, after the main treatment has been accomplished with the transference frame appropriate to the motherhood constellation, a problem individual to one or both parents reemerges as the dominant feature. In such cases individual psychotherapy or couples therapy, with its own appropriate transference framework, is then indicated as a follow-up.

mother at the time of treatment. If the dominant psychic organization of the mother is found to be the motherhood constellation, then there must be alterations in technique and in the therapeutic framework to facilitate the commonalities discussed in chapter 10.

SOME IMPLICATIONS FOR FATHERS AND THE NUCLEAR FAMILY

It is worth distinguishing "new parents"[4]—parents who believe in, seek after, and sometimes achieve equality between mother and father in caregiving—from "traditional parents," who place less value on that equality and accordingly do not realize it. Both kinds of fathers can provide the practical support that frames and protects the mother in her early relationship with the infant. The "new father" can also participate with her in virtually all the caregiving tasks. And he can do both well. There are two things that he cannot do well, however, and that the traditional father does not try to do. First, he cannot richly and expertly advise, teach, and model for the mother a wide array of caregiving information, attitudes, and techniques, since he is as inexperienced in parenting as she is (or more so). He will thus be inadequate for this aspect of the support matrix. Second, while he can validate and appreciate the mother in her caregiver role, he cannot do so as well as a personally selected, "legitimate" maternal figure. He is simply not entitled by history and experience to do so. His appreciation as a husband, father, and man is of great importance, but it is of a different order and can satisfy only a part of the mother's need for psychological "holding."

These considerations pose certain problems that are aggravated for "new" families. For instance, a woman who values her career and wants to keep that door either partly or fully open greatly appreciates the husband's sharing of the caregiving. Often his help is reassuring more because it promises to make her later reentry into work easier, and less because she needs a coparent, or even the extra support, now. In fact, many mothers, "new" ones included, may not want to lose the special early mother-infant relationship, at least for a while. The "new" husband is then left with half the work and less than half the gratification, unless he can be gratified in supporting the mother in her parental role—a more traditional form.

There is another potential problem. If the extended family is functionally nonexistent, much of the mother's need for real or fantasized support,

---

[4]I am borrowing, in the main, the definition and terms given by Frascarolo-Moutinot (1994).

encouragement, education, and validation falls on the husband. He becomes maternalized in part. And furthermore, even when he is willing, he is unable to meet the need. He becomes a failed or inadequate maternal substitute. The long-range consequences of becoming maternalized and partially failing at it for the evolution of the "new nuclear family" remain to be seen.

Would these sorts of problems disappear if the mother's main caregiving and parental figure had been both parents—that is, a "new family"? That also remains to be seen. Social movement in that direction is slow despite the preferences of many modern parents. The intergenerational drag is a conservative force (Frascarolo-Moutinot, 1994).

Finally, if the father is the primary caregiver, will he also develop a motherhood constellation? After all, his primary caregiver was (most probably) his mother. Or will the necessity to identify with his father alter this situation very much? The answers to these questions will become clearer in time.

The motherhood constellation remains, by far, the prevailing psychic organization for mothers, for the immediate future. So whether or not it is desirable from a sociocultural point of view, it is what must be taken into account therapeutically, now.

CHAPTER 12

Some Wider Implications for Other Clinical Situations

W E CAN NOW return to one of the central questions that was posed in the introduction. Is the outcome of the encounter between traditional psychotherapies and the new clinical situation of parent-infant relationship disturbances relevant for other clinical situations, populations, and approaches? What follows is a discussion of several points bearing on these wider applications.

The Applicability of the Serial Brief Treatment Format Beyond the Parent-Infant Clinical Situation

It frequently happens that adult former patients who have completed "successful" treatments run into previously unexpected life crises, such as divorce or the death of a parent. Either they find themselves forced to deal with feelings and motivations that they never had to deal with before—in quantity or quality—or they find that previously effective ways of coping are proving unsuccessful in this new context. In either case they return for a second treatment, to reapply, in a sense, the gains of the initial therapy to the new situation and enlarge the treatment effect. A large part of the motive to return to treatment is the clear feeling that the first one worked well.

This situation for adults is perhaps not different in kind from the conditions at the beginning of life that require longitudinal working through, and it raises the issue of a basic view of development during the entire life span, from the clinical point of view. If the major work of development, in a large sense, is accomplished in early adulthood and can be (more or less) stabilized for a lifetime by giving the patient in therapy the self-righting processes to deal with all further developments, then one does not need the notion of longitudinal working through. But if one sees life-span development as a never-ending series of transformations that cannot be anticipated or sufficiently prepared for, even by getting the coping machinery in good order, then the only difference between infancy—or adolescence, for that matter—and any other period or phase of the life span is one of degree, that is, rate of internal change and rate of encountering drastically new contexts. The need for a working-through process over time is then seen as normative, and the timing of therapy may need to adjust to it in the form of some variation of the serial-treatment format. Such reapplications of treatment, in this light, are neither retreatments nor second treatments. They are simply the continuation of a single treatment across discontinuities in a life span.

Specificity and Cultural Variability

It came as no surprise that as far as therapeutic outcome was concerned, there were no striking differences among the various clinical approaches. This has been the experience with almost all forms of psychotherapeutic treatment.

Where the various approaches probably have their largest differential effect is on the subpopulations they can attract to come for treatment, induce to enter into the therapeutic process, and hold in that therapy. In other words, it appears that the biggest difference lies in the nature of the therapeutic framework and relationship with the therapist, rather than in the therapeutic technique proper (in the strict sense) or in the type or severity of psychopathology, per se. It makes sense that it is the therapeutic relationship—in particular the therapeutic alliance itself—that is the most culturally sensitive aspect of any treatment approach, since it is there that the nature of the relationship between the therapist and patient is most revealed.

These cultural considerations, however, are not minor. Recent thinking (e.g., Nathan, 1986) suggests that within culturally mixed populations, therapy must be conducted in the cultural mode that the patient lives in. To be effective, it must utilize the local language and metaphor and share the basic assumptions, values, and practices of the culture. This makes immediate common sense for recognizable cultural groups, but it is perhaps equally true for the divergent beliefs and assumptions about therapy within the same overall culture. For the purposes of therapeutic efficacy, these differences in belief may need to be considered cultural. There are different "therapy cultures" in our society.

Therapists working with parents and infants have become extremely aware of how the particular therapy culture influences the nature of the therapeutic alliance they seek to establish. For example, being disadvantaged and uneducated tends to go with a particular therapy culture. The nature of the therapeutic alliance to be established is always an open, conscious therapeutic issue. And this is especially so in the presence of the motherhood constellation. The cumulative experience of parent-infant psychotherapists has helped us to see more clearly that the cultural differences in treatment involve the therapeutic alliance more than any other aspect of the treatment approach.

There is one final question concerning the equal effectiveness of the various treatment approaches. What consequences should these findings have on public policy? A shortsighted political and economic answer would be to conduct only the therapeutic approach that costs the least to perform and have it done by professionals who are the most cost-effective to train. A more farsighted scientific answer would be that different therapeutic approaches, even if they do not differ in treatment outcome, can, as the subject of clinical research, teach very different things about the psychopathologies being treated and the therapeutic process of change. Moreover, each approach has something different and valuable to offer in the overall training of psychotherapists of all persuasions. Also, different approaches will attract and keep in treatment different subgroups, as pointed out above. Some compromise between science, training, and economics will be needed.

While I fully believe that at present we cannot predict which approach will be best for which particular patient, it is obvious that any approach is likely to run into problems at times and fail. What to do then? Ideally the patient should be referred to someone with a different approach. (Therapists would then have to remain open to the value of other approaches.) Or the therapist might be trained in several approaches and be able to switch approaches. Can therapists learn and effectively practice several approaches well? Most are skeptical, but in the domain of parent-infant therapies I am less skeptical. I believe that the range of problems encountered and solutions possible is limited. I can well imagine a three- or four-year training exclusively for parent-infant mental health specialists who could learn to move flexibly from one approach to another as needed while still holding in mind the need for a measure of continuity in the therapeutic alliance.

Moving Into and Out of the Motherhood Constellation

The existence of something like a motherhood constellation has implications for all therapies in which a woman seeks treatment for reasons unrelated to being a mother. It often happens that the woman becomes pregnant or has a child during the course of treatment, but the central aim of the therapy rests with the original motives for treatment and the original technique of therapy. In light of her entrance into the motherhood constellation, what does one do?

Frequently the therapist and patient contrive to leave all motherhood issues out of the treatment or to bring them in only to the extent that they bear on the issues raised anyway. They may try to decompress an acute infant-related problem so that the "normal" therapy can proceed as before. Leaving mother-baby issues out of the treatment can be done if the treatment was intended to be highly focused therapy. Addressing these issues only to push them aside and continue the main treatment goal creates a kind of compartmentalization. What frequently happens is that as motherhood constellation issues grow in importance, the other, originally pressing issues pale in importance. Therapy is either interrupted for unclear reasons or limps along on a reduced motivation. Because of this situation, some psychoanalysts have suggested an official interruption in treatment (e.g., during the pregnancy and for several months after) until the pervasive lifelong issues can again reoccupy center stage without the intrusion of a pressing current reality—in effect, until the motherhood constellation has largely passed. This is a drastic solution, but it implicitly recognizes the workings of something like a motherhood constellation.

The third solution is to continue the treatment and not leave the motherhood issues out of the treatment. This approach may be difficult, however, if the nature of the therapeutic alliance established for the general treatment is not compatible with one appropriate for the motherhood constellation. On the one hand, if the originally established alliance cannot be altered, the therapist cannot address the issues specific to the motherhood constellation. On the other hand, if the therapeutic alliance is altered, will the therapist and patient ever be able to return to the form of alliance needed (by that approach) to treat the original issues later on?

I don't believe there is a general solution here. Case-by-case compromises must be found, often with some shifting back and forth. It will be easier to find solutions, however, when these issues are held in mind.

A second implication is more theoretical. The motherhood constellation partakes of both a life-course phase or task or issue and something like a psychological complex—that is, a mental organization, whatever that might be. Life-course phases are generally assumed to be concerned with general issues appropriate to an age period and to the social-cultural conditions operating during that age period. These phases have largely been modeled on the idea of developmental phases as global organizations, such as for psychodynamics (with issues like independence, trust, and autonomy) or for cognitive stages (sensorimotor, operational, symbolic, and so on). The basic assumption is of a fairly pervasive and uniform, general, organizing view that colors all aspects of life during a phase.

In contrast to these assumptions, current researchers in developmental psychology, ethology, and the cognitive sciences tend to argue against large general stages and to think in terms of specific mental organizations that are designed and adapted for particular tasks and domains with separate evolutionary consequences (e.g., Cosmides & Tooby, 1994; Spelke, 1994).[1]

So far, I have presented the motherhood constellation as a sort of powerful interloper—a visiting form of mental organization that comes on the scene, takes center stage, and then goes, leaving the psychic world as it was before, organized into the large, already accepted, fundamental mental organizations such as the Oedipal complex. (I will continue to use the Oedipal complex as the example, but I could just as well have used personality organizations or others.) The alternative view is that both the motherhood constellation and the Oedipal complex are simply separate, task-specific mental organizations with different evolutionary functions for overall survival. The apparent dominance or pervasiveness of either one is only a reflection of the ecological human conditions that people find themselves in at different life points. It is not a reflection on the universality, strength, or profundity of one mental organization compared with the other.

Generally, mothers of any age who are in psychotherapy and who have passed well beyond the early phases of parenting—their children are in

---

[1]For instance, depending on whether a toddler's immediate task is to discover "where he is" (i.e., to orient himself) or "where it is" (i.e., to discover a hidden object), the salience and use of different visual cues (color versus geometry) will be quite different. That is to say, the child will appear to have different capacities in these two situations. His mental organization will in some ways be different depending on the exact task at hand. This shift in emphasis is fully compatible with and inspired by the current view in cognitive science of a more modular mind.

school or independent—periodically have very acute and intense concerns about their mothering, both past and present. After all, some of the basic concerns of the motherhood constellation never disappear. (I am reminded of that nightly announcement on a New York City TV channel that appears to seize all mothers from age 16 to 96: "It is 10 o'clock. Do you know where your children are?") As these concerns in the older mothers get attended to therapeutically, it is usually not necessary to reestablish the therapeutic framework appropriate to the acute motherhood constellation if one is treating a problem mainly centered in the past. Sometimes, on the other hand, it is useful to reapply the motherhood constellation therapeutic framework, at least for a time.

We are witnessing a reshuffling of what we mean by instincts, drives, and motivations, on one hand, and complexes, mental organizations, stages, life phases, and life tasks, on the other hand. This is inevitable since these two groups of concepts are interdependent, and altering one will force changes in the other.

The motherhood constellation is an attempt to shift in the direction from general life phases to more domain- and task-specific, evolutionarily relevant mental organizations and still stay clinically useful. The concept may have to be fractionalized more to be scientifically valid, but that will always be at the risk of becoming clinically less useful. And a larger question remains to be answered: To what extent are these reflections relevant not only for the motherhood constellation but equally so for other motivated life-span phenomena of clinical and survival interest?

A final implication of the motherhood constellation concerns the psychology of women and of men. I prefer to not address these issues here, as they would take us too far afield.

The Place of Action in the Theory and Practice of Psychotherapy

What weight is given to actions as against mental events (desires, thoughts, fantasies) in psychotherapy theories? In a sense, the answer to this question goes far in distinguishing the major therapeutic approaches. Most psychodynamic and cognitive therapies have focused mainly on thinking and representing (in all its forms) and less on acting. At its origin, psychoanalysis had to establish its basic tenets by confining itself to mental phenomena, both theoretically and technically (e.g., barring acting in the consulting room, so as to produce thinking—about acting). One of the main consequences of this emphasis has been greater interest in intrapsychic phenomena than in interpersonal events, and in fantasized interactions than in real ones. For example (and paradigmatically), Freud's second seduction theory presumed that the little girl was never actually seduced in historical fact, rather that she wished it, fantasized it, and repressed both the wish and the fantasy.

It is in the same spirit that the ideas of Melanie Klein and many who have followed her have emphasized infants' original (primary) fantasies, rather than their observable interactive experience, in forming their psychic reality.[2]

Far at the other end of the spectrum are those behavioral therapies that in their exclusive focus on actions or responses have been uninterested in the mental structures that mediated the responses, let alone in the subjective experiences that accompany them. Similarly, one wing of the family or group therapies inspired by systems theory has strongly emphasized the actions and interactions of the group at the expense of the intrapsychic mental phenomena, which are seen almost as theoretical obstacles to viewing interactive patterns—just as, in a mirror fashion, some psychoanalysts consider actions an obstacle to viewing mental events.

In spite of these polarities and (often historically corrective) exaggerations, it is clear to most that both actions and mental phenomena must be considered and reconciled. It is the dialectic between the two that is finally most interesting and productive theoretically.

It is on just this issue that the encounter with preverbal infants and their parents contributes to this dialectic between action and thought in the clinical realm. This encounter has forced those most interested in intrapsychic mental phenomena to become more aware of and interested in actions and has forced those most interested in actions and behavior to look at the mental phenomena that give rise to and accompany them. This growing redefinition of the field of vision and interest is a general consequence of this encounter. There are some more specific ones.

The recent clinical experience with sexual abuse in childhood suggests that very important psychopathological origins may lie in real interactions and, just as important, that to make therapeutic progress and get past the defenses of dissociation it is necessary to uncover or reconstruct the actual

---

[2]Some psychoanalytic thinkers are interested in infants' actions, not in and of themselves, but rather only as forerunners of thinking or language. Similarly, the very mental structuring of experience has been viewed as possible only in, and due to, the absence of action or absence of an object to act upon. (If one could achieve the aim directly through physical action, there would be no need to think.) The opposite view is that it is action and objects to act upon that structure experience and permit its representation. (Absence only recalls or reevokes these representations; it does not structure them.)

original interactive experiences. The act and the interaction have become, once again, potentially "real" traumas.

If this is the case for child sexual abuse, will it also prove to be the case for other clinically important life situations or events, such as maternal depression, parental neglect, family violence, or severe compulsive behavior or anxiety states in the parent? Once this door has been opened (or reopened) in adult therapies, it is hard to know how large a world exists on the other side. But it is clear that progress in describing that world is highly dependent on the descriptive reach and precision of infant observers and clinicians of parent-infant interactions. After all, whatever the trauma (or just plain origin) was, if it really happened, and we want to reconstruct it, at least in part and to the limited extent that is possible, we need a general idea of what we are looking for. And that will only come from observing and thinking about actions and interpersonal interactions as a structuring experience for infant (and later adult) mental life. The idea is not to establish actual points of historical origin that will serve as sure endpoints for the reconstructive journey, but rather to provide a general map to aid in a search for a good, workable narrative.

It is in this quest that the microanalytic interview mentioned in chapter 3 takes on some of its possible utility. It provides a way of exploring lived interactive experience, putting considerable emphasis on actions and using the examination of actions and interactions to evoke memories and representations of previous such experiences. It is a way of asking, "What really happened to you and around you, then?"

There is nothing new about this sort of inquiry except that the microanalytic interview is rigorous about keeping the inquiry centered on the lived experience in question. Most therapists use some version of this kind of technique from time to time to find out what actually happened. And, interestingly, most supervisors of therapy often use such a technique in their supervision. The sorts of questions they ask beginning therapists— "And then what exactly did you say?" "And how did the patient take that? What did she do when you said it?" "Was there a long pause there?" "And how did you feel just then?"—are attempts to reconstruct the experience of the session. It is curious that in this situation the therapist and supervisor act as if what happened in the session is sometimes more important and knowable than what happened in the patient's life. In any event, it is clear that the encounter of traditional psychotherapies with the preverbal infant and mainly nonverbal parenting behaviors has given a new impetus to, perspective on, and perhaps the germ of some techniques for a reconsideration of the act, the interaction, and their recovery.

These reconsiderations may permit us to take a fresh look at a variety of clinical phenomena. For instance, when a patient, after a usually long struggle with his or her state of transference, says to the therapist something like, "I love you," what is to be made of it? It is considered a mental event, a verbalization of an action tendency, the mental manifestation of a set of desires. It is thus not in itself "acting out." Yet is that true? When the patient said, "I love you," was the voice quality softened? Was the body tensed? Did the patient look at the therapist a split second too long, or avoid looking with clear head aversion? Are these not acts? And is not the speech-*act* of saying "I love you" a kind of "performative" that, pragmatically speaking, is an action? What is the act, and what are the mental phenomena behind the act? The answer is not so clear (see Stern, 1993). There are certainly a myriad such ambiguous phenomena in therapy, and they have been insufficiently considered in relation to therapeutic theories.

Historically psychoanalysis has considered dreams, free associations, symptoms, and slips of the tongue as privileged routes into the unconscious. The encounter with infants and parent-infant psychotherapy makes it clear that actions, too, can provide a privileged route. The act can have a transparency revealing the underlying motivation that the word may not. Also that act may show much that could never reach consciousness or never get put into words. For instance, the fleeting succession of facial expressions and body movements can often provide a window into the wishes (and thoughts about those wishes) just as much as words can and at times much more. Techniques that focus mainly on behavior, such as the microanalytic interview, and the methods of behavioral observation and analysis provide the means for pursuing the route of action.

Reconstructing the Immediate and Long-Term Past

Reconstructing the past is a part of most psychotherapies. The encounter with infancy and parenting may provide some leads in several areas: situating nonverbal memories and experiences, finding patterns in clinical material, and providing a representational structure to use clinically in thinking about how things ordinarily happen.

SITUATING NONVERBAL MEMORIES

The clinical exploration and therapeutic use of nonverbal memories has generally been problematic. The therapies that privilege the word and symbol often have had trouble in pursuing and then integrating nonverbal memories. Similarly, the therapies that have arisen to address this lack (e.g., hands-on therapies) have been able to evoke isolated nonverbal experiences and memories but often have been less successful in integrating this material into the intricate story line of a life history.

The encounter with infancy, where so much is nonverbal, has forced us to grapple with these problems. The temporal feeling shape and its use as the temporal backbone of the protonarrative envelope are concepts that have been designed for precisely this purpose of integrating nonverbal and affective experience into the story line of a narrated life. By nonverbal memories or experiences I mean affective experiences (e.g., sadness) especially those that fall into the category of vitality affects (e.g., exploding, fading, accelerating, immediacy, etc.). This also includes such phenomena as feeling physically bold or tentative, vulnerable or invincible, and so on. In fact, most of the clinically relevant feelings concern the temporal contours of traditional affects (e.g., the speed and force with which a feeling of sadness descends and takes over, or the sense of an unchanged level of anger that seems to stretch unendingly into the future, or an explosion of dangerous joy).

The advantage of a concept such as the protonarrative envelope is in large part in the assumption it makes. It supposes that an isolated nonverbal memory belonged (and belongs) to a specific lived event or type of event and that recovering the event and the place of the nonverbal in the whole experience is simply the expected routine work of therapeutic exploration. Nonverbal material is not thought to have any special status when compared with perceptions, sensations, or words. It is another part of an experienced whole that helps establish the local or specific happening. It is conceptualized to leads to and from an interpersonal life event consisting of agents with desires and goals committing actions at given times and places. It creates in the therapist's mind and secondarily in the patient's mind a mental set and a structure for working toward an integration of nonverbal feelings into the plot line of a life.

FINDING PATTERNS IN CLINICAL MATERIAL

Because babies do not speak or understand language, the usual verbal content of clinical material recedes in importance and the nonverbal form carries most of the sense of events. This is often equally true where language is present but the therapy must get behind what is said. For instance, if a patient or couple in therapy complains of repeated severe arguments, at some point the therapy will have to unpack the form of the arguments. The pattern might be: husband provokes wife → wife counterattacks → husband threatens physically → wife retreats → wife has depression → husband feels guilt → wife exacts revenge. These arguments could have as their local apparent content anything from household chores to sex to money. It is recognizing the form or patterns that transcend the myriad possible instantiations that leads the way to change. The same is true for transference patterns.

The experience of watching parent-infant interaction is an excellent training ground for recognizing the pragmatics of interactions, verbal or nonverbal. One gets less caught up in the local content. Emphasizing the form and patterns renders more evident "what this is really about" that is the pragmatics. And it is there that the major currents of the transference or the core conflictual themes will be discovered. Therapeutically we want to know what someone wants to happen or thinks is happening between you.

THE SCHEMA-OF-BEING-WITH AS A NOTION FOR EXPLORING HOW THINGS ORDINARILY HAPPEN

Therapists readily distinguish two different kinds of experience that take on clinical importance. There are the unusual, especially revealing, symbolic, or traumatic events that are marked as special, at least by their departure from the ordinary. And there are the ordinary events that generally pass without notice or, when they are noticed, need no comment. The unusual events take on their meaning and markedness only against the background of the ordinary—that is, the expectable or the canonical. This division into background and marked events is widely used. Episodic autobiographical memories arise as specific deviations from expected happenings. The need to create and tell a narrative is assumed to result from a specific problem or trouble or unusualness in the smooth flow of life events.

The marked, unusual life events have occupied a very prominent place in clinical thinking, for all the obvious reasons. The ordinary canonical events have received far less attention. One of the interesting outcomes of the encounter of traditional clinical theories with the new population of young infants has been the need to pay greater attention to the daily ordinary events, for at least three reasons. First, with infants we can take for granted only a small amount of basic background knowledge about how the world-at-large works and how a particular family or mother works. Second, we usually do not know how to differentiate what is ordinary from what is extraordinary for an infant. And third, many of the basic social and emotional patterns between people in a family fall into the class of the ordinary yet play a huge role in structuring the representational world: What expectably happens when someone is hungry, or tired, or upset, or crying, or hurt, or laughing? What happens at separations big and small, bedtime, an evening out, retreats to read the newspaper? What happens at reunions big and small? How do arguments unfold and resolve? What happens when you feel loving, playful, slighted, ignored, dismissed? This is the world of the ordinary or canonical. But what is considered ordinary or the canon is unique to each family or person.

The schema-of-being-with is an attempt to delineate a representational form to deal with these kinds of ordinary interpersonal experiences—that is, "what it is like to be with someone in a certain way," where the "certain way" could be ordinary or special. It could be defined largely in terms of a particular motivational system (or drive) being activated or equally well in terms of those situations where it is difficult to pinpoint which motivational system is most activated (e.g., being alone in someone's presence or what happens on the way to Grandma's house on Sundays). It is an open structure designed to capture the local conditions (who? where? why? when? what? and how?) that make up bounded moments of being with.

The kind of lived experiences that adult patients tell about in therapy consist largely of episodes with others, episodes that are ordinary or variants of ordinary for them. When similar lived experiences are repeated, they become represented as expectable life happenings. The therapist can recategorize these representations into our usual groupings of representations: of others, of self, of self-objects, of motivational states, and so on. But while these categories may be clinically useful in the therapist's mind, they need not exist for the patient or for anyone else. The schema-of-being-with is more closely related to the experience. Clinically speaking, it generally captures what experiences with others feel like to a patient. It has the very important added advantage of being limited to the sensed phenomena of the lived experience and not including more abstract notions.

There are several reasons why this limitation to the sensed experience is advantageous. First, we cannot know what really happened during someone's infancy, and we cannot tell if a reconstruction is therapeutically good because it is historically true or because it provides a coherent narrative. Furthermore these two versions of reality can only approximate each other, at best. The reconstructive process, then, cannot and should not know exactly where it is going. Not only do reconstructions proceed in several directions at the same time, but the same experience is likely to be used over and over again to lead the search in different directions. The exact same set of experiences or representations may be used to constitute specific representations of others, later of self, and at another time of a motivational state. What is needed is a representation that locates the subjectively lived experience so that it can be used over and over for reconstructive ends that are not inherent in the experience itself. This is the essence of the schema-of-being-with. It is an essential piece of the mental landscape that can be read and reread differently but still remains a locatable real experience that permits an unfettered and multiple exploration of the past. It allows for a reconstructive search that ends up not treating a theory but treating a patient with very specific life experiences.

For all forms of therapy that use the past, what is most needed are search strategies to explore the past. In good part, the treatment is the search. The answers that one comes upon during the search can be seen as terminal points of the therapeutic voyage. They are just as much or even more signposts that mark the process of the journey. The encounter of traditional psychotherapies with infants and with parent-infant treatments has given—and promises to give—therapists of all persuasions new ideas for their therapeutic search strategies and new vantage points for viewing the early terrains into which treatment may voyage.

References

Ainsworth, M. D. S. (1974). Mother-infant attachment and social development. In M. Richards (Ed.), *The interrogation of the child into the social world*. Cambridge: Cambridge University Press.

Ainsworth, M. D. S., Blehard, M. C., Waters, E., & Wall, S. (1978). *Patterns of attachment*. Hillsdale, N.J.: Erlbaum.

Ammaniti, M. (1991). Maternal representations during pregnancy and early infant-mother interactions. *Infant Mental Health Journal, 12*(3), 246–255.

Ammaniti, M. Stability and change of maternal representations between pregnancy and the period after birth. Submitted for publication.

Ammaniti, M., Baumgartner, E., Candelori, C., Perucchini, P., Pola, M., Tambelli, R., & Zampino, F. (1992). Representations and narratives during pregnancy. *Infant Mental Health Journal, 13*(2), 167–182.

Ammaniti, M., & Stern, D. N. (Eds.). (1994). *Psychoanalysis and development: Representations and narrations* (M. Ammaniti and R. Nicolson, Trans.). New York: New York University Press. (Original work published 1991).

Astington, J. W., Harris, P. L., & Olson, D. R. (Eds.). (1988). *Developing theories of mind*. Cambridge: Cambridge University Press.

Aulangier, P. (1985). Hallucinating withdrawal. Is it the same thing as autistic withdrawal? *Lieux de l'enfance, 3*, 53–59.

Bachmann, J. P., & Robert-Tissot, C. (1992). Le raisonnement du clinicien dans les indications aux psychothérapies brèves mère-bébé. *Psychothérapies, 12*(2), 99–109.

Baddeley, A. D. (1986). *Working memory*. Oxford: Oxford University Press.

Barnard, K. E., Booth, C. L., Mitchell, S. K., & Telzrow, R. W. (1988). Newborn nursing models: A test of early intervention to high-risk infants and families. In E. Hibbs (Ed.), *Children and families: Studies in prevention and intervention*. Madison, Conn.: International Universities Press.

Barnard, K. E., Hammond, M. A., Sumner, G. A., Kang, R., Johnson-Crowley, N., Snyder, C., Spretz, A., Blackburn, S., Brandt, P., & Magyaru, D. (1987). Helping parents with pre-term infants: Field test of a protocol. *Early Child Development and Care*, 27(2), 256–290.

Barnard, K. E., Morisset, C. E., & Spieker, S. (1993). Preventive interventions: Enhancing parent-infant relationships. In C. H. Zeanah (Ed.), *Handbook of infant mental health*. New York: The Guilford Press.

Bartlett, F. C. (1964). *Remembering: A study in experimental and social psychology*. Cambridge: Cambridge University Press.

Beck, A. T., Rush, A. J., Shaw, B. F., & Emery, G. (1979). *Cognitive theory of depression*. New York: Guilford Press.

Beebe, B., Jaffe, J., Feldstein, S. (1992). Mother-infant vocal dialogues. *Infant Behavior and Development: Abstracts*, May, 15.

Beebe, B., Jaffe, J., Feldstein, S., Mays, K., & Alson, D. (1985). Interpersonal timing: The application of an adult dialogic model to mother-infant vocal and kinesic interaction. In T. Field and N. Fox (Eds.), *Infant Social Perception*. New York: Ablex.

Beebe, B., & Stern, D. N. (1977). Engagement-disengagement and early object experiences. In M. Freedman and S. Grand (Eds.), *Communicative structures and psychic structures*. New York: Plenum Press.

Benedek, T. (1959). Parenthood as a developmental phase: A contribution to libido theory. *Journal of the American Psychoanalytic Association*, 7(3), 389–417.

Bennett, S., Sackler-Lefcourt, I., Haft, W., Nachman, P., & Stern, D. N. (in press). The activation of maternal representations.

Benoit, D., Parker, K. C. H., & Zeanah, C. H. (in press). Mothers' representations of their infants assessed prenatally: Stability and association with infant attachment classification. *Journal of Child Psychology and Psychiatry*.

Berthoud-Papandropoulou, I., & Veneziano, E. (1989). La signification énonciative dans les débuts du langage. *Archives de Psychologie*, 57, 271–281.

Bertoncini, J., Bijeljac-Babic, R., Blumstein, S., & Mehler, J. (1987). Discrimination in neonates of very short CVs. *Journal of the Acoustical Society of America*, 82, 31–37.

Bertoncini, J., Bijeljac-Babic, R., Jusczyk, P. W., Kennedy, L. J., & Mehler, J. (1988). An investigation of young infants' perceptual representations of speech sounds. *Journal of Experimental Psychology: General*, 117, 21–33.

Bick, E. (1964). Notes of infant observation in psycho-analytic training. *International Journal of Psychoanalysis*, 49, 484–486.

Bion, W. R. (1963). *Eléments de psychanalyse*. Paris: Presses Universitaires de France. Collection Bibliothèque de Psychanalyse.

Bion, W. R. (1967). *Second thoughts*. London: Karnac.

Block, J. (1991). *Motherhood as metamorphosis*. New York: Plume (Penguin).

Bloom, L. (1973). *One word at a time: The use of single word utterances before syntax.* The Hague: Mouton.

Bowlby, J. (1969). *Attachment and loss: Vol. 1. Attachment.* New York: Basic Books.

Bowlby, J. (1973). *Attachment and loss: Vol. 2. Separation: Anxiety and anger.* New York: Basic Books.

Bowlby, J. (1980). *Attachment and loss: Vol. 3. Loss: Sadness and depression.* New York: Basic Books.

Brazelton, T. B. (1984). *To listen to a child.* Reading, Mass.: Addison-Wesley.

Brazelton, T. B. (1992). *Touchpoints.* New York: Guilford Press.

Brazelton, T. B. (1994). Touchpoints: Opportunities for preventing problems in the parent-child relationship. *Acta Paediatrica,* suppl., *394,* 35–39.

Brazelton, T. B., Yogman, M., Als, H., & Tronick, E. (1979). Joint regulation of neonate-parent behavior. In E. Tronick (Ed.), *Social interchange in infancy* (pp. 7–22). Baltimore: University Park Press.

Bretherton, I. (1984). Representing the social world in symbolic play: Reality and fantasy. In I. Bretherton (Ed.), *Symbolic play: The development of social understanding* (pp. 1–41). New York: Academic Press.

Bretherton, I., & Waters, E. (Eds.). (1985). Growing points of attachment theory and research. *Monographs of the Society for Research in Child Development, 209*(50).

Brown, R. (1973). *A first language: The early stages.* Cambridge: Harvard University Press.

Bruner, J. (1990). *Acts of meaning.* Cambridge: Harvard University Press.

Burke, K. (1945). *Grammar of motives.* New York: Prentice-Hall.

Byng-Hall, J. (1986). Family scripts: A concept which can bridge child psychotherapy and family therapy thinking. *Journal of Child Psychotherapy, 12*(2), 3–13.

Byng-Hall, J. (in press). *Family scripts.* New York: Guilford Press.

Byng-Hall, J., & Stevenson-Hinde, J. (1991). Attachment relationships within a family system. *Infant Mental Health Journal, 12*(3), 187–200.

Call, J. D., Galenson, F., & Tyson, R. L. (Eds.). (1983). *Frontiers of infant psychiatry, Vol. 1.* New York: Basic Books.

Case, R., Marini, Z., McKeough, A., Dennis, S., & Goldberg, J. (1986). Horizontal structure in middle childhood: Cross domain parallels in the course of cognitive growth. In I. Levin (Ed.), *Stage and structure: Reopening the debate* (pp. 1–39). Norwood, N.J.: Oblex.

Céllerier, G. (1976). La genèse historique de la cybernétique ou la téléonomie, est-elle une catégorie de l'entendement? *Revue européenne des sciences sociales, 14*(38/39), 273–290.

Céllerier, G. (1992). Le constructivisme génétique aujourd'hui. In B. Inhelder & G. Céllerier (Eds.), *Le cheminement des découvertes de l'enfant.* Lausanne: Delachaux et Niestlé.

Chodorow, N. (1978). *The reproduction of mothering.* Berkeley and Los Angeles: University of California Press.

Churchland, P. M. (1984). *Matter and consciousness.* Cambridge: MIT Press.

208   *References*

10.

Cichetti, D., & Cohen, D. J. (Eds.). (in press). *Manual of developmental psychopathology, Vol. I.* New York: Wiley.

Clark, G. N., & Seifer, R. (1983). Facilitating mother-infant communication: A treatment model for high-risk and developmentally delayed infants. *Infant Mental Health Journal, 4,* 67–82.

Clarkson, M. G., Clifton, R. K., Swain, I. U., and Perris, E. E. (1989). Stimulus duration and repetition rate influence newborn's head orientation toward sound. *Developmental Psychobiology, 22,* 683–705.

Clarkson, M. G., Swain, I. U., Clifton, R. K., & Cohen, K. (1991). Newborn's head orientation toward trains of brief sounds. *Journal of the Acoustical Society of America, 89,* 2411–2420.

Clynes, M. (1978). *Sentics.* Garden City, N.Y.: Anchor Books.

Collis, G. M., & Schaffer, H. R. (1979). Synchronization of visual attention in mother-infant pairs. *Journal of Child Psychiatry, 16,* 315–320.

Corboz, A. (1986). Echanges du père avec la dyade mère-bébé dans une famille décompensée au post-partum. In G. Garrone, A. Jablensky, & J. Manzano (Eds.), *Jeunes parents psychotiques et leurs enfants* (pp. 141–146). Villeurbanne: SIMEP.

Corboz-Warnery, A., & Fivaz-Depeursinge, E. (in press). L'observation du "Jeu Triade Lausanne" et son utilisation thérapeutique. *Perspectives Psychiatriques.*

Corboz-Warnery, A., Fivaz-Depeursinge, E., Gertsch-Bettens, C., & Favez, N. (1993). Systemic analysis of triadic father-mother-baby interactions. *Infant Mental Health Journal, 14,* 298–316.

Corboz-Warnery, A., Forni, P., & Fivaz, E. (1989). Le jeu à trois entre père, mère et bébé: Une méthode d'analyse des interactions visuelles triadiques. *Neuro-psychiatrie de l'Enfance, 37*(1), 23–33.

Cosmides, L., & Tooby, J. (1994). Beyond tuition and instinct blindness: Toward an evolutionarily rigorous cognitive science. *Cognition, 5,* 41–77.

Cramer, B. (1993, March). *Mother-baby interactions: In reality and in fantasy.* Paper presentation at the Third International Psychoanalytic Association Standing Conference on Psychoanalytic Research: The observed child and the reconstructed child, London.

Cramer, B., & Palacio-Espasa, F. (1993). *La pratique des psychothérapies mères-bébés: Études clinique et technique.* Paris: Presses Universitaires de France.

Cramer, B., Robert-Tissot, C., Stern, D. N., Serpa-Rusconi, S., De Muralt, M., Besson, G., Palacio-Espasa, F., Bachmann, J.-P., Knauer, D., Berney, C., & d'Arcis, U. (1990). Outcome evaluation in brief mother-infant psychotherapy: A preliminary report. *Infant Mental Health Journal, 11*(3): 278–300.

Cramer, B., & Stern, D. N. (1988). Evaluation of changes in mother-infant brief psychotherapy: A single case study. *Infant Mental Health Journal, 9*(1), 20–45.

Crittenden, P. M. (1981). Abusing, neglecting, problematic and adequate dyads: Differentiating by patterns of interaction. *Merrill-Palmer Quarterly, 27,* 201–218.

Darbellay, E. (1992). La composante de la temporalité comme critère d'analyse des NIGHT FANTASIES d'Elliot Carter. In P. Albèra, V. Barras, & C. Russi (Eds.), *Entretiens avec Elliot Carter*. Genève: Contrechamps.

De Beauvoir, S. (1953). *The second sex*. New York: Knopf.

Dennett, D. C. (1987). *The intentional stance*. Cambridge: MIT Press.

Dennett, D. C. (1991). *Consciousness explained*. Boston: Little, Brown.

De Ribaupierre, A., & Bailleux, C. (1994). Developmental change in a spacial task of attentional capacity: A comparison of two modes of response. *International Journal of Behavioral Development*, 17(1), 5–35.

Deutsch, H. (1945). *The psychology of women: A psychoanalytic interpretation: Vol. 2. Motherhood*. New York: Grune and Stratton.

Dolto, F. (1971). *Psychanalyse et pédiatrie*. Paris: Editions du Seuil.

Edelman, G. M. (1987). *Neural Darwinism*. New York: Basic Books.

Edelman, G. M. (1989). *The remembered present: A biological theory of consciousness*. New York: Basic Books.

Emde, R. N. (1980). Toward a psychoanalytic theory of affect: I. The organizational model and its propositions. In S. Greenspan & G. Pollock (Eds.), *The course of life: Psychoanalytic contributions toward understanding personality development: Vol. 1. Infancy and childhood*. Washington, D.C.: U.S. Government Printing Office.

Emde, R. N. (1983a). The pre-representational self and its affective core. *The Psychoanalytic Study of the Child*, 38, 165–192.

Emde, R. N. (Ed.). (1983b). *René A. Spitz: Dialogics from infancy: Selected paper*. New York: International Universities Press.

Emde, R. N. (1988). Development terminable and interminable: 1. Innate and motivational factors from infancy. *International Journal of Psychoanalysis*, 69, 23–42.

Emde, R. N. (1994). Three roads intersecting: Changing viewpoints in the psychoanalytic story of Oedipus. In M. Ammaniti & D. N. Stern (Eds.), *Psychoanalysis and development: Representations and narratives*. New York: New York University Press.

Emde, R. N., Biringen, Z., Clyman, R. B., & Oppenheim, D. (1991). The moral self of infancy: Affective core and procedural knowledge. *Developmental Review*, 11, 251–270.

Emde, R. N., & Harmon, R. J. (Eds.). (1984). *Continuities and discontinuities in development*. New York: Plenum Press.

Emde, R. N., & Sorce, J. F. (1983). The rewards of infancy: Emotional availability and maternal referencing. In J. D. Call, E. Galenson, & R. Tyson (Eds.), *Frontiers of infant psychiatry, Vol. 2*. New York: Basic Books.

Erikson, E. H. (1950). *Childhood and society*. New York: Norton.

Fava Vizziello, G. M., Antonioli, M., Cocci, V., & Invernizzi, R. (1992). Dal mito al bambino reale. In M. Ammaniti (Ed.), *Gravidanza e maternità tra rappresentazioni e narrazioni*. Roma: Il Pensiero Scientifico.

Fava Vizziello, G. M., Antonioli, M., Cocci, V., Invernizzi, R., & Cristante, F. (1993). From pregnancy to motherhood: The structure of representative and narrative change. *Infant Mental Health Journal*, 14(1), 4–16.

Fava Vizziello, G. M., & Stern, D. N. (Eds.). (1992). Dalle cure materne all'interpretazione. Milan: Raffaello Cortina Editore.

Field, T. (1982). Interaction coaching for high-risk infants and their parents. In H. A. Moss, R. Hess, & C. Swift (Eds.), *Prevention in human services: Vol. 1. Section 4. Early intervention programs for infants* (pp. 5–24). New York: Hayworth Press.

Field, T. (1987). Affective and interactive disturbances in infants. In J. D. Osofsky (Ed.), *Handbook of Infant Development* (pp. 972–1005). New York: Wiley.

Fivaz, E., Fivaz, R., & Kaufmann, L. (1982). Encadrement du développement, le point de vue systémique. Fonctions pédagogique, parentale, thérapeutique. *Cahiers Critiques de Thérapie Familiale et de Pratique de Réseaux,* 4(5), 63–74.

Fivaz, E., Martin, D., & Cornut-Zimmer, B. (1984). Holding interactions in a clinical family. In J. D. Call, E. Galenson, & R. L. Tyson (Eds.), *Frontiers of infant psychiatry, vol. 2* (pp. 502–521). New York: Basic Books.

Fivaz-Depeursinge, E. (1987). *Alliances et mésalliances dans le dialogue entre adulte et bébé: La communication précoce dans la famille.* Neuchâtel-Paris: Delachaux et Niestlé.

Fivaz-Depeursinge, E. (1991). Documenting a time-bound, circular view of hierarchies: A microanalysis of parent-infant dyadic interaction. *Family Process, 30,* 101–120.

Fivaz-Depeursinge, E., Corboz-Warnery, A., & Frenck, N. (1990). Modèles et techniques d'intervention thérapeutique pendant les premières années de vie. *L'Approche Systémique, 10,* 1–49.

Fivaz-Depeursinge, E., Stern, D. N., Bürgin, D., Byng-Hall, J., Corboz-Warnery, A., Lamour, M., & Lebovici, S., with R. Emde, discussant (1994). The dynamics of interface: Seven authors in search of encounters across levels of description of an event involving a mother, father and baby. *Infant Mental Health Journal, 15,* 69–89.

Fonagy, P., Steele, M., Moran, G. S., Steele, H., & Higgit, A. C. (1991). Measuring the ghost in the nursery: A summary of the main findings of the Anna Freud Centre–University College London parent-child study. *Bull. Anna Freud Centre, 14,* 115–131.

Fonagy, P., Steele, M., Steele, H., Moran, G. S., & Higgit, A. C. (1991). The capacity for understanding mental states: The reflective self in parent and child and its significance for security of attachment. *Infant Mental Health Journal, 13,* 200–217.

Foucault, M. (1977). Nietzsche, genealogy, history. In D. F. Bouchard (Ed.), *Language, counter-memory, practice: Selected essays.* Ithaca, N.Y.: Cornell University Press.

Fraiberg, S. (Ed.). (1980). *Clinical studies in infant mental health.* New York: Basic Books.

Fraiberg, S., Adelson, E., & Shapiro, V. (1975). Ghosts in the nursery: A psychoanalytic approach to the problems of impaired infant-mother relationships. *Journal of the American Academy of Child Psychiatry, 14,* 387–421.

Frank, J. D., & Frank, J. B. (1991). *Persuasion and healing: A comparative study of psychotherapy* (3rd Ed.). Baltimore and London: Johns Hopkins University Press.

Frascarolo-Moutinot, F. (1994). *Engagement paternel quotidien et relations parents-enfant.* Unpublished doctoral dissertation, Faculté de Psychologie et des Sciences de l'Education, Université de Genève, Switzerland, Thesis No. 207.

Freud, S. (1895). *Project for a scientific psychology.* In J. Strachey (Ed.), *The standard edition of the complete psychological works of Sigmund Freud* (Vol. 1, pp. 317–). London: Hogarth Press. (Original work published 1895.)

Freud, S. (1912). Recommendations to physicians practicing psycho-analysis. In J. Strachey (Ed.), *The standard edition of the complete psychological works of Sigmund Freud* (Vol. 12). London: Hogarth Press. (Original work published 1912.)

Freud, S. (1914a). On the history of the psycho-analytic movement. In J. Strachey (Ed.), *The standard edition of the complete psychological works of Sigmund Freud* (Vol. 14). London: Hogarth Press.

Freud, S. (1914b). Remembering, repeating and working-through. (Further recommendations on the technique of psycho-analysis.) In J. Strachey (Ed.), *The standard edition of the complete psychological works of Sigmund Freud* (Vol. 14). London: Hogarth Press.

Freud, S. (1915a). Observations on transference-love. In J. Strachey (Ed.), *The standard edition of the complete psychological works of Sigmund Freud* (Vol. 12). London: Hogarth Press.

Freud, S. (1915b). Repression. In J. Strachey (Ed.), *The standard edition of the complete psychological works of Sigmund Freud* (Vol. 14). London: Hogarth Press. (Original work published 1915.)

Freud, S. (1938). An outline of psycho-analysis. In J. Strachey (Ed.), *The standard edition of the complete psychological works of Sigmund Freud* (Vol. 23, pp. 174–). London: Hogarth Press. (Original work published 1938.)

Frijda, N. H., Mesquita, B., Sonnemans, J., & Van Goozen, S. (1991). *The duration of affective phenomena or emotions, sentiments and passions.* In K. T. Strongman (Ed.), *International review of studies on emotion* (Vol. 1, pp. 187–225). New York: Wiley.

Gautier, Y., Lebovici, S., Mazet, P., & Visier, J.-P. (Eds.). (1993). *Tragédies à l'aube de la vie.* Paris: Païdos/Recherche, Bayard Editions, INSERM.

Gendlin, E. T. (1992). The primacy of the body, not the primacy of perception. *Man and World, 01,* 341–353. Netherlands: Kluwer Academic Publishers.

Gergely, G., Nàdasdy-Gergely, C., & Birò, S. (in press). Taking the intentional stance at 12 months of age. *Cognition.*

Gertsch-Bettens, C., Corboz-Warnery, A., Favez, N., & Fivaz-Depeursinge, E. (1992). Les débuts de la communication à trois: Interactions visuelles triadique entre père, mère et bébé. *Enfance, 46,* 323–348.

Gilligan, C. (1982). *In a different voice: Psychological theory and woman's development.* Cambridge: Harvard University Press.

Green, A. (1986). *On private madness.* London: The Hogarth Press and the Institute of Psychoanalysis. (Original work published 1983.)

Greenspan, S. I. (1981). *Psychopathology and adaptation in infancy and early childhood.* New York: International Universities Press.

Greenspan, S. I., Lourie, R., & Nover, R. (1979). A developmental approach to the classification of psychopathology in infancy and early childhood. In J. Noshpitz (Ed.), *The basic handbook of child psychiatry* (pp. 157–164). New York: Basic Books.

Grossmann, K. E., & Grossmann, K. (1991). Attachment quality as an organizer of emotional and behavioral responses in a longitudinal perspective. In C. M. Parkes, J. Stevenson-Hinde, & P. Marris (Eds.), *Attachment across the life cycle* (pp. 93–114). London: Tavistock/Routledge.

Haynal, A. (1989). *Controversies in psychoanalytic method: From Freud and Ferenczi to Michael Balint* (Elizabeth Holder, Trans.). New York: New York University Press. (Original work published 1988.)

Hinde, R. A. (1979). *Towards understanding relationships.* London: Academic Press.

Hinde, R. A. (1982). *Ethology, its nature and relations with other sciences.* New York: Oxford University Press.

Hinde, R. A., & Stevenson-Hinde, J. (Eds.). (1988). *Relationships within families: Mutual influences.* Oxford: Clarendon Press.

Hofer, M., & Hofer, L. (1994). *Monica revisited.* Paper presented at the Annual American Psychiatric Association Meeting. May 25, 26, Philadelphia, Pa.

Horowitz, M. J. (1987). *States of mind: Configurational analysis of individual psychology.* New York: Plenum Medical Book.

Horowitz, M. J. (Ed.). (1991). *Person schemas and maladaptive interpersonal patterns.* Chicago: University of Chicago Press.

Houzel, D. (1985). Le monde tourbillonnaire de l'autisme. *Lieux de l'Enfance, 3,* 169–183.

Isaacs, S. (1989). The nature and function of phantasy. In J. Riviere (Ed.), *Developments in psychoanalysis.* London: Karnac Books. (Original work published 1952.)

Jaffe, J., Feldstein, S., Beebe, B., Crown, C., & Jasnow, M. (Monograph in preparation). Interpersonal timing and infant social development. New York: State Psychiatric Institute.

Kaye, K. L. (1992, May). *Nonsense syllable list learning in newborns.* Poster presented at the International Conference on Infant Studies (ICIS), Miami, Fla.

Keefer, C. H. A mother-centered interactive newborn examination (unpublished manuscript).

Kernberg, O. (1984). *Severe personality disorders: Psychotherapeutic strategies.* New Haven: Yale University Press.

Klinnert, M. D., Campos, J. J., Sorce, J. F., Emde, R. N., & Svejda, M. (1983). Emotions as behavior regulators: Social referencing in infancy. In R. Plutshik and H. Kellerman (Eds.), *Emotion: theory, research and experience, Vol. 2.* New York: Academic Press.

Kohut, H. (1971). *The analysis of the self.* New York: International Universities Press.

Kohut, H. (1977). *The restoration of the self.* New York: International Universities Press.

Kreisler, L. (1981). *L'enfant du désordre psychosomatique.* Toulouse: Privat.

Kreisler, L., & Cramer, B. (1981). Sur les bases cliniques de la psychiatrie du nourrisson. *La psychiatrie de l'enfant, 24,* 1–15.

Kreisler, L., Fain, M., Soulé, M. (1974). *L'enfant et son corps.* Paris: Presses Universitaires de France.

Labov, W. (1972). *Language in the inner city.* Philadelphia: University of Pennsylvania Press.

Lamour, M. (1988). Quand la relation est en danger. *Le Groupe Familial, 118,* 61–67.

Langer, S. K. (1967). *Mind: An essay on human feeling, Vol. 1.* Baltimore, Md.: Johns Hopkins University Press.

Laplanche, J., & Pontalis, J. B. (1988). *The language of psychoanalysis.* London: Karnac Books and the Institute of Psycho-analysis. (Original work published 1967.)

Lebovici, S. (1980). Névrose infantile, névrose de transfert. *Revue Française de Psychanalyse, 5–6,* 743–857.

Lebovici, S. (1983). *Le nourrisson, la mère et le psychanalyste: Les interventions précoces.* Paris: Le Centurion.

Lebovici, S. (1988). Fantasmatic interactions and intergenerational transmission. *Infant Mental Health Journal, 9,* 10–19.

Lebovici, S. (1993). On intergenerational transmission: From filiation to affiliation. *Infant Mental Health Journal, 14,* 260–272.

Lebovici, S., & Weil-Halpern, F. (Eds.). (1989). *Psychopathologie du bébé.* Paris: Presses Universitaires de France.

Leslie, A. M. (1987). Pretense and representation: The origins of "theory of mind." *Psychological Review, 94,* 412–426.

Leslie, A. M. (1988). Some implications of pretense for mechanisms underlying the child's theory of mind. In J. W. Astington, P. L. Harris, & D. R. Olsen (Eds.), *Developing theories of mind* (pp. 19–46). New York: Cambridge University Press.

Leslie, A. M., & Happé, F. (1989). Autism and ostensive communication: The relevance of metarepresentation. *Development and Psychopathology, 1*(3), 205–212.

Lewis, M., & Miller, S. M. (Eds.). (1990). *Handbook of developmental psychopathology.* New York: Plenum Press.

Lewkowicz, D. J. (1989). The role of temporal factors in infant behavior and development. In I. Levin & D. Zakay (Eds.), *Time and human cognition: A lifespan perspective* (pp. 9–62). North Holland: Elsevier Science Publishers.

Lewkowicz, D. J. (1992). The development of temporally based intersensory perception in human infants. In F. Macar et al. (Eds.), *Time, action and cognition* (pp. 33–43). The Netherlands: Kluwer Academic Publishers.

Lichtenberg, J. (1989). *Psychoanalysis and motivation.* Hillsdale, N.J.: The Analytic Press.

Lieberman, A. F., & Pawl, J. H. (1993). Infant-parent psychotherapy. In C. Zeanah

(Ed.), *Handbook of infant mental health* (pp. 427–442). New York, Boston: Guilford Press.

Luborsky, L., & Crits-Christoph, P. (1990). *Understanding transference: The core conflictual relationship theme model.* New York: Basic Books.

Mahler, M. S., Pine, F., & Bergman, A. (1975). *The psychological birth of the human infant.* New York: Basic Books.

Main, M., & Cassidy, J. (1988). Categories of response to reunion with the parent at age six: Predictable from infant attachment classification and stable over a one month period. *Development Psychology, 24,* 415–426.

Main, M., & Goldwyn, R. (1985). Adult attachment classification and rating system. Unpublished manuscript, University of California, Berkeley.

Main, M., Kaplan, N., & Cassidy, J. (1989). Security in infancy, childhood and adulthood: A move to the level of representation. In I. Bretherton & E. Waters (Eds.), Growing points in attachment theory and research (pp. 66–106). *Monographs of the Society for Research in Child Development, 50.*

Mandler, J. M. (1979). Categorical and schematic organization in memory. In C. R. Puff (Ed.), *Memory organization and structure* (pp. 259–299). New York: Academic Press.

Mandler, J. M. (1983). Representation. In J. H. Flavell & E. M. Markman (Eds.), *Cognitive development* (pp. 420–494). Vol. 3 of P. Mussen (Ed.), *Handbook of Child Psychology,* 4th ed. New York: Wiley.

Mandler, J. M. (1988). How to build a baby: On the development of an accessible representational system. *Cognitive Development, 3,* 113–136.

Mandler, J. M. (1992). How to build a baby: II. Conceptual primitives. *Psychological Review, 99,* 587–604.

Manzano, J., & Palacio-Espasa, F. (1990, November). Concepts théoriques fondamentaux à propos des psychothérapies mère-bébé. Paper presented at the Symposium de Psychiatrie Infantile de Genève, Geneva, Switzerland.

Maturana, H. R., & Varela, F. J. (1979). *Autopoiesis and cognition: The realization of the living.* Dordrecht, Boston, and London: D. Reidel.

McDonough, S. C. (1991). Interaction guidance: A technique for treating early relationship disturbances in parents and children. In J. Gomes-Pedro (Ed.), *Bebe XXI.* Lisbon, Portugal: Condor Press.

McDonough, S. C. (1992). Treating early relationship disturbances with interaction guidance. In G. Fava Vizziello & D. N. Stern (Eds.), *Models and techniques of psychotherapeutic intervention in the first year of life.* Milan: Raffaello Cortina.

McDonough, S. C. (1993). Interaction guidance: Understanding and treating early infant-caregiver relationship disorders. In C. Zeanah (Ed.), *Handbook of infant mental health* (pp. 414–426). New York: Guilford Press.

McHale, S. M., & Huston, T. L. (1984). Men and women as parents: Sex role orientations, employment and parental roles with infants. *Child Development, 55,* 1349–1361.

Meisels, S. J., Dichtelmiller, M., & Llaw, F. R. (1993). A multidimensional analysis of early childhood intervention programs. In C. Zeanah (Ed.), *Handbook of infant mental health.* New York: Guilford Press.

Meisels, S. J., & Shonkoff, J. P. (1990). *Handbook of early childhood intervention.* Cambridge: Cambridge University Press.

Meltzoff, A. N. (1994, June). Representation of persons: A bridge between infant's understanding of people and things. Paper presented at the Ninth International Conference on Infant Studies, Paris.

Murray, L. (1988). Effects of post-natal depression on infant development: Direct studies of early mother-infant interaction. In I. Brockington and R. Kumer (Eds.), *Motherhood and mental illness, Vol. 2.* Bristol: John Wright.

Murray, L. (1992). Impact of post-natal depression on infant development. *Journal of Child Psychology and Psychiatry, 33*(3), 543–561.

Nachman, P., Sackler-Lefcourt, I., Haft, W., Bennett, S., & Stern, D. N. Maternal identification: A description of the process in real time. Unpublished manuscript.

Nathan, T. (1986). *La folie des autres.* Paris: Dunod.

Nelson, K. (Ed.). (1986). *Event knowledge: Structure and function in development.* Hillsdale, N.J.: Erlbaum.

Nelson, K. (1988). The ontogeny of memory for real events. In M. Neisser & W. Winograd (Eds.), *Remembering reconsidered: Ecological and traditional approaches to the study of memory.* New York: Cambridge University Press.

Nelson, K., & Greundel, J. M. (1981). Generalized event representation: Basic building blocks of cognitive development. In M. E. Lamb & A. L. Brown (Eds.), *Advances in developmental psychology, Vol. 1.* Hillsdale, N.J.: Erlbaum.

Osofsky, J. D., Hann, D., Biringen, Z., Emde, R. N., Robinson, J., & Little, C. (1990). Emotional availability: Strengths and vulnerabilities in development. In C. Rovee-Collier (Ed.), *Abstracts of papers presented at the Seventh International Conference on Infant Studies,* Montreal (p. 64). Norwood, N.J.: Ablex.

Papoušek, M., Papoušek, H. (1981). Musical elements in the infant's vocalization: Their significance for communication, cognition and creativity. In L. P. Lipsitt (Ed.), *Advances in infancy research.* Norwood, N.J.: Ablex.

Parke, R. D., Power, T. G., & Gottman, J. M. (1979). Conceptualizing and quantifying influence patterns in the family triad. In M. E. Lamb, S. J. Suomi, & G. R. Stephenson (Eds.), *Social interaction analysis: Methodological issues* (pp. 231–251). Madison: University of Wisconsin Press.

Parks, C. M., Stevenson-Hinde, J., & Marris, P. (Eds.). (1991). *Attachment across the life cycle.* London: Routledge.

Parloff, M. B. (1988). Psychotherapy outcome research. In R. Michels & J. B. Lippincott (Eds.), *Psychiatry, Vol. 3.* New York: Basic Books.

Pascual-Leone, J. (1987). Organismic processes for new-Piagetian theories: A dialectical causal account of cognitive development. *International Journal of Psychology, 22,* 531–570.

Patterson, D. M., and Barnard, K. E. (1990). Parenting of low birth weight infants: A review of issues and interventions. *Infant Mental Health Journal, 11,* 37–56.

Person, E. S., Hagelin, A., & Fonagy, P. (Eds.). (1993). *On Freud's "observations on transference-love."* International Psychoanalytic Association, Contemporary Freud: Turning Points and Critical Issues Series. New Haven: Yale University Press.

Piaget, J. (1952). *The origins of intelligence in children*. New York: International Universities Press.

Piaget, J. (1954). *The construction of reality in the child*. New York: Basic Books (Originally published 1937.)

Piontelli, A. A. (1992). *From fetus to child*. New Library of Psychoanalysis, 15, Ed. E. B. Spillius. London: Tavistock/Routledge.

Pourrinet, J. (1993, September). Observation d'un bébé dans sa famille. Paper presented at the 13th Journées bretonnes de psychothérapie d'enfants, Pont-L'Abbé, France.

Premack, D. (1990). The infant's theory of self-propelled objects. *Cognition, 36,* 1–16.

Premack, D., & Woodruff, G. (1978). Does a chimpanzee have a theory of mind? *Behavioral and Brain Sciences, 1,* 515–526.

Reiss, D. (1989). The represented and practicing family: Contrasting visions of family continuity. In A. Sameroff & R. N. Emde (Eds.), *Relationship disturbances* (pp. 191–214). New York: Basic Books.

Rexford, E. N., Sander, L. W., & Shapiro, T. (1976). *Infant psychiatry: A new synthesis*. New Haven: Yale University Press.

Ricoeur, P. (1977). The question of proof in Freud's psychoanalytical writings. *Journal of American Psychoanalytic Association, 25,* 835–871.

Ricoeur, P. (1983–1985). *Temps et récit* (Vols. 1–3). Paris: Editions du Seuil.

Robertson, J. (1958). *Young Children in Hospitals*. New York: Basic Books.

Robert-Tissot, C., Rusconi-Serpa, S., Bachmann, J. P., Besson, G., Cramer, B., Knauer, D., de Muralt, M., Palacio-Espasa, F., & Stern, D. N. (1989). Le questionnaire "Symptom check-list," évaluation des troubles psycho-fonctionnels de la petite enfance. In S. Lebovici, P. Mazet, & J. P. Visier (Eds.), *L'évaluation des interactions précoces entre le bébé et ses partenaires* (pp. 179–215). Paris: Eshel; Genève: Médecine et Hygiène.

Rosch, E., & Floyd, B. B. (Eds.). (1978). *Cognition and categorization*. Hillsdale, N.J.: Erlbaum.

Rovee-Collier, L., & Fagen, J. W. (1981). The retrieval of memory in early infancy. In L. P. Lipsitt (Ed.), *Advances in infancy research, Vol. 1*. Norwood, N.J.: Ablex.

Rumelhart, D. D., McClelland, J. L., & the PDP Research Group (1986). *Parallel distributed processing: Explorations in the microstructure of cognition*. Cambridge: Bradford/MIT Press.

Sameroff, A. J., & Emde, R. N. (Eds.). (1989). *Relationship disturbances*. New York: Basic Books.

Sameroff, A. J., & Fiese, B. H. (1990). Transactional regulation and early intervention. In S. J. Meisels & J. P. Shankoff (Eds.), *Handbook of early childhood intervention* (pp. 119–149). Cambridge: Cambridge University Press.

Sameroff, A. J., Seifer, R., Barocas, B., Lax, M., & Greenspan, S. (1987). IQ scores of 4 year old children: Social environmental risk factors. *Pediatrics, 79*(3), 343–350.

Sander, L. W. (1962). Issues in early mother-child interaction. *Journal of American Academy of Child Psychiatry, 1,* 141–166.

Sander, L. W. (1964). Adaptive relationships in early mother-child interaction. *Journal of American Academy of Child Psychiatry, 3,* 231–264.

Sandler, J. (1985). Towards a reconsideration of the psychoanalytic theory of motivation. *Bulletin of the Anna Freud Center, 8,* 223–243.

Sandler, J. (1987). *Projection, identification, projective identification.* New York: International Universities Press.

Sandler, J., & Sandler, A. M. (in press). *Internal objects revisited.*

Schafer, R. (1981). Narration in the psychoanalytic dialogue. In W. J. T. Mitchell (Ed.), *On narration.* Chicago: University of Chicago Press.

Scherer, K. R. (1984). On the nature and function of emotion: A component process approach. In K. R. Scherer & P. Ekman (Eds.), *Approaches to emotion.* Hillsdale, N.J.: Erlbaum.

Scherer, K. R. (1986). Vocal affect expression. *Psychological Bulletin, 99*(2), 143–165.

Scherer, K. R. (1993). Neuroscience projections to current debates in emotion psychology. *Cognition and Emotion, 7*(1), 1–41.

Shank, R. C. (1982) *Dynamic memory: A theory of reminding and learning in computers and people.* New York: Cambridge University Press.

Shank, R. C., & Abelson, R. (1977). *Scripts, plans, goals and understanding.* Hillsdale, N.J.: Erlbaum.

Singer, J. L., & Salorey, P. (1991). Organized knowledge structures and personality. In M. J. Horowitz (Ed.), *Person schemas and maladaptive interpersonal patterns* (pp. 33–80). Chicago: University of Chicago Press.

Soulé, M., & Golse, B. (Eds.). (1992). *Les traitements des psychoses de l'enfant et de l'adolescent.* Paris: Païdos/Recherche, Bayard Editions.

Spelke, E. (1994). Initial knowledge: Six suggestions. *Cognition, 50,* 431–445.

Spence, D. P. (1976). Clinical interpretation: Some comments on the nature of the evidence. *Psychoanalysis and Contemporary Science, 5,* 367–388.

Spence, M. J. (1992, May). *Infant's discrimination of novel and repeatedly experienced speech passages.* Poster presented at the Ninth International Conference on Infant Studies (ICIS), Miami, Fla.

Sroufe, L. A. (1983). Infant-caregiver attachment and patterns of adaptation in pre-school: The roots of maladaptation and competence. In M. Perlmutter (Ed.), *Minnesota Symposium in Child Psychology, 16,* 41–81. Hillsdale, N.J.: Erlbaum.

Sroufe, L. A., & Waters, E. (1977). Heart-rate as a convergent measure in clinical and developmental research. *Merrill-Palmer Quarterly, 23,* 3–28.

Steimer-Krause, E. (1992, March). Transference and non-verbal behaviors. Paper presented at the meetings of the International Psychoanalytic Association, Standing Committee on Psychoanalytic Research, London.

Stern, D. N. (1971). A micro-analysis of mother-infant interaction: Behavior regulating social contact between a mother and her 3½-month-old twins. *Journal of the American Academy of Child Psychiatry, 10*, 501–517.

Stern, D. N. (1977). *The first relationship: Infant and mother.* Cambridge: Harvard University Press.

Stern, D. N. (1985). *The interpersonal world of the infant: A view from psychoanalysis and developmental psychology.* New York: Basic Books.

Stern, D. N. (1989). The representation of relational patterns: Some developmental considerations. In A. Sameroff & R. N. Emde (Eds.), *Relationship disorders.* New York: Basic Books.

Stern, D. N. (1990). *Diary of a baby.* New York: Basic Books.

Stern, D. N. (1991). Maternal representations: A clinical and subjective phenomenological view. *Infant Mental Health Journal, 12*(3), 174–186.

Stern, D. N. (1993). Acting versus remembering in transference love and infantile love. In E. S. Person, A. Hagelin, & P. Fonagy (Eds.), *On Freud's observations on transference-love* (pp. 172–186). International Psychoanalytic Association, Contemporary Freud: Turning Points and Critical Issues Series. New Haven: Yale University Press.

Stern, D. N. (1994a). L'enveloppe pré-narrative: Vers une unité fondamentale d'expérience permettant d'explorer la réalité psychique du bébé. *Journal de la Psychanalyse de l'Enfant, 14*, 13–65.

Stern, D. N. (1994b). One way to build a clinically relevant baby. *Infant Mental Health Journal, 15*(1) 9–25.

Stern, D. N. (1994c). Ce que comprend le bébé. In O. Bourguignon & M. Bydlowski (Eds.), *La recherche clinique en psychopathologie.* Paris: Presses Universitaires de France.

Stern, D. N., Hofer, L., Haft, W., & Dore, J. (1984). Affect attunement: The sharing of feeling states between mother and infant by means of intermodal fluency. In T. Field & N. Fox (Eds.), *Social perception in infants* (pp. 249–268). Norwood, N.J.: Ablex.

Stern, D. N., Robert-Tissot, C., Besson, G., Rusconi-Serpa, S., de Muralt, M., Cramer, B., & Palacio-Espasa, F. (1989a). L'entretien "R," une méthode d'évaluation des représentations maternelles. In S. Lebovici, P. Mazet, & J. P. Visier (Eds.), *L'évaluation des interactions précoces entre le bébé et ses partenaires* (pp. 151–177). Paris: Eshel; Genève: Médecine et Hygiène.

Stern, D. N., Robert-Tissot, C., de Muralt, M., & Cramer, B. (1989b). Le KIA-profil, un instrument de recherche pour l'évaluation des états affectifs du jeune enfant. In S. Lebovici, P. Mazet, & J. P. Visier (Eds.), *L'évaluation des interactions précoces entre le bébé et ses partenaires.* Paris: Eshel; Genève: Médecine et Hygiène.

Stern-Bruschweiler, N., & Stern, D. N. (1989). A model for conceptualizing the role of the mother's representational world in various mother-infant therapies. *Infant Mental Health Journal, 10*(3), 142–156.

Stevenson-Hinde, J. (1990). Attachment within family systems: An overview. *Infant Mental Health Journal, 11*(3), 219–227.

Stoleru, S., & Moralès-Huet, M. (Eds.). (1989). *Psychothérapies mère-nourrisson dans les familles à problèmes multiples*. Paris: Presses Universitaires de France.

Strauss, M. S. (1979). Abstraction of prototypical information by adults and ten-month-old infants. *Journal of Experimental Psychology: Human Learning and Memory, 5*, 618–632.

Sullivan, H. S. (1953). *The interpersonal theory of psychiatry*. New York: Norton.

Swain, I. U. (1992, May). Newborn response to auditory stimulus complexity. Paper presented at the Ninth International Conference on Infant Studies (ICIS), Miami, Fla.

Thelen, E. (1990). Dynamical systems and the generation of individual differences. In J. Colombo & J. W. Fagen (Eds.), *Individual differences in infancy: Reliability, stability and prediction*. Hillsdale, N.J.: Erlbaum.

Tomkins, S. S. (1962). *Affect, imagery, consciousness: Vol. 1. The positive affects*. New York: Springer.

Tomkins, S. S. (1963). *Affect, imagery, consciousness: Vol. 2. The negative affects*. New York: Springer.

Trad, P. V. (1990). *Infant previewing: Predicting and sharing interpersonal outcome*. New York: Springer.

Trevarthen, C. (1979). Communication and cooperation in early infancy: A description of primary intersubjectivity. In M. M. Bullowa (Ed.), *Before speech: The beginning of interpersonal communication*. New York: Cambridge University Press.

Trevarthen, C. (1980). The foundations of intersubjectivity: Development of interpersonal and cooperative understanding in infants. In D. Olsen (Ed.), *The social foundations of language and thought: Essays in honor of J. S. Bruner* (pp. 316–342). New York: W. W. Norton.

Trevarthen, C. (1982). The primary motives for cooperative understanding. In G. Butterworth & P. Light (Eds.), *Social cognition: Studies on the development of understanding* (pp. 77–109). Brighton, England: Harvesters Press.

Trevarthen, C. (1989). Signs before speech. In T. A. Sebeok & J. Umiker-Sebeok (Eds.), *The semiotic web*. Berlin: Mouton de Gruyter.

Trevarthen, C. (1993). The function of emotions in early infant communication and development. In J. Nadel & L. Camaioni (Eds.), *New perspectives in early communicative development*. London: Routledge.

Tronick, E., Als, H., Adamson, L., Wise, S., & Brazelton, T. B. (1978). The infant's response to entrapment between contradictory messages in face-to-face interaction. *Journal of Child Psychiatry, 17*, 1–13.

Tronick, E. Z., & Cohn, J. (1989). Infant-mother face-to-face interaction: Age and gender differences in coordination and the occurrence of miscoordinations. *Child Development, 60*, 85–91.

Tustin, F. (1984). Autistic shapes. *International Review of Psychoanalysis, 11*, 279–290.

Tustin, F. (1990). *The protective shell in children and adults*. London: Karnac Books.

Von Cranach, M., Kalbermatten, U., Indermühle, K., & Gugler, B. (1982). Goal-direction action. *European Monographs in Social Psychology,* New York: Academic Press.

Vygotsky, L. S. (1962). *Thought and language.* (E. Haufmann & G. Vakar, Eds. and Trans.). Cambridge: MIT Press.

Weinberg, M. K., & Tronick, E. Z. (1994). Beyond the face: An empirical study of infant affective configurations of facial, vocal, gestural and regulatory behaviors. *Child Development, 65,* 1495–1507.

Wertheim, E. S. (1975). Person-environment interaction: The epigenesis of autonomy and competence: I. Theoretical considerations (normal development). *British Journal of Medical Psychology, 48,* 1–8.

Winnicott, D. W. (1957). *Mother and Child: A primer of first relationship.* New York: Basic Books.

Winnicott, D. W. (1965). *The maturational process and the facilitating environment.* New York: International Universities Press.

Winnicott, D. W. (1971). *Playing and reality.* New York: Basic Books.

Zeanah, C. H. (Ed.). (1993). *Handbook of infant mental health.* New York: Guilford Press.

Zeanah, C. H., Anders, T. F., Seifer, R., & Stern, D. N. (1989). Implications of research on infant development for psychodynamic theory and practice. *Journal of the American Academy of Child and Adolescent Psychiatry, 2*(5), 657–668.

Zeanah, C. H., & Barton, M. L. (1989). Introduction: Internal representations and parent-infant relationships. *Infant Mental Health Journal, 10,* 135–141.

Zeanah, C. H., & Benoit, D. (in press). Clinical applications of a parent perception interview in infant mental health. *Child and Adolescent Psychiatric Clinics of North America.*

Zeanah, C. H., Keener, M. A., & Anders, T. F. (1986). Adolescent mothers' prenatal fantasies and working models of their infants. *Psychiatry, 49,* 193–203.

Zeanah, C. H., Keener, M. A., Stewart, L., & Anders, T. F. (1985). Prenatal perception of infant personality: A preliminary investigation. *Journal of the American Academy of Child Psychiatry, 24,* 204–210.

Zeanah, C. H., Mammen, O. K., & Lieberman, A. F. (1993). Disorders of attachment. In C. H. Zeanah (Ed.), *Handbook of infant mental health.* New York: Guilford Press.

Zeanah, C. H., & McDonough, S. C. (1989). Clinical approaches to families in early intervention. *Seminars in Perinatology, 13,* 513–522.

Zelazo, P. R., Brody, L. B., & Chaika, H. (1984). Neonatal habituation and dishabituation of headturning to rattle sounds. *Infant Behavior and Development, 7,* 311–321.

Index

Note: Page numbers followed by *n* indicate material in footnotes.